Bloom's Modern Critical Views

CONTEMPORARY POETS
New Edition

Edited and with an introduction by
Harold Bloom
Sterling Professor of the Humanities
Yale University

BLOOM'S
LITERARY CRITICISM
An imprint of Infobase Publishing

Bloom's Modern Critical Views: Contemporary Poets—New Edition

Copyright © 2010 by Infobase Publishing
Introduction © 2010 by Harold Bloom

Bloom's Literary Criticism
An imprint of Infobase Publishing
132 West 31st Street
New York NY 10001

Library of Congress Cataloging-in-Publication Data
   Contemporary poets / edited and with an introduction by Harold Bloom. — New ed.
     p. cm. — (Bloom's modern critical views)
   Includes bibliographical references and index.
   ISBN 978-1-60413-588-6 (hardcover)
   1. American poetry—20th century—History and criticism.   I. Bloom, Harold.
   PS325.C67 2009
   811'.5'09—dc22

                              2009025032

Bloom's Literary Criticism books are available at special discounts when purchased in bulk quantities for businesses, associations, institutions, or sales promotions. Please call our Special Sales Department in New York at (212) 967-8800 or (800) 322-8755.

You can find Bloom's Literary Criticism on the World Wide Web at
http://www.chelseahouse.com.

Contributing editor: Pamela Loos
Cover designed by Takeshi Takahashi

Printed in the United States of America
IBT IBT 10 9 8 7 6 5 4 3 2 1

This book is printed on acid-free paper.

Contents

Editor's Note

The introduction is a revised and condensed version of an essay written in partnership with David Bromwich more than a quarter century ago. It sets the background of American poetic tradition that still informs the poets surveyed here: Merwin, Ashbery, Rich, Simic, Glück, Hollander, Graham, and Howard.

Marjorie Perloff precisely and sympathetically finds in W.S. Merwin our equivalent of Thomas Gray, who is a permanent poet, after which Stephen Paul Miller attempts to see John Ashbery as a political poet, which I find surprising. Adrienne Rich, who most certainly is political, is studied by Barbara L. Estrin as a poet of outrage.

Roger Gilbert gives a broad survey of the contemporary scene, while the late Anthony Hecht, one of our major poets, welcomes Charles Simic to that company and Linda Gregerson celebrates the originality of Louise Glück.

David Bromwich returns with a subtle appreciation of John Hollander's extraordinarily heightened poetic consciousness, after which Jorie Graham's perceptiveness is detailed by Willard Spiegelman.

Richard Howard's reincarnation of Robert Browning is praised by Langdon Hammer, while Adam Kirsch completes this volume by analyzing current fashions in the criticism of verse.

HAROLD BLOOM

Introduction

"Ask the fact for the form," Emerson said, but the history of American poetry has tended to illustrate a rival quest, which is to beg the form for the fact. Emerson urged the American bards to emulate his Merlin, who mounted to paradise by the stairway of surprise, but even the greatest among Emerson's immediate progeny, Whitman and Dickinson, chose to present their poetic selves through repetitive modes of continuous and overwhelming formal innovation. American poetry since the end of World War II is an epitome of this reverse Emersonianism: No other poets in Western history have so self-deceivingly organized themselves along the supposed lines of formal divisions. The mimic wars of "closed" against "open" formers have masqueraded as conflicts between spiritual stances and ideological commitments: Closed form, governed by metric and stanza, could thus be writ large as a settled insulation from experience, whereas open form, freestyle and full of vatic self-confidence, reduced all experience to a chaos. And yet if we stand back now, we behold mostly a welter of wholly shared anxieties that unite the feuding camps.

The poets who were gathered together at their first full strength circa 1945 would include Robert Penn Warren, Richard Eberhart, Theodore Roethke, Elizabeth Bishop, Robert Lowell, John Berryman, Delmore Schwartz, J. V. Cunningham, Randall Jarrell, Richard Wilbur, Charles Olson, and Robert Duncan. They had as predecessors the most formidable group of poets in the American tradition, one that began with Edwin Arlington Robinson and Frost and proceeded through Pound, Eliot, Moore, Williams, Stevens, Ransom, and Jeffers down to a somewhat younger trio of e. e. cummings, Hart Crane, and Allen Tate. Almost all the poets born in the first two decades of the twentieth century seem

1

diminished today when juxtaposed very closely with those born in the last two or three decades of the nineteenth. Great achievement by the fathers sometimes exacts a price from the children, and something of the current strength of American poets born during the 1920s may derive from the sorrows and sacrifice of the middle generation of Roethke, Berryman, Jarrell, Lowell, and others.

We can distinguish two formal strains in the important American poets born during the closing decades of the nineteenth century. If we examine American poetic practice as opposed to theory in the nineteenth century, we see that the main British line of Spenserian-Miltonic poetry, which emerges as the romantic tradition, was carried on through Bryant, Poe, Longfellow, Timrod, and Lanier, while native strains were invented most plainly by Whitman and more subtly by a gnomic group that includes Emerson, Thoreau, Melville, and, most grandly, Dickinson. The two strains, those of the English romantic and the Emersonian gnomic, met and mingled in Robinson and Frost.

A third strain of Whitmanian innovation ended in the major outburst of 1915 and afterwards. The immediate influence of Whitman here—on Edgar Lee Masters, Vachel Lindsay, Carl Sandburg—was not fructifying, though these poets continue to be popular, and their simplified idiom has much to do with the recent development of a quasifolk music. However, a Whitmanian element in Pound, Williams, and even Eliot today seems far more central and vitalizing than the European influences so directly exalted by Eliot and Pound themselves and by their followers. An even more elusive Whitmanian influence, wholly divorced from formal considerations, was crucial for Stevens, whose major formal inheritance is as close to Wordsworth, Keats, and Tennyson as ever Bryant, Poe, and Longfellow were.

Despite its enormous range and power, Stevens's poetry has waited until the late 1960s and early 1970s to find a strong disciple in John Ashbery, whose own work took a turn away from surrealism and automatic writing in *The Double Dream of Spring, Three Poems*, and a number of uncollected lyrics. In Ashbery's best poems we look back through Stevens to Whitman in the employment of a long line, and in a rather oblique use of the cataloguing effect. There is a similar background for poets whose middle range of ancestry and poetic temperament appears to be occupied by Eliot. For instance, W.S. Merwin began during the mid-1960s to experiment with a celebratory kind of neoprimitivism: in *The Moving Target* and *The Lice*, broken syntax is making the dissociation Eliot saw as historically unfortunate but necessary. Yet Merwin has recovered the consolatory strain that belonged to Whitman and decisively affected *The Waste Land* and *Four Quartets*, though Eliot in his own quite ambivalent public pronouncements had tried to eliminate Whitman from the acceptable "tradition" of poetry in the English language.

These cases illustrate the emergence during the past few years of a transcendentalism that has always been essential to American poetry but was for a time anxiously rejected by its surest descendants. The poets of the generation of Roethke-Lowell-Wilbur began with the sober admonition of Eliot and Auden; they were to return to closed forms and forsake metrical innovation. They, together with their younger followers in the 1950s—Ashbery, Merwin, James Dickey, James Merrill, Anthony Hecht, James Wright, Louis Simpson, Richard Howard, John Hollander—discovered in their various ways that neither closed nor open forms could be anything but an evasion. Poets who came into their force somewhat later, such as Gary Snyder, A.R. Ammons, Galway Kinnell, and Mark Strand, were less troubled by constraints of form and so could start more comfortably from the fact. In short, never having labored under the illusion that there was some crosscultural modern idiom to which they ought to aspire, they declared themselves from the first to be successors of Emerson and Whitman.

Among the closed formers, it is Auden rather than Eliot who has been the steadiest influence. His idiom is still going strong in the most recent work of Merrill, Howard Moss, and Wilbur, had a determining effect on the early efforts of Hollander and Howard, and never left Jarrell. What separates the American disciples of Auden from many of their British counterparts is a revision of Auden's characteristic irony, which (as Donald Davie has remarked in a slightly different context) begins to realize in it the attitude that nature strikes in confronting man: not merely a man's own pose in confronting himself. This shift is evident also in matters of detail. Wilbur can be representative: His early and late poems look very nearly the same, but their technical evenness covers a progress away from the metaphysical conceits that used to lie thick on his pages. Similarly, Jarrell in his last work moved to the Wordsworthian pathos that had been his theme all along and wrote increasingly in a loose iambic that allowed for much of the "inclusiveness" he had explicitly admired in Whitman. Howard in his most recent volumes has written dramatic monologues after the manner of Browning, while Hollander has tended to favor syllabics or else a highly enjambed accentual verse. Such a list might go on: The point is that poets who had their beginning in Auden, and whose early work can often be mistaken for Auden's, have by whatever route found a resting place in the native tradition.

Our emphasis ought to fall on a Wordsworthian-Whitmanian *subjectivity* that is just and inevitable. Against this stands the mode of confessional verse, a matrix that has produced W.D. Snodgrass, Sylvia Plath, Anne Sexton, and many other figures. Confessional poetry owes its genesis to Lowell, whose earliest writing looked like a late metaphysical pastiche for which his only precursors might be Edward Taylor and Allen Tate. In *Life Studies,* Lowell opened himself to the type of free verse pioneered by Williams, while using the form, as Williams had not done, to write his own life's story by way of the strictly clinical facts. In later works, Lowell has put the same subject, himself, under a still more minute examination, reverting to the format of a diary and adopting the form of a fourteen-line entry written in flat pentameter. He is certainly the poet central to this movement, or tendency, in American poetry, and, though he has been a less imposing as well as a less domineering presence, he seems to be the logical successor to Eliot in the poetry of belief or anxious unbelief, which ranges itself against the poetry of vision. Although the issue of form is as always bogus, the larger opposition here will probably be lasting.

Critics have ordinarily associated Lowell in this phase with the later work of Berryman, which belongs more appropriately to a consideration of Pound's influence. Berryman's *Dream Songs* have much of the terseness that Pound asked to be communicated from the tone of a poem to its prosody, and their way of setting an expressionistic personal stance over against imagistic hardness was also anticipated by Pound. It is only in his last and less individually realized songs that Berryman approaches Lowell.

Iris Murdoch has observed that imagism itself was never more than a fantastically stripped-down version of late romanticism: Personality was being reduced to its smallest points of perception without ever being expunged, so that a large claim for the self was at all events implicitly maintained. There was never any "extinction of personality," in Eliot's phrase. Pound recognized this when he embarked on his own private quest poem, the enormous and deliberately uncompleted *Cantos*, and his followers have taken roughly the same path. The Black Mountain School, including primarily Olson, Duncan, and Robert Creeley, can be counted among his most faithful. Olson's own epic was composed largely in Poundian cadences, though he professed to write according to a different rationale. Thus, projective verse is the name given to his exhortation to future bards to write by "field"—that is, using all the resources of a typewriter to complicate what the eye sees on the written page—and at the same time to plan their metric according to breath—that is, with a respect for the full and varied possibilities of exhalation helped by the human voice. Olson felt that he was licensed in principle as in practice by the metric of Shakespeare's later plays.

As all the manifestos show, there is an obscure but profound spiritual kinship that binds together Williams, Pound, Olson, and a much younger poet, Allen Ginsberg. The self-discoveries of Ginsberg, Gregory Corso, Lawrence Ferlinghetti, William Everson, and a host of lesser eminences, who were first heard from in the mid-1950s, are occasionally referred to as making a San Francisco Renaissance. The advent of the Beat Poets and the writing

Duncan issued out of San Francisco may be set under the rubric of this event. Since the Beat Poets were noisiest in being reborn, have stayed active through their connection with Ferlinghetti's publishing enterprise, and compose the largest subset of this group, they have a special claim on our attention. In one sense, these poets are Whitman's authentic heirs: They have his expansiveness, his belief in the democracy of the spirit, his sexual frankness, and they sing of the open road. But the myth has become a mystique in their hands, which merely to invoke is apparently to justify. In much of Ginsberg's work during the late 1950s and early 1960s, the elliptical image-making faculty of Williams has also been brought to bear, and it is to be noted that Williams associated himself with this poet's Whitmanian incarnation at its most aggressive pitch. At least one current in Williams's own poetry, however, ran directly contrary to Whitman, for Williams tended to freeze any given image in order to isolate it for contemplation, rather than immersing its solitariness in some wider flow of reverie. This is where the style of a poet and the deepest facts of his or her personality intersect, and on this point of style a disciple far truer to Williams than any of the "Howl"-Whitmanians has been Denise Levertov.

Williams's habit of regarding a poem as "observations," enlivened by the colloquial diction of Pound, helped to encourage Marianne Moore in one generation and Elizabeth Bishop in the next. An ingratiating element in both of these poets is that they seem to claim nothing for their role or for their craft. The type of syllabic verse invented by Moore makes the prose of life concede very little to the poetry and sets nervousness very high among the faculties that aid perception. Similar qualities, though with a certain loosening as to form and a less jagged conception of what a poem ought to be, are notable throughout Bishop's work. The "mad exactness" that has often been remarked in her poetry is itself an exacting discipline and may eventually be viewed as a corrective reaction against the thaumaturgical excesses of the modern tradition.

Another kind of reaction against modernism accounts for the group of New York poets in which Frank O'Hara, Kenneth Koch, James Schuyler, and Ashbery figure as significant names. The opéra bouffe of American silent films as well as a native surrealism is at work in the writing of this school: O'Hara's *Second Avenue* can be considered an exemplum of the new mode thereby brought into being, which might be described as comic phantasmagoria. Such a poetics is in the last degree an urban phenomenon and will be found irrevocably at odds with the school of pre-Wordsworthian, or indeed as it likes to be thought—prehistorical clarity that we connect with the names of James Wright and Robert Bly.

Sooner or later, as has been noted, the proliferation of schools and methods must be understood as an impediment, not an aid, to appreciation. There are two innovations that have some importance: first, the definitive sloughing off of the Georgian diction by Pound, Frost, and a few others. That the advance took place at a certain time and place has come to seem a truism, yet it holds within it an essential truth. There is also, a bit later, Williams's reassertion in free verse of the full range of ambiguity made possible by enjambment, when, as John Hollander has indicated, the rhetorical flexibility of that particular feature of English poetry had been allowed to lapse after Milton in the poetry of the late romantics and the Victorians. But, once we have taken these into account, the arguments within and between self-proclaiming schools are at best misleading. In the strongest and most characteristic poetry of the late 1960s and early 1970s, a transcendental synthesis of the various native strains seems to be developing, and what is emerging is clearly an expressionistic and severe version of American romanticism. At any rate, that is our safest generalization as we trace the continuity of individual careers. Thus Simpson, who was once allied with Bly and the Midwest clarifiers, appears in his liveliest work to have been relatively free of their defining impulse. Ashbery, sometimes categorized quite simply as one of the New York poets, instead moves together with Schuyler in an enormous ambience that includes the otherwise very diverse Merrill, Wright, Hecht, Ammons, Merwin, Hollander, Alvin Feinman, Kinnell, Strand, and many others, who are visionary, as Emerson prophesied they must be. The *stance* of all these poets makes impossible an expression in either closed- or open-phrased fields, and each has been compelled, in order to escape the fall into the confessional, to perform a deliberate curtailment of the revisionary impulse toward an endlessly journalistic scrutiny of himself, while simultaneously asking the fact for the form.

For what, finally, can poetic form mean to an American? Every American poet who aspires to strength knows that he or she starts in the evening land, realizes he or she is a latecomer, fears to be only a secondary person.

> Solitary,
> Patient for the last voices of the dusk to die down, and the dusk
> To die down, listener waiting for courteous rivers
> To rise and be known

> ... but in the large view, no
> lines or changeless shapes: the working in and out, together
>   and against, of millions of events: this,
>   so that I make
>   no form of
>   formlessness

Suspended somewhere in summer between the ceremonies
Remembered from childhood and the historical conflagrations
Imagined in sad, learned youth—somewhere there always hangs
The American moment.
                              Burning, restless, between the deed
And the dream is the life remembered

In new rocks new insects are sitting

With the lights off
And once more I remember that the beginning

Is broken

No wonder the addresses are torn

Glad of the changes already and if there are more it will never be
    you that minds
Since it will not be you to be changed, but in the evening in the
    severe lamplight doubts come
From many scattered distances, and do not come too near.
As it falls along the house, your treasure
Cries to the other men; the darkness will have none of you, and
    you are folded into it like mint into the sound of haying.

These are five representative poets of their generation (James Wright,
A.R. Ammons, John Hollander, W.S. Merwin, and John Ashbery, respectively); the excerpts have been taken at random from an anthology. Every
passage, whether in tone, in cognitive aim, or in human stance, shows the
same anxiety: to ask the fact for the form, while being fearful that the fact
no longer has a form. This is what Geoffrey Hartman has called "the anxiety
of demand": that which can be used can be used up. The generation of poets
who stand together now, mature and ready to write the major American verse
of the twenty-first century, may yet be seen as what Stevens called "a great
shadow's last embellishment," the shadow being Emerson's.

MARJORIE PERLOFF

Apocalypse Then:
Merwin and the Sorrows of Literary History

Merwin's sixth book of poems, *The Lice*, appeared in 1967 at the height of the war in Vietnam. Reviewing the book for the *Yale Review*, Laurence Lieberman declared:

> If there is any book today that has perfectly captured the peculiar spiritual agony of our time, the agony of a generation which knows itself to be the last, and has transformed that agony into great art, it is W. S. Merwin's *The Lice*. To read these poems is an act of self-purification. Every poem in the book pronounces a judgment against modern man—the gravest sentence the poetic imagination can conceive for man's withered and wasted conscience: our sweep of history adds up to one thing only, a moral vacuity that is absolute and irrevocable. This book is a testament of betrayals; we have betrayed all beings that had power to save us: the forests, the animals, the gods, the dead, the spirit in us, the words. Now, in our last moments alive, they return to haunt us.[1]

Extreme claims, these, especially now that a younger generation is proclaiming that it is the last, even as its poets are writing in a "cool" mode, very different from Merwin's.[2] The apocalyptic consciousness of the six-

From *W. S. Merwin: Essays on the Poetry*, edited by Cary Nelson and Ed Folsom, pp. 122–44.

9

ties had no use for the lessons of history: to write, as Merwin presumably did, about what Altieri calls "the other side of despair," to "make loss itself the ground for numinous awareness that might suffice for the attentive imagination"[3]—this, it was assumed, was to write "the New Poetry" or "Poetry in Open Forms" or "Postmodern Poetry"—a radical poetry that questions the assumptions of modernism. Thus Merwin holds a place of honor in Stephen Berg and Robert Mezey's 1969 anthology, *Naked Poetry*, an anthology that grew out of "the firm conviction that the strongest and most alive poetry in America had abandoned or at least broken the grip of traditional meters and had set out, once again, into 'the wilderness of unopened life.'"[4] In his own statement "On Open Form" for *Naked Poetry*, Merwin himself insisted: "I am a formalist, in the most strict and ortho-dox sense," but that statement could be—and was—safely ignored, for on the same page the poet remarked: "In an age when time and technique encroach hourly . . . on the source itself of poetry, it seems as though what is needed for any particular nebulous unwritten hope that may become a poem is not a manipulable, more or less predictably recurring pattern, but an unduplicatable resonance, something that would be like an echo except that it is repeating no sound" (p. 271).

I find the logic of this statement puzzling: why is ours, more than any other period in history, "an age when time and technique encroach hourly on the source itself of poetry"? And in what sense can any good poem in the late twentieth century have an "unduplicatable resonance"? Never mind: Merwin's "echo . . . repeating no sound" became, for "the generation which knows itself to be the last," a kind of *nouveau frisson*. Reviewing *The Carrier of Ladders* (1970), Richard Howard, whose *Alone with America* devotes more space to Merwin than to any of its other forty poets, declared that "the real goal of these poems . . . [is] a quality of life which used to be called visionary, and which must be characterized by its negatives, by what it is not, for what it is cannot be spoken."[5] And in what is a very different study, Paul Carroll's *Poem in Its Skin* (1968), a book that submits to close reading ten new poems by "the generation of 1962," a generation to which Carroll refers as "Bar-barians inside the City Gates," and which includes Allen Ginsberg, Frank O'Hara, Robert Creeley, and John Ashbery, Merwin was called "the prince of the new poets": "In many of his most recent lyrics, one feels as if taken into a country where all is poetry—pristine, totally natural, miracles everywhere. Listen to this brief poem called 'Dead Hand': Temptations still nest in it like basilisks. / Hang it up till the rings fall."[6]

Merwin as New Visionary—this view was codified by Karl Malkoff in his *Crowell's Handbook of Contemporary American Poetry* (1973). Again, Mer-win gets more space than any other poet of his generation (the only two poets who receive more than Merwin are Lowell and Roethke) and is called "the representative poet of his time, having gone through a process that is not only common to many of his contemporaries, but a microcosm of the history of modern verse as well."[7] That history, as Malkoff sees it, is the movement "from the formal to the free, from the traditional to the innovative." The poems of *A Mask for Janus* (1952) are "monuments to orderly vision," but by the time he wrote the final section of *The Drunk in the Furnace* (1960), with its more realistic family poems, somewhat in the vein of Lowell, Merwin had emerged "as a practitioner of open form": "the syntax is frequently fragmented, the language is less precious, less archaic, and much tougher" (p. 213). The "new spareness" of the sixties poems, a "language . . . simple but capable of bearing much weight" (p. 215), paradoxically brings Merwin back to the beginnings of his career: "It is as if he had not developed his style by metamorphosis, but rather by a stripping down, so that what we have now in the later poems are the bare elements of his earliest verse reduced to their essential forms" (p. 216). A similar case was made by Cary Nelson in a challenging essay called "The Resources of Failure: W. S. Merwin's Deconstructive Career" (1977): "[Merwin's] recent work offers us what remained after he rigorously pruned the excesses of his first poems and then turned what was left back on itself. The result has been a poetry of extraordinary force, a poetry that inherits the despair of the century but gives it a prophetic new form, a form that ruthlessly deconstructs its own accomplishments."[8]

But even as Merwin's "prophetic new form" was being hailed by the critics, dissenting voices were beginning to question it: Nelson himself, for that matter, remarks that "Merwin's desolate landscapes are pervaded with a sense of uneasy expectation. The apocalypse in our past survives only as a kind of vague dread, as if it were only about to occur" (p. 104). The same point was made more emphatically by Harold Bloom in a 1973 essay called "The New Transcendentalism: The Visionary Strain in Merwin, Ashbery, and Ammons." Like Malkoff, Carroll, and Howard, Bloom calls Merwin "the indubitably representative poet of my generation," but although he admires Merwin's attempt to make himself into "an American visionary poet," he concludes that "Merwin's predicament . . . is that he has no Transcendental vision, and yet feels impelled to prophesy":

The poignance of his current phase is the constant attempt at self-reliance, in the conviction that only thus will the poet *see*. Merwin's true precursors are three honorable, civilized representative poets: Longfellow and MacLeish and Wilbur, none of whom attempted to speak a Word that was his own Word only. In another time, Merwin would have gone on with the cultivation of a more continuous idiom, as he did in his early volumes, and as Longfellow did even in the Age of Emerson. The pressures of the quasi-apocalyptic nineteen-sixties have made of Merwin an American Orphic bard despite the sorrow that his poetic temperament is not at home in suffering the Native Strain. No poet legitimately speaks a Word whose burden is that his generation will be the very last. Merwin's litanies of denudation will read very oddly when a fresh generation proclaims nearly the same dilemma, and then yet another generation trumpets finality.[9]

One may want to quarrel with Bloom's list of legitimate precursors, but his prediction that the poet's "litanies of denudation" will read oddly to the next generation has already come true: indeed, the very same year that Bloom published his essay, two young poet-critics, both political activists, submitted the premises of poems like "The Asians Dying" to severe questioning. In an essay called "Language against Itself: The Middle Generation of Contemporary Poets," Alan Williamson argued that poets like Merwin, Galway Kinnell, James Wright, and Gary Snyder had turned the search for poetic vision into a kind of "ecological survival technique."[10] As "the first generation to confront concentration camps and the atomic bomb, the fully revealed destructiveness of civilized man, while still in the process of growing up," this generation of poets, so Williamson argues, turned inward, concentrating on "the lessons to be learned from animals, Indians, primitive or peasant cultures, the wilderness as well as simple Wordsworthian solitary works; and thus a whole new repertory of characteristic subjects is created" (pp. 56–57). Merwin and Kinnell, Bly and Wright have a "shared penchant for putting the 'I' in the simplest of possible sentence structures, pronoun/active or linking verb, with no modifiers before or between. The 'I' becomes numb, neutral, universal: a transparency through which we look directly to the state of being or feeling" (p. 58). Indeed, Merwin, by Williamson's account, denies his natural sensibility which is ethereal rather than "concrete or earthly," forcing his poetry to "develop toward the same tactics as his contemporaries' (the simple, quasi-narrative sentence, the isolated word, the numb 'I'), toward the same loyalties, political and symbolic, and above all, toward the same stress on the inadequacy of language" (p. 65). And Williamson quotes three lines from "The Gods" (*L*, 30)

My blind neighbor has required of me
A description of darkness
And I begin I begin but. . . .

James Atlas's essay, published in the same collection, is called "Diminishing Returns: The Writings of W. S. Merwin." Like Williamson, Atlas objects to the poet's "disembodied voice, addressing some unknown Other," to his excessive use of animism (e.g., "the horizon / Climbs down from its tree") which imbues the poems with "Surrealist confusion" (p. 76). What Lieberman calls "a testament of betrayals" is considered by Atlas to be a curious withdrawal from the meaning of political experience. For although Merwin may follow writers like Barthes in believing that only a language of disruption can measure our current history, he "still resists the real significance of what he practices; the disruption of language is no more than a device in *The Lice* (1967) and *The Carrier of Ladders* (1970). Monotonous, interminable, self-imitative, each poem exudes unbearable exhaustion; none supports a close analysis" (p. 78). And Atlas submits "The Night of the Shirts" to some basic questions ("Where is 'here'?" "What is 'it'?" "What is 'the same story'?"), concluding that "excessive transmutation of our 'modern dilemmas' has caused us to misinterpret them; what there should be more of at this time are critiques, poems that situate us in the world, or elaborate on real conditions" (p. 79).

Ironically, then, the very qualities in the poetry that were singled out for praise during what Bloom calls the "quasi-apocalyptic" sixties, have been cited by certain articulate poet-critics, who came of age in just this period, as its defects. For Howard, Merwin's poetry embodies a quality "which used to be called visionary, and which must be characterized by its negatives, by what it is not, for what it is cannot be spoken." To which the student of Wittgenstein might retort: "Whereof one cannot speak, thereof one must be silent." A compelling case against Merwin's rhetoric—or, more accurately, against the rhetoric of "mysterious, bardic hush" as it appears in the poetry of Bly and Wright as well as that of Merwin, has been made by Robert Pinsky in *The Situation of Poetry* (1977). Here is Pinsky on "Whenever I Go There" from *The Lice*:

Whenever I go there everything is changed

The stamps on the bandages the titles
Of the professors of water

The portrait of Glare the reasons for
The white mourning

In new rocks new insects are sitting

With the lights off
And once more I remember that the beginning

Is broken

No wonder the addresses are torn

To which I make my way eating the silence of animals
Offering snow to the darkness

Today belongs to few and tomorrow to no one.
  (*L*, 24)

It is possible to think the way this poem proceeds—elliptical,
allusive, dark, introspective, abrupt, intimate—as a "contemporary"
mode distinct from ... more traditional method[s].... For that
reason, some explicit exposition ... may be helpful. "There"
seems to be an internal place and a region of the mind which the
poet chooses repeatedly to visit; knowledge of that place seems
necessary to his imaginative life. But "habit" or expectation is
useless in this place which never repeats itself. If "there" is the
starting place for one's poems, or most valued perceptions, it is
an absolute starting place: remembered categories and labels, if
not quite discarded, must be subjected to new learning.... To
put it more simply, each time the poet meditates upon—say—the
fact that in some cultures mourners wear white, his sense of the
reasons must be new.

  The life there is hidden in a nearly impenetrable darkness,
and the effort even to describe it is awkward, somewhat farcical,
cruelly exposed.[11]

The voice that here, and in related poems, refuses the limitations of the
conscious mind is characterized by Laurence Lieberman as one that "filters
up to the reader like echoes from a very deep well, and yet ... strikes his ear
with a raw energy—a sustained inner urgency" (p. 260). Richard Howard
similarly observes that "All the poems [in *The Lice*] appear to be written from
one and the same place where the poet has holed up, observant but withdrawn, compassionate but hopeless, isolated yet the more concerned ... by
the events of a public world" (pp. 441–42). Pinsky is more skeptical: "Whenever I Go There," he suggests, may well be *about* difficulty, about the need to
renounce habits and expectations, but Merwin's "elliptically 'beautiful' phrases

fall with a stylistic ease which we do not question even while we are questioning whether those phrases mean anything":

> ... in a sense this poem embodies an extreme Romanticism: a pursuit of darkness, of silence, of the soul moving in ways so unlike abstract thought that it burrows into or 'eats' its immobile paradise. On the other hand, the Romanticism is qualified by the form of the last line

> Today belongs to few and tomorrow to no one

> which, despite the absence of end punctuation, is a summarizing abstract formula. You could nearly call it a moral ... in fact the action of this poem, as with most of [Merwin's] best poems, is to create a generic experience. (pp. 93–94)

Which is to say that the poem "moves in a resolutely elliptical way from image to atomistic image, finally reaching a kind of generalization-against-generalizing" (p. 164).

Cautiously stated as this is, Pinsky's charge is serious: he is saying that Merwin's rhetoric of vision is contradicted by a curiously non-visionary penchant for summarizing moral statement, for the formulated abstract truth. Such questioning of the Merwinian mode is not an isolated case. A decade after Paul Carroll referred to Merwin as the "prince of poets," the British poet Andrew Waterman, reviewing *The Compass Flower* (1977) for the *Times Literary Supplement*, wrote, "Merwin ... whose poetry has been admired in America for twenty-five years, offers a depressing case of extreme regression. ... Merwin's is simply banal and devitalized writing ... [its] enervation of language, sick-lily ingenuous tone, and sentimentality are all self-consciously perpetrated."[12] If this dismissal sounds unduly harsh—and of course it is—we should remember that a critic as different in outlook from Pinsky and Waterman as Harold Bloom, who has declared himself to be "not unsympathetic to [Merwin's] work" (p. 128), concludes his discussion of the poetry with the statement, "Merwin seems condemned to write a poetry that is as bare of true content as it is so elegantly bare in diction and design" (p. 129).

It seems, then, that what was regarded a short decade ago as the epitome of "Naked Poetry," as "an Eliotic process of negative mysticism as the way to achieve a 'Poverty' beyond even love,"[13] now looks, to many readers, suspiciously like the Poetic Diction that the "naked poets" were supposedly repudiating. How this process came about, how one generation's "prince of poets" could become, in the words of Turner Cassity, "a very talented practitioner in a very tired tradition,"[14] is my subject.

II

Throughout the sixties and well into the early seventies, the debate between modernism and postmodernism in poetry (or "closed" versus "open" poetry, or poetry as "product" versus poetry as "process") revolved around two questions: the question of verse form ("fixed" versus "free") and the question of "transcendence" versus "immanence" or "presence." Thus, when in the last section of *The Drunk in the Furnace* (1960) Merwin turned from the traditional meters and stanzas of his first three books to the flexible blank verse of the final, more personal section, James Dickey hailed the change with the announcement that "With tools like these ["an odd kind of roughed-up, clunking diction and meter"] and with the discoveries about himself that this book shows him intent on making, Merwin should soar like a phoenix out of the neat ashes of his early work."[15] And soar like a phoenix Merwin did: by the time he published *The Moving Target* (1963), whose poems are written in short, abrupt free-verse units, critics like Richard Howard could speak of "an entirely different mastery of style." "On the page," said Howard, "the generally unpunctuated poems look as though they had been exploded, not written down, the images arranged so that the lines never enclose but instead *expose* them" (p. 436). And in their introduction to *Naked Poetry*, Stephen Berg and Robert Mezey take it as a given that to break "the grip of traditional meters" is to "set out . . . into 'the wilderness of unopened life'" (p. xi). By such an account, Merwin, who had renounced the villanelle and sestina, the rondel and ballad stanza of his first books for the hushed and impassioned free verse of *The Moving Target*, could be nothing less than a creator of the New.

Two things were safely ignored at the time. First, Merwin's free verse, which may have seemed enormously innovative when read against the background of the formalism of the fifties—the mode, say, of Richard Wilbur or Allen Tate or Howard Nemerov—was nowhere as explosive as the free verse Pound and Williams were writing by 1916, a free-verse model carried on by Zukofsky and Oppen in the thirties, and by Olson into the late forties and early fifties. Second, it should have struck the critics as slightly odd that a poetry so seemingly explosive—the poetry of "the wilderness of unopened life"—was routinely published in the *New Yorker*, *Poetry*, the *Hudson Review*, and *Harper's*—hardly the organs of the avant-garde. *The Moving Target* has gone through eight printings between 1963 and 1979; *The Lice*, eleven printings between 1967 and 1981. Eleven of the sixty-three poems in *The Lice* first appeared in the *New Yorker* and eighteen in *Poetry*. In the case of Merwin's subsequent volumes, this ratio has increased: in *The Compass Flower* (1977), eighteen out of sixty-one poems—almost one-third—were published in the *New Yorker*. How is it that readers of the *New Yorker*, coming across a poem like "The Asians Dying" on a glossy page between those gorgeous ads for fur coats and diamonds and resorts in St. Croix, were not put off by the newness of lines like

When the forests have been destroyed their darkness remains
The ash the great walker follows the possessors
Forever,
(*L*, 63)

by their evident strangeness?

This is a question to which I shall return, but for the moment let me consider the more difficult question of Merwin's poetics of immanence. It has been argued, most notably by Charles Altieri in his important book *Enlarging the Temple*, that whereas the great modernists—Yeats, Eliot, Stevens—adopt the Coleridgean "commitment to the creative, form-giving imagination and its power to affect society, or at least personal needs for meaning, by constructing coherent, fully human forms out of the flux of experience," postmodern poets follow Wordsworth in developing "an essentially immanentist vision of the role of poetry": "Here poetic creation is conceived more as the discovery and the disclosure of numinous relationships within nature than as the creation of containing and structuring forms. Hence its basic commitment is to recovering familiar realities in such a way that they appear dynamically present and invigorate the mind with a sense of powers and objective values available to it" (p. 17). And again, "In the symbolist aesthetic, especially in the enervated forms of it practiced in the 1950s, the central focus is on the mind's powers to balance opposites and to take up a perspective from which the mind can judge and interpret what it presents. In the aesthetics of presence, on the other hand, poems do not present direct experience but the direct aesthetic illusion of direct experience that depends on style and form as means of seeing the word freshly" (p. 24). And Altieri quotes Robert Duncan's essay, "Towards an Open Universe": "Central to and defining the poetics I am trying to suggest here is the conviction that the order man may contrive or impose upon the things about him or upon his own language is trivial beside the divine order or natural order he may discover in them."[16]

Where does Merwin fit into this scheme? If a postmodern poet like Duncan can discover "natural order" in the "things about him," Merwin, so Altieri argues, is one of his "fallen counterparts" in that "at the very moment of intense awareness of presence there is produced a terrifying self-consciousness of all that cannot be made present or numinously 'here'" (p. 19). This very sense of emptiness or "absence" now becomes "the source of more complex and satisfying modes of inhabiting the other side of despair, however bleak that territory might be. . . . Merwin makes loss itself the ground for numinous awareness that might suffice for the attentive imagination."

It is this sense of loss that accounts for Merwin's penchant for abstract language and surreal image. Altieri says, "The illusory present is more insubstantial than the darkness or painful sense of absence it replaces. Moreover, the language one uses to fix those particulars, or even to comfort oneself by lamenting their passing, eventually mocks one with its inadequacies and its absences" (p. 194). Or, as Cary Nelson puts it, "The challenge Merwin sets himself in his best work . . . is to become the anonymous figure who announces the harmonizing dissolution of the language" (p. 79). Such recurrent words as "silence," "emptiness," and "distance," already present in Merwin's earliest poems, are undercut in the later work, in which language is turned back on itself so as to measure "the loss of any real historical possibility" (p. 90). Indeed, Merwin's "formal self-subversions" mirror our own; they draw out the "inadequacies . . . of the language we share" (p. 92).

My difficulty with these readings is that the sense of loss, of absence, of "the harmonizing dissolution of the language," so interestingly discussed by Altieri and Nelson, seems to me to be asserted rather than explored. Unlike Beckett, to whom he has frequently been compared,[17] Merwin rarely invents a fictional situation in which emptiness, darkness, the failure of the language to mirror "reality" are actually *experienced* by someone. It is time to look at a concrete example.

FOR THE ANNIVERSARY OF MY DEATH

Every year without knowing it I have passed the day
When the last fires will wave to me
And the silence will set out
Tireless traveller
Like the beam of a lightless star

Then I will no longer
Find myself in life as in a strange garment
Surprised at the earth
And the love of one woman
And the shamelessness of men
As today writing after three days of rain
Hearing the wren sing and the falling cease
And bowing not knowing to what
    (*L*, 58)

Karl Malkoff, who calls this "one of the most striking poems in the collection [*The Lice*]," provides an analysis which is worth pondering:

> The central idea of the poem is simple: each year contains the date
> on which the poet will finally die, each year he unknowingly passes
> the anniversary of his death. But the implications of this premise
> are complex. They involve nothing less than the total breakdown
> of conventional modes of apprehending time. Viewing time *sub
> specie aeternitatis* . . . Merwin labels the linear sense of time—that
> is, time as inexorable, unfolding, continual movement—as illusory.
> The "beam of a lightless star" is in one sense a metaphor of
> Merwin's own language of silence, the silence of death, the silence
> of meaninglessness. A beam emanating from a lightless star also
> suggests that from a sufficiently detached perspective, a dead star
> can appear still alive. . . . This is a fine symbol of the poet's eternal
> longings. And it is a fine symbol of time as relative in a world of
> absolute being.
>
> Merwin perceives that his death has already taken place in
> precisely the sense that the present exists eternally. The temporal
> distinction is false. In the second stanza, however, he sets up new
> distinctions to replace the old. He will no longer "Find myself
> in life as in a strange garment." He will lose his divisive percep-
> tions that isolate him from the rest of being. Merwin's response
> is characteristically ambivalent. He will no longer be "surprised
> at the earth / And the love of one woman." The uncomfortable
> world of time and change is also the realm of specifically human
> satisfactions. It is finally to this human universe that Merwin
> must return. (pp. 214–15)

I have cited this reading at such length because it strikes me as wholly
typical of what we might call a sixties reading of sixties poetry. What Malkoff goes on to call "the hallmark of Merwin's 'new style'" is that his images
consist "not of detailed description, but rather of actions and essential types."
Indeed, the types become "almost allegorical. . . . But like all modern allegory,
it is not supported by an ordered universe; it is grounded in nothingness"
(p. 215). Here Malkoff unwittingly contradicts his own reading of the text,
for what he has just shown, painstakingly and convincingly, is that Merwin's
allegory, far from being "grounded in nothingness," is grounded in the familiar paradox that time is at once linear and eternal. "Viewing time *sub specie
aeternitatis*," the linear view is illusory, as the symbolic "beam" of the lightless

star, shining millions of miles from its dead source, suggests. On the other hand, to lose one's linear sense of time is, as the poet says in the second stanza, to lose one's humanity, one's ability to be "surprised at the earth / And the love of one woman." A paradox as neat as any Cleanth Brooks discovered in Wordsworth's "It Is a Beauteous Evening" or Yeats's "Among School Children." Yeats, for that matter, had pondered a similar time/eternity paradox as early as "The Stolen Child."

How, then, is the poem different from the late modernist lyric of the fifties, including Merwin's own early work? For one thing, the "I" is not a persona but quite simply the poet himself—here is a point of departure that seemed much more striking to readers of the sixties than it does to us today. For another, the imagery does not have the texture of W. K. Wimsatt's "concrete universal," of the metaphysical conceit dear to the New Critics. Merwin's language is "simple," if by simple we mean familiar: everyone knows what "day" means, or "fire" or "silence" or "traveller" or "three days of rain." It is also curiously abstract: most of the generic nouns are preceded by an article but not by an adjectival modifier: "the day," "the silence," "the earth," "the beam," "the love," "the shamelessness." In the rare cases when the noun does have a modifier, the adjective works to increase the sense of abstraction—"the tireless traveller," "strange garment," "last fires," "lightless star." Accordingly, the landscape of the poem seems to be mysterious; it has repeatedly been called "dreamlike" or "surreal," even though both these terms are probably misnomers: in a dream, one doesn't think in terms of "Every year" or "Then I will no longer / Find myself" or "today writing after three days of rain"; and "surreal" refers, not to something vaguely mysterious and blurred, but to a landscape, whether in the verbal or the visual arts, in which objects, people, actions, or situations that cannot conceivably coexist in the "real world" are brought together, as in Magritte's painting *Collective Invention* (in which a fish with the lower torso and legs of a woman—a sort of reverse mermaid—is seen lying on a naturalistically painted beach beside the ocean).

But whatever term we use to describe Merwin's images, it is true that they are unlike, say, John Crowe Ransom's metaphors in "The Equilibrists." If "Lemuel's Blessing" is, as Paul Carroll argues, again a poem built around a single paradox ("one who is an archetype of civilized tribal values petitions in a traditionally communal form of prayer that he be allowed to exist outside of civilized communal values . . . and come to share as deeply as possible the nature and characteristics of the wolf" pp. 146–47), that paradox is nevertheless framed differently from Ransom's, an allegorical mode having replaced the symbolist mode of the moderns. This difference aside, Merwin's poetry carried on the tradition of the well-made poem of the fifties. For what distinguishes a poem like "For the Anniversary of My Death" from the "undecidable" texts of a Beckett on the one hand, as from its modernist predecessors on the other, is the marked authorial control that runs counter to the lip-service paid to "bowing not knowing to what." Far from being a poem of *dis-covery*, a text whose "echo repeats no sound," "For the Anniversary of My Death" is characterized by a strong sense of closure.

Consider, for example, the stanzaic division. The first stanza (five lines) describes what happens "Every year"; the second (eight lines) refers to "Then" (when I will be dead). The first concentrates on the silence of eternity, beyond "the last fires," the eternity symbolized by the beam of the lightless star. The second recalls, even as does the final stanza of Yeats's "The Stolen Child," what will be lost when death ends the inexorable forward movement of time, when the "strange garment" of life is shed: namely, the love of one woman, the shamelessness of men, the singing of the wren, the falling of rain, and, yes, the "bowing not knowing to what," which is to say, "bowing" to the premonition of death one has in moments of transition, as when a three-day rain comes to an end.

Does the language "mock the poet with its absences"? Not really, or at least its mockery seems to take place only on the surface. The first line quickly gives the game away: since there is obviously no way to know on what day of the year one will die, the phrase "without knowing it" strikes a rather self-important note. This is the language, not of dream or of mysterious Otherness, but of calculation: the setting up of a hypothetical situation that brings the time/eternity paradox into sharp relief. Again, the reference to "death" as the moment when "the last fires will wave to me" seems to me the very opposite of "spare" (a word regularly applied to Merwin's poetry by his admirers); it is a gestural, a decorative metaphor reminiscent of Dylan Thomas rather than René Char.[18] Indeed, lines 2–5, with their heavy alliteration and assonance, their repetition and slow, stately movement, have the authentic Thomas ring:

> When the last fires will wave to me
> And the silence will set out
> Tireless traveller
> Like the beam of a lightless star

The language of the second stanza is increasingly abstract, conceptual, formulaic, recalling, as Bloom points out, the conservative rhetoric of poets like Longfellow or MacLeish. To call life "a strange garment," to define one's humanity in terms of "the love of one woman" and the need to wrestle with "the shamelessness of men"—such locutions have the accent of the Sunday sermon rather than the surrealist lyric. Given this context, the "bowing not knowing to what" in the unpunctuated last line is a predictable closural device: it points us back to the title with its recognition that one of the days now lived through will, one year, be the day of the poet's death.

The poem's closure is reflected in its formal verse structure. Merwin's heavily end-stopped lines, each followed by a brief rest or hush, are lightly stressed, anapests predominating as in

> Like the beam of a lightless star

or

> And bowing not knowing to what

but in many lines the pattern is complicated by an initial trochee:

> Évery yéar without knówing it
> Tíreless tráveller
> Héaring the wrén síng.

Syntactic parallelism—"And the silence will set out," "And the love of one woman," "And the shamelessness of men"—provides a further ordering principle. And although the stress count ranges between two and five (and syllable count between five and thirteen), the lines are organized tightly by qualitative sound repetition: Merwin's patterning is extremely intricate, as in the alliteration of *t*'s, *r*'s, and *l*'s in "<u>T</u>i<u>rel</u>ess <u>tr</u>ave<u>ll</u>er," the assonance and consonance in "<u>F</u>i<u>nd</u> my<u>self</u> in <u>l</u>i<u>f</u>e," and the internal eye rhyme in "And b<u>owing</u> not k<u>nowing</u> to what."

"For the Anniversary of My Death" is thus a very elegant, well-made poem; it has a finish that would be the envy of any number of poets, and its theme is certainly universal—just mysterious enough to arrest the reader's attention, yet just natural enough (this is the way we all feel about death sometimes) to have broad appeal. It is, I think, this blend of strangeness and a clear-sighted literalness that makes a poem like "The Asians Dying" memorable. Consider the lines

> Rain falls into the open eyes of the dead
> Again again with its pointless sound
> When the moon finds them they are the color of everything
>   (*L*, 63)

We don't usually think of rain falling precisely into open eyes, let alone "the open eyes of the dead." The image is an odd one and yet the third line has a kind of photographic accuracy: in the moonlight, the dead bodies, clothed in khaki, would indeed blend with the colors of the forest ground, and so theirs is "the color of everything." Add to this the irony—a rather heavy-handed irony, I think—of Merwin's implication that, in our world, the color of death has become "everything," and you have an intricate enough layering of meanings, which is not to say that Merwin's construction is in any way radical or subversive. Indeed, I submit that nothing in "The Asians Dying" has the startling modernity of

> I was neither at the hot gates
> Nor fought in the warm rain
> Nor knee deep in the salt marsh, heaving a cutlass,
> Bitten by flies, fought.

Cary Nelson has rightly noted Merwin's debt to Eliot (p. 119), but it is a good question whether "Gerontion" doesn't capture what Lieberman calls "the peculiar spiritual agony of our time" at least as well as do poems like "The Asians Dying."

In Merwin's poems of the early seventies, fragmentation of syntax, abstraction, and ellipsis become, as the critics have noted, more marked; these are "difficult" poems in that their nouns are generic and that their spatial and temporal adverbs usually have ambiguous referents. Of *The Carrier of Ladders*, Richard Howard writes: "They are intimate poems, but not in the least personal—there are no persons here, nor even personifications. There are presences, and they support processes which afford the speaking voice an access to prophecy, by which I mean the capacity not to predict the future but rather to release the present: *'key / unlocking the presence / of the unlighted river / under the mountains.'* For Merwin, for the poet who is the one voice raised in Merwin's book, anyone or anything can be the 'key'—another person, his own body, an event, a landscape—the key to darkness, to unconditional life" (p. 444). Let us see how this "unconditional life" is released in "Beginning of the Plains":

> On city bridges steep as hills I change countries
> and this according to the promise
> is the way home
>
> where the cold has come from
> with its secret baggage

in the white sky the light flickering
like the flight of a wing

nothing to be bought in the last
dim shops

before the plain begins
few shelves kept only by children
and relatives there for the holiday
who know nothing

wind without flags
marching into the city
to the rear

I recognize the first hunger
as the plains start
under my feet
   (*CL*, 80)

"Beginning of the Plains" is the sort of Merwin poem often called Kaf-kaesque:[19] in a nightmare vision, the poet must climb city bridges "as steep as hills," must "change countries" in a journey that will paradoxically bring him "home," a home dreaded with the premonition that "the cold has come from [it] / with its secret baggage." As he sets out on his journey, the poet passes "dim shops / before the plain begins," but there is "nothing to be bought" in these, only a "few shelves kept only by children / and relatives there for the holiday / who know nothing." The nature of the holiday is not specified but it doesn't matter, for the holiday is, in any case, not destined for him. Rather, he must proceed on his lonely pilgrimage, driven "to the rear" by a "wind without flags," that is to say an empty air mass, one in which nothing flutters, nothing has life. As the poet is swept along by this wind, his exile begins: "I recognize the first hunger / as the plains start / under my feet."

It would be an interesting exercise to study how a poem like "Be-ginning of the Plains" "deconstructs," to use Cary Nelson's word, earlier journey poems like "Anabasis I," the opening poem of *A Mask for Janus*, which has passages like the following:

Silence about our silence grew;
Beached by the convenient stream

Night is familiar when it comes.
On dim gestures does the mind
Exorcise abandoned limbs,
Disbodied, of that other hand

Estranged almost beyond response.
    (*MJ*, 3)

In the later poem, Merwin has abandoned the complex modification and inversion of his first experiments with poetic syntax; he has also purged his language of recondite words like "Disbodied." But the journey into "silence" and "night" has not appreciably changed; it is the journey of life, the eternal Pilgrim's Progress, even if the 1970 poem presents that journey in more abstract, more seemingly mysterious terms, the "I" now being overheard as if speaking in a trance: "I see x, I do y, then I must do z. . . ."

The Kafkaesque rhetoric of "Beginning of the Plains" does not, for all the stress on absence, go very deep. In a Kafka journey, as in a Beckett one, there are very concrete, specific signposts, signposts that yield particular meanings, even as those meanings are undercut by other contradictory signs. But what is indeterminacy in Kafka is mere vagueness here: we don't know *where* the poet must journey or why or in what "city" he now finds himself, but the nature of the journey is nevertheless easily understood. The traveler is afraid, for the projected journey is fraught with danger, pain, and hunger. Moreover, this is not a journey for which one can prepare: "nothing to be bought in the last / dim shops / before the plain begins." One must simply go up those "bridges steep as hills"; there is no choice. It is the familiar allegory of pilgrimage—*nel mezzo del cammin di nostra vita.*

But the working out of this allegory involves Merwin in a certain contradiction between form and meaning. What Howard calls the "key" to the "unconditional life" is found, formally speaking, all too easily. We are told that the journey is difficult, that the beginning of the plains marks a frightening threshold, but the poem unfolds without struggle in what is a continuous narrative made up of simple declarative sentences ("I change countries"; "I recognize the first hunger") and noun phrases ("few shelves kept only by children"; "wind without flags"). Again, the sound structure is reassuring: the nicely measured end-stopped lines with their lightly stressed anapests ("and relatives there for the holiday") foreground intricate patterns of sound repetition:

in the white sky the light is flickering
like the flight of a wing

Here we have not only end-rhyme, but internal rhyme ("white"/"light"/
"flight"), assonance of both short and long *i*'s, and alliteration of *f*'s, *l*'s,
and *w*'s; the chiming recalls, say, Poe rather than Beckett. Interestingly,
when Beckett does, in some of the late prose, use such sound patterns, it is
for parodic effect, an effect quite unlike Merwin's solemn, low-key, evenly
pitched speech. Indeed, "Beginning of the Plains" presents a progress to
a goal:

> I recognize the first hunger
> as the plains start
> under my feet

The "first hunger" marks the turn: the journey, we know, has begun. Punctuated or not, Merwin's last two lines, four syllables each, seem to close the
box with the click of a spring on the off-rhyme "start"/"feet."

"Beginning of the Plains" thus makes a series of statements about experience that are curiously at odds with what Howard calls "an access to prophecy" and Bloom, "the Native Strain, the American Orphic vision." Unlike
Char or Beckett or Kafka, but like the three poets Bloom cites—Longfellow,
MacLeish, and Wilbur (and I would add E. A. Robinson)—Merwin sets up
his poems so that they press toward generalization even if the generalization
to be made is only that we must recognize the nothing that is. Indeed, John
Bayley, in a review of *Writings to an Unfinished Accompaniment* (1973), puts
his finger on the problem when he says, referring to the book blurb which
reprints the previously cited statement by Richard Howard as well as an even
more extravagant one by Adrienne Rich:

> W. S. Merwin seems to me a poet of civility and civilisation, and
> as such a beautifully sensitive and accomplished one. What can
> Adrienne Rich mean by saying that he "has been working more
> privately, profoundly and daringly than any other American poet
> of my generation? . . . It was not *daring* of Gray to write "The
> curfew tolls the knell of parting day," though if he had written
> "The curfew strikes the hour of parting day," he would have failed
> to produce a line of good poetry. . . . Merwin's poetry, I would
> have thought, is of a kind not at all common today and decidedly
> interesting: it is the poetry of a kind of inner cultivation, requiring
> an audience with something of the same degree of experience
> and refinement, with expectations and pre-knowledge of what is
> going on.[20]

Precisely. That audience is the audience of the *New Yorker* and *Poetry*, of the *Hudson Review* and the *Yale Review*; it is this audience that has kept Merwin's poems in print, unlike almost anyone else's poems one can cite today, going through countless editions in their elegant Atheneum jackets. It is an audience that recognizes that, like Gray, Merwin almost never writes a bad line of poetry: "wind without flags," for example, conveys precisely and economically the sense of emptiness Merwin wants to depict.

Merwin's poetry, Bayley suggests, "is both extremely solitary and extremely fastidious, and yet it seems to need and call for the presence of a roomful of invisible understanders in something of the same way . . . early Augustan poetry needed the presence of that receptive coffeehouse society . . . who were alert to their manifestation of intellectual fine breeding, and concerned to be pleased with it" (p. 117). I think this is a very telling point. From the time that he won the Yale Younger Poets Award for *A Mask for Janus* in 1952 through the mid-seventies—that is to say, for a twenty-five-year span—Merwin could count on that "roomful of invisible understanders"who shared his fastidiousness, his good breeding, his elegant ways of distancing and yet bringing to mind the pain and emptiness of living in a bad time. It was an audience to whom the poet could say, as he does in "Avoiding News by the River," "Milky light flows through the branches / Fills with blood / Men will be waking," and count on their instant response to his circumspect reference to the bloodshed in Vietnam.

But viewed more dispassionately, Merwin, as Bayley puts it, "is not strong meat" (p. 117), and it was inevitable that before long the younger generation, who had been in college and hence more or less on the barricades when the Vietnam War was coming to its climax, would be less well-bred, less receptive to the measured abstractions, the careful distancing in Merwin's poetry about war and suffering and loss. Two things happened. On the one hand, for poets like Robert Pinsky and Alan Williamson, Merwin's elegance came to represent a thinly disguised evasiveness, a turning of one's back on the real world. As Turner Cassity puts it, "I know of no poems from which the apparatuses of industrial revolution have been more rigidly excluded" (p. 295). On the other hand, more experimental writers like the L-A-N-G-U-A-G-E poets of New York and San Francisco or the performance poets associated with Jerome Rothenberg's *New Wilderness Letter* are creating a decentered and playfully deconstructed universe—an undecidability—that exists on the other side of Merwin's "unduplicatable resonance."

In his recent work, Merwin seems to be trying to meet this avant-garde on its own ground: he has, for instance, written a group of poems in long, prosaic lines, whose spacing is meant to mark the pauses in natural speech in what looks superficially like David Antin's "talk poems":

> Something continues and   I don't know what to call it
> though the language is full of suggestions
> in the way of language
>   but they are all anonymous
> and it's almost your birthday   music next to my bones

Surely this is writing against the grain, the flippant tone ("though the language is full of suggestions / in the way of language") not according with the more familiar Merwin locutions of lines 8–9:

> the leaks in the roof go on dripping   after the rain has passed
> smell of ginger flowers   slips through the dark house

locutions that would seem more at home in his usual free-verse stanzas:

> the leaks in the roof go on dripping
> after the rain has passed
> smell of ginger flowers
> slips through the dark house.

Merwin's poetry has, in many ways, suffered at the hands of his admirers, who have championed it as a "testament of betrayals," a key prophetically unlocking the door of the present. But apocalypse has never been the métier of this fastidious poet, whose gift is perhaps less for revelation than for delicate resonance. Here is a short poem called "Dusk in Winter":

> The sun sets in the cold without friends
> Without reproaches after all it has done for us
> It goes down believing in nothing
> When it has gone I hear the stream running after it
> It has brought its flute it is a long way
>   (L, 49)

Here, in the compass of five lines, Merwin deftly debunks the pathetic fallacy, the human belief that the sun either does or does not have "friends," that it might "reproach" us for "all it has done for us." All one can do, Merwin implies, is to define how it feels to watch the sun go down—its look and its sound—for the sun has no importance beyond itself or, to quote Wallace Stevens, "beyond ourselves." "When it has gone I hear the stream running after it"—here Merwin defines a commonly experienced aural illusion, an intuition that in nature all things are related. That intuition is confirmed by the last line which stands out both visually and aurally: a run-on sentence made up of ten monosyllables with a delicate echo structure of short *i*'s and *t*'s, the second clause trailing off at the line end—"long way"—thus crossing the basic iambic pentameter rhythm with anapest and spondee:

it has brought its flute it is a long way

The flute metaphor, precisely conveying the dying fall of stream and sun, reinforces this special sound effect. The poem thus ends on the carefully planned downbeat that we have come to recognize as the authentic Merwin signature. It is a signature ill at ease with phrases like "prophecy" or "negative mysticism" or "naked poetry" or "the opening of the field." As for being one of the "Barbarians inside the City Gates," surely Merwin himself knows better. As he puts it in "The Cold before the Moonrise":

If there is a place where this is the language may
It be my country
    (*L*, 46)

Notes

1. Reprinted in Laurence Lieberman, *Unassigned Frequencies* (Urbana: University of Illinois Press, 1977), p. 257.

2. For a good overview of the difference between sixties and seventies poetry, see Stanley Plumly's two-part article, "Chapter and Verse," in *American Poetry Review*; Part 1: "Rhetoric and Emotion," 7 (Jan./Feb. 1978), 21–42; Part 2: "Image and Emblem," 7 (May/June 1978), 21–32.

3. Charles Altieri, *Enlarging the Temple* (Lewisburg, [Pa.]: Bucknell University Press, 1979), p. 19. The section on Merwin is revised in this collection as "Situating Merwin's Poetry since 1970."

4. Stephen Berg and Robert Mezey, eds., *Naked Poetry* (Indianapolis: Bobbs-Merrill Co., 1969), p. xi.

5. Richard Howard, *Alone with America: Essays on the Art of Poetry in the United States since 1950* (New York: Atheneum, 1969; enlarged ed. New York: Atheneum, 1980), p. 444. All references are to the second edition unless specified. In the first edition, Merwin gets thirty-two pages, closely followed by John Hollander (thirty-one) and James Dickey (twenty-three). Some other figures to measure against these: John Ashbery (nineteen), Robert Creeley (nine), Allen Ginsberg (seven), Denise Levertov (thirteen), Frank O'Hara (sixteen).

6. Paul Carroll, *The Poem in Its Skin* (Chicago: Big Table, 1968), pp. 219–20.

7. Karl Malkoff, *Crowell's Handbook of Contemporary American Poetry* (New York: Thomas Y. Crowell, Co., 1973), p. 208.

8. Cary Nelson, "The Resources of Failure: W. S. Merwin's Deconstructive Career," p. 80 (revised from *Our Last First Poets* [Urbana: University of Illinois Press, 1981]).

9. Harold Bloom, *Figures of Capable Imagination* (New York: Seabury Press, 1976), pp. 124, 127.

10. Alan Williamson, "Language against Itself: The Middle Generation of Contemporary Poets," in *American Poetry since 1960: Some Critical Perspectives*, ed. Robert Shaw (Cheadle Hulme: Carcanet Press, 1973), p. 56.

11. Robert Pinsky, *The Situation of Poetry: Contemporary Poetry and Its Traditions* (Princeton: Princeton University Press, 1977, pp. 92–93.

12. Andrew Waterman, "The Illusions of Immediacy," *Times Literary Supplement*, July 29, 1977, p. 836.

13. Altieri, "Situating Merwin's Poetry," p. 172.

14. Turner Cassity, "Dresden Milkmaids: The Pitfalls of Tradition," *Parnassus*, 5 (Fall/Winter 1976), 300.

15. James Dickey, *Babel to Byzantium* (New York: Farrar, Straus and Giroux, Inc., 1968), p. 143.

16. Altieri, *Enlarging the Temple*, pp. 38–39; quoting Robert Duncan, "Towards an Open Universe," in *Poets on Poetry*, ed. Howard Nemerov (New York: Basic Books, 1966), p. 139.

17. See Nelson, "Resources of Failure," p. 90; Robert Peters, *The Great American Poetry Bake-Off* (Metuchen, N.J.: Scarecrow Press, 1979), pp. 259, 267.

18. For the Char connection, see Howard, *Alone with America*, p. 435, and cf. Altieri, *Enlarging the Temple*, p. 196: "Merwin is so disturbing in large measure because his roots are European—in poets like Rilke and Follain who have developed numerous variations on the *via negativa* as the way of enduring presence." It should be noted that Altieri's discussion of Merwin, although not published before *Enlarging the Temple* (1979), was framed, as are the other chapters in the book, prior to 1970.

19. See, for example, Harvey Gross, "The Writing on the Void: The Poetry of W. S. Merwin," *Iowa Review*, 1 (Summer 1970), 105.

20. John Bayley, "How to Be Intimate without Being Personal," *Parnassus*, 2 (Fall/Winter 1973), 116–17.

STEPHEN PAUL MILLER

Periodizing Ashbery and His Influence

"Self-Portrait in a Convex Mirror" and Watergate are doubles. Just as the Nixon administration intertwines efforts to imperialize the presidency and unite all of the nation's surveillance operations under it, so Ashbery's poem creates a mirror world that traps its subject in his own surveillance or self-portraiture. Just as Nixon's efforts lead his administration to self-destruction through a series of surveillance mishaps that highlight America's ambivalence toward presidential authority, so Ashbery's poem leads a fictive character to destroy himself, his round mirror world, and his and the poem's expected subject matter.

Both the poem and the political scandal undermine the strong and, indeed, monolithic configurations they posit. Ashbery uses the second half of "Self-Portrait in a Convex Mirror" to shatter the first half of the poem's self-replenishing and all-encompassing vision of a subjectivity ensnared by the "surveillance mechanism" of the convex mirror. Similarly, Nixon himself, in the Watergate affair, is ultimately the chief target of his own surveillance mechanism.

Ashbery's poem is first published in the August 1974 issue of *Poetry*, the same month that Richard Nixon resigns his office, and correspondences between the poem and the Watergate drama are as rife as they are obvious. "Self Portrait in a Convex Mirror" is written in the guise of a meditation

From *The Tribe of John: Ashbery and Contemporary Poetry*, edited by Susan M. Schultz, pp. 146–67. © 1995 by the University of Alabama Press.

31

that overthrows its object of meditation, and during the midseventies, Nixon serves as an "object of meditation" that is banished.

A discussion of Ashbery's use of the convex mirror trope can shed light on the workings of both phenomena. Put simply, a convex mirror is a perfect surveillance mechanism. An ordinary, flat mirror and a convex mirror of the same size are quite different. The sixteenth-century painter Francesco Parmigianino uses a convex mirror to capture the image of everything in his studio in one view so that he can transmute this likeness appearing on his protruding three-dimensional mirror into one on a two-dimensional curved wooden surface. The result is Parmigianino's famed 1524 *Self-Portrait in a Convex Mirror*, which Ashbery describes in his major long poem of the same name. Parmigianino cannot achieve the all-encompassing effect of his round painting with a flat, conventional mirror. Although a convex mirror creates images that are obviously distorted and that therefore cannot render the same kind of mimetically "correct" images that a flat mirror does, nonetheless a convex mirror must capture everything before it. No one can stand at an angle too oblique from a convex mirror's perimeter to avoid being observed by another occupant of the same room.

The convex mirror therefore conveys a notion of supreme surveillance. Any extensive discussion of Ashbery's "Self-Portrait in a Convex Mirror" must account for this major feature of convex mirrors. As Ashbery organizes "Self-Portrait in a Convex Mirror" around the central trope of a surveillance mechanism, so one can also organize a consideration of the Watergate affair around the central trope of another surveillance mechanism: undisclosed audiotaping. Furthermore, Parmigianino—in Ashbery's characterization, Richard Nixon—is undone by his own surveillance systems. Ashbery revives poetic topos in his poetry, and the Nixon administration seeks to apply almost monarchical presidential powers. What is the connection? Perhaps American culture ends an era of expansion by constructing surveillance devices that serve to monitor and delimit American culture through the agency of traditional organizing principles like subject matter and the presidency.

"It seems appropriate to mark the definitive end of the '60's,' in the general area of 1972–74," says Fredric Jameson.[1] This kind of precise periodization, however, does not concern me here so much as the wider contention that contemporaneous cultural productions as significant as the ones considered here should, at some point in the critical literature of each phenomenon, be discussed in relation to one another.

One might easily postulate direct influence., After all, even as referentially evasive a poet as Ashbery could hardly have avoided the Watergate narrative that was in the air during this period. One could imagine the Watergate Senate hearings on Ashbery's television while he was writing "Self-Portrait in a Convex Mirror." However, this avenue of inquiry holds limited promise. First, a problem of verifiability seems insurmountable. How could one ever be sure what part of the poem Ashbery was writing when Alexander Butterfield publicly revealed the existence of Nixon's self-espionage? Indeed, in terms of "influence," how crucial was this moment of July 16, 1973? Did not John Dean earlier, during his televised testimony before the Ervin Senate Committee, note his suspicion that he was being taped in the Oval Office? Did not Dean's Senate testimony describe the Nixon administration's proclivity toward surveillance and its attempts to control all federal surveillance agencies and use them for base political ends? Was not surveillance and self-surveillance embedded in the logic of the affair?

Even if Ashbery could be trusted to divulge accurate, day-by-day records of his progress in the writing of "Self-Portrait in a Convex Mirror," a task fraught with much room for error in itself, how could we ever be sure how the poem reflects the poet's responses to the unfolding scandal? How could the poet himself be sure? When I first told Ashbery about my parallel between Watergate and "Self-Portrait in a Convex Mirror," he responded with incredulous humor. "You're comparing me to Nixon," he said jocularly. "Someday you'll get yours. . . . Oh, Nixon was a great president. I wish he was still president." Years later, Ashbery himself cited Oliver North's Iran-Contra arms and money flow-chart placard as an inspiration for *Flow Chart* (1990).

John Ashbery is indeed one of our most political poets. His customary evasions of logical and thematic closure allow his poetry to register cultural nuances and patterns that poetries of more overt narrative or thematic intent might overlook. The paradox here of course is that strong partisan and referential designs can limit a literary work's political expressiveness.

By the term "political," I mean here the "political unconscious" as articulated by Fredric Jameson, a concept which has much in common with Louis Althusser's notions of ideological state apparatuses, Jacques Lacan's "real," and Michel Foucault's epistemes. The political unconscious, according to Fredric Jameson, is the ideological limitation embedded in a society's cultural mindset. Because of these limits, or, as Jameson calls them, horizons, all literature is ideological and political. Additionally, all literature is primarily political because it is only through the language of culture, in its broadest sense, that the contradictions of economic and political power and inequity can be dynamically yet unconsciously reconciled. Put simply, culture is a cover-up. However, this does not necessarily involve a conspiracy or even a cause-and-effect relationship as much as a kind of "structural causality."[2] Althusser's term, cited by Jameson, refers to a system of causality in which the whole of a culture expresses itself in its parts as cultural phenomena. For both Jameson and Althusser, the totality of a culture is found everywhere in that culture.

However, a critic requires "interpretive master code[s]" to unlock these cultural codes, making clear that culture is indeed cultural and historical, not naturally, divinely, or otherwise transcendentally given.[3]

Jameson maintains that Althusser facilitated an interpretive mode that is not reductive. Since everything that can be interpreted is political, nothing is excluded from a political interpretation. In a radical departure for a Marxist, economic considerations are no longer chief determinants. Theories of how culture produces itself must help account for any given part of the whole. Jameson argues that it is no longer possible to understand cultural and literary phenomena distinct from a theory of the cultural and the social powers that hold them in place. This is not to say that close and specific observation and reading are not necessary, but rather to say that one must not renounce the responsibility to theorize associations within the cultural whole. When one energetically enters this general and theoretical realm, one inevitably opens oneself to criticisms of overgeneralizing and of ignoring laws of causality. Causality does constitute our most comfortable mode of accountability. It allows us to identify those who are "outside" of an effect or a result. But causal analysis also allows us to evade total cultural responsibility and, by extension, ourselves. For too long, literary critics have been too conveniently comfortable with their limitations. We must dare to be general in a manner that does not close and reduce our readings of texts and phenomena but rather sharpens our powers of specificity.

Althusser lists every conceivable manner of culture as "ideological state apparatuses."[4] Every function that it is possible for culture to fulfill, such as education and entertainment, is an ideological state apparatus because cultural phenomena serve the limits of conceivable reality so that this reality does not threaten the existing social hierarchy. This hierarchy is deeply entrenched, protecting the most essential workings of social division, inequity, and repression. Althusser bases his notion of culture as an aggregate of ideological state apparatuses on Lacan's category of the "real order." For Lacan, the real is the unknowable limit on our imaginations and symbolic workings.

According to Althusser, even "revolutionary" art assists these limits. Yet it does so in a way that betrays the political realities that it is based upon. What virtue is there for art in a culture wherein all cultural phenomena serve repressive ends? Art works, Althusser posits, because it "accounts" for modes of cultural production. To perceive art is to distance oneself from the ideological horizons of reality so as to make that reality visible. Althusser elaborates upon the relationship between art and ideologically determined reality:

> This relationship is not one of identity but one of difference. I believe that the peculiarity of art is to "make us see" [*nous donner à voir*], "make us perceive," "make us feel," something which alludes

> to reality. . . . What art makes *us see*, and therefore gives to us in the form of *"seeing," "perceiving,"* and *"feeling"* (which is not the form of *knowing*) is the *ideology* from which it is born, in which it bathes, from which it detaches itself as art, and to which it *alludes*. . . . They make us "perceive" (but not know) in some sense *from the inside*, by an *internal distance*, the very ideology in which they are held.[5]

Successful art, even abstract art, offers its audience the opportunity to note the workings of culture. Thus art can be a kind of spy. Indeed, since art is inescapably political, overt content is not necessary, and abstract art, better camouflaged, can be a more successful double agent.

I am thus not arguing that Ashbery's poetry is rawly realistic. More significantly, I contend that a typical Ashbery poem is effective as a poem and cultural product because it clarifies the workings of that poem's historical period and our present understanding of that period. As Harold Bloom notes, Ashbery's poetry is often organized by the evocation of an Emersonian "Beautiful Necessity."[6] By surrendering to a given reality with abandon, the opposition between determinism and freedom is bypassed. The achievement of "Soonest Mended," Bloom says of one of Ashbery's great poems of the sixties, "is to have told a reductive truth, yet to have raised it out of reductiveness by a persistence masked as the commonal.[7] "Soonest Mended" achieves a liberated and liberating complexity by accepting simplicity, yet seeing through it.

Bloom attributes this freedom within limitations to an acceptance of approaching middle age. Undeniably, "Soonest Mended" concludes upon a tone of acceptance. The speaker, however, accepts a planned regression within his middle-aged years. He accepts and even welcomes "the charity of the hard moments as they are doled out" (DDS 19).

> To reduce all this to a small variant,
> To step free at last, minuscule on the gigantic plateau—
> This was our ambition: to be small and clear and free.
>   (17)

But the speaker also implements "fantasy" and "loose" (18) imprecision into his limitations:

> this is action, this not being sure, this careless
> Preparing, sowing the seeds crooked in the furrow,
> Making ready to forget, and always coming back
> To the mooring of starting out, that day so long ago.
>   (19)

The speaker associates wisdom, in addition to "action," with youth:

> probably thinking not to grow up
> Is the brightest kind of maturity for us, right now at any rate.
>   (19)

The "right now" of "Soonest Mended" is the midsixties. The poem negotiates with the romantic imperative of its era. It begins by alluding to life
outside mainstream culture: "Barely tolerated, living on the margin / In our
technological society, we were always having to be rescued" (17). Within this
framework, pseudo-reassurance recurrently arrives in the form of a comic-
book-like hero:

> there always came a time when
> Happy Hooligan in his rusted green automobile
> Came plowing down the course, just to make sure everything was
> O.K.,
> Only by that time we were in another chapter and confused
> About how to receive this latest piece of information.
> *Was* it information?
>   (17)

Conventional, industrial ("a rustling of coils," "rusted, green automobile")
reassurances are no longer credible in the sixties. "We" are in the context of
"another chapter." What the previous age has to tell us is not applicable and
indeed may not even be "information." We are little served by our former
selves: "Weren't we rather acting this out / For someone else's benefit?" (17).
Accustomed reconciliations lose their bases.

As "summer's energy wanes," so does the desire to simplify:

> no longer
> May we make the necessary arrangements, simple as they are.
> Our star was brighter perhaps when it had water in it.
> Now there is no question even of that, but only
> Of holding on to the hard earth so as not to get thrown off.
>   (17)

Glamorous stars no longer hold "water." The speaker reconciles himself to
his crisis of disillusionment by noting a psychic opening that is to be the
poem's turning point. At the end of the first of two verse paragraphs, the
speaker owns up to the limits of his discourse:

> We are all talkers
> It is true, but underneath the talk lies
> The moving and not wanting to be moved, the loose
> Meaning, untidy and simple like a threshing floor.
>   (18)

After this "untidy and simple" observation, "the clarity of the rules dawn[s]" "for the first time." The speaker is "shock[ed]" by his alienation: "*They* were the players, and we who had struggled at the game / Were merely spectators." This realization comes "almost a quarter of a century later" (18). Since "Soonest Mended" is a midsixties poem, this alienation begins with the cold war. What we think of as the heart of the sixties lies at the chronological center of the cold-war era. In the sixties, realities put forward by the military-industrial complex are severely doubted. Appropriately, the speaker appeals to "fantasy."

We live in a fantasy with very real applications, a "fantasy [that] makes it ours, a kind of fence-sitting / Raised to the level of an esthetic ideal" (18). One thinks of Ashbery's poetic development. Bloom maintains that *The Double Dream of Spring* is Ashbery's first mature collection of poetry not to rely on ellipses, or the apparent omission of subject matter. The critic attributes this to Ashbery's more open confrontation with the American Romantic tradition. I would explain this observation in a manner that does not contradict Bloom's explanation but rather accounts for it in a more encompassing and political context. The sixties is a moment when the American Romantic tradition seemed pervasive in counterculture America. Ashbery's native tradition approaches him from the "outside." His poems can talk more directly to his audience. With *The Double Dream of Spring*, Ashbery's poetry becomes more openly Romantic and less disjunctively modernist. We are reminded of the difficulties inherent in Trilling's dubbing of the sixties as a "modernism on the streets." Modernism can so easily be linked with an elitism that is counter to sixties ideals, if not realities.

As "solid" "reality" fades, the speaker no longer needs to hide his uncertainty. In the sixties, it becomes more positive not to define one's identity or be very certain of what one knows:

> These were moments, years,
> Solid with reality, faces, nameable events, kisses, heroic acts,
> But like the friendly beginning of a geometrical progression
> Not too reassuring, as though meaning could be cast aside some day
> When it had been outgrown. Better, you said, to stay cowering
> Like this in the early lessons, since the promise of learning

> Is a delusion, and I agreed, adding that
> Tomorrow would alter the sense of what had already been
> learned,
> That the learning process is extended in this way, so that from
> this standpoint
> None of us ever graduates from college,
> For time is an emulsion.
>   (18–19)

The speaker coyly identifies himself with college-aged baby boomers. Time and age are, after all, liquid. Conformity to a fantastic reality is no conformity at all. We have learned the arts of "conforming to the rules and living / Around the home" from "avatars" (19), suggesting spiritual leaders, such as Meher Baba, who were relatively popular in America during the sixties for their appeals to an admixture of the everyday and the apocalyptic. Similarly, "Soonest Mended" achieves a "hazardous" romanticism by positing the incredible as a given. After all, if the sixties were as an age of the antihero, it follows that heroism could be found everywhere.

It is difficult to say that "Soonest Mended" could only have been written in the sixties. Much of what we identify as the sixties is of course filtered through other decades. However, "Soonest Mended" uniquely synthesizes motifs and tropes that are particularly strong in the mid and late sixties. It attains a kind of originality by accepting and focusing on its historical material. The more the poem accepts its affinities to the wider cultural text, the freer and more unique it seems.

I do not claim to be able to determine what Ashbery intends to signify. In terms of influence, it would be possible to engage in such source findings, since three of the younger poets that I discuss—David Shapiro, David Lehman, and Thomas Fink—have written about Ashbery. However, I do not claim that Ashbery directly influenced another poet that I discuss, Cherríe Moraga. I claim a wider cultural connection among all of these poets.

As may be apparent by now, the writings of Michel Foucault establish a theoretical basis for relating my close readings of poetry to cultural conditions. Foucault meticulously studies textual details to construe the code of a hidden but prevailing epistemological framework that allows a text to function within its respective time and culture. Foucault terms these epistemological systems epistemes.

Epistemes form the rules and limits through which a culture's modes of knowledge and culture are made possible. Hence, epistemes are detectable in all cultural phenomena. But since, according to Foucault, we discover epistemes through a close textual scrutiny that is attentive to tropological regularities and configurations, epistemes are particularly observable in poetry when we juxtapose poetic texts with contexts that are perhaps unrelated to any authorial intentions. Foucault was aware that epistemes can be used as an overly reductive tool. He thus pointed out that epistemes are in constant flux. Since the historian must be sensitive to small distinctions, close reading is essential. As Ashbery's "Fragment" puts it:

It would not be good to examine these ages
Except for sun flecks, little, on the golden sand
And coming to reappraisal of the distance.
    (DDS 81)

The analysis of epistemes within relatively small units of time is an antidote to the uncritical synopses of post–World War II American culture prevalent in the press and the media today. Perhaps our most important political work is to render ourselves members of a community who are critically helpful and accountable to one another in all facets of our public discourse. What do we as critics, aesthetic issues aside, really do if we do not build communicative bridges about all manner of cultural phenomena among ourselves, students, and the larger public?

It is not my intention to pin poems too neatly to a decade. Of course, decades do overlap. However, it would be more misleading to avoid what they represent than to grasp them within a problematized framework. How can a critic ignore the tropes and mind-sets prevailing in an era? It is the critic's job to bring the political unconscious to consciousness in a manner that must be unique and seemingly fictional because it has never existed as consciousness before. According to Jameson, history is text. Yet history is not a text until it is made so by those who interpret it. A critic acting on this premise will always be faulted when a creative reading is equated to a false reading. Jameson's words in this regard bear citation:

I happen to feel that no interpretation can be effectively disqualified on its own terms by a simple enumeration of inaccuracies or omissions, or by a list of unanswered questions. Interpretation is not an isolated act, but takes place within a Homeric battlefield, on which a host of interpretive options are either openly or implicitly in conflict. If the positivistic conception of philological accuracy be the only alternative, then I would much prefer to endorse the current provocative celebration of strong misreadings over weak ones. As the Chinese proverb has it, you use one ax handle to hew another: in our context, only another, stronger interpretation can overthrow and practically refute an interpretation already in place.[8]

It is too easy to discount history by saying that its application is too obvious. It sometimes seems that we must strenuously labor to keep recent history and Ashbery's poetry from shedding light on one another. For example, few long poems emblematize and explain the sixties as well as "Fragment," another Ashbery poem of the midsixties. One might apply this passage to both the poem and its era:

> That coming together of masses coincides
> With that stable emptiness . . .
>
> . . . .
>   winking with it
> To tablelands of disadumbrated feeling
> Treetops whose mysterious hegemony concerns
> Merely, by opening around factors of accident
> So as to install miscellaneous control.
>   (DDS 79)

Ashbery's "Fragment" describes its own "mysterious hegemony," based in large part upon avoiding a too explicit hegemony and continuity or "coming together of masses coincid[ing] / With that stable emptiness" (79). The sixties would not have been possible without general prosperity. This prosperity, however, is met with ambivalence. In "Fragment," the articulation of an unspecified, empty merger is perhaps a product of "disadumbrat[ing] feeling," which is affected by the paradoxical mix of order and disorder in the "install[ation]" of "miscellaneous control." Indeed, fifteen pages later, when the poem says "Anomaly had spoken" (94), there is no doubt but that the poem has demonstrated this.

This anomaly is also an irreconcilable distance between lovers. The speaker often addresses a beloved that he seems destined to lose. He takes solace, however, in the notion that an impending reality will bring his love back to him. The poem, however, sometimes loses faith in the power of wish fulfillment. "Fragment" exposes the inherent contradictions of a sixties counterculture that questions the surplus production of the Western consumerist culture that it relies on. An inability to transcend consumerist values was never more acutely felt than in the sixties. Apocalyptic prospects cannot fructify. We are separated from the day's "flame-colored phenomena." "Expressions of hope" are "too late." The poem foresees the sixties to be like a love affair that goes nowhere: "This information was like a road no one ever took." Millionaires are "bent on turning everyday affairs into something tragic" (88).

Jameson speculates that during the sixties our economy was stuck in a prolonged transition from industrial to postindustrial, service, and multinational modes. Economic systems lost regulatory power. A sense of economic reality was thus suspended, and all things appeared possible. By the midseventies, however, reality had irrefutably returned.

Jameson's premise, whether it is correct or not, speaks to our mythology of the late sixties and following periods. Each era can be described by its relationship to "reality." We seemed to move from the suspended reality of the sixties, to a return to and ambivalence toward reality in the seventies, to an apparent eighties' affirmation of reality and a contradictory denial of its responsibilities, and to the severe disappointment and anger of the nineties. We have not yet adjusted to the promises and the conflicts of the sixties. It sometimes seems that everything was thrown up in the air then and has not yet fallen. Clint Eastwood's film *In the Line of Fire* (1993), for instance, plays upon this cultural suspicion: Playing the character of a secret service agent who had been President Kennedy's favorite protector, Eastwood claims that Kennedy was "different" from the fictional president he is now defending. Indeed, he claims that everything was different then. Now there is nothing but game-playing. He wonders if the world would still hold definitive meaning if he had been able to prevent Kennedy's assassination. The agent's alienation is so great that he attaches little import in itself to protecting the president. More important, he feels that he must do his job as if it had tangible meaning. He and the would-be assassin played by John Malkovich differentiate themselves from one another in this respect. The professional assassin, trained by the CIA after Kennedy's death, sees what he is trying to do as a mere game. Eastwood's character insists to him that doing a job is not the same as playing a game. Reacting against sixties and postsixties ruptures with reality, he elegantly expresses nostalgia for presixties reality.

The sixties can be described as an unguarded gap between two dominant capitalistic modes, before capitalism coheres into a multinational system that more seamlessly and less obviously engulfs the world. In the words of "Fragment," the sixties are a "multicolored / Parentheses." It is "love in short periods" that "puts everything out of focus" (81).

"Fragment" begins with a simple description of the end of an order that occurs near the start of spring: "The last block is closed in April." "Intrusions" come between the speaker and the object of his address, his apparent former lover. His lover's seeming permission will elude him. He will attain only "sympathy." The poem's remorse is here reminiscent of Ashbery's poetry of the early and mid fifties, collected in *Some Trees* (1956). Much of this poetry seems to mourn the irreconcilability of society's ever coming to terms with gay identity in McCarthyite America. One thinks of "the men" in "*Le livre est sur la table*" who "live in boxes. / The sea protects them like a wall" (SPs 28). In "Fragment," however, the speaker finds powerful solace in a supposition that is similar to the aesthetic "fence-sitting" (DDS 18) of "Soonest Mended" yet also maneuvers against a closeted affection and identity. "Fragment" posits a "moment's commandment" that does not allow any room for the decision to "withdraw" (78) love.

The second of the poem's fifty ten-line stanzas posits a new and happier "reality," in which his lover's face is "the only real beginning." The speaker moves "beyond the gray." He escapes the closed system of "friendship / With self alone." He "open[s] out." What seems like "fiction" sustains him. By the beginning of the third stanza, he turns another "page." "Other sounds are heard." "Propositions hitherto omitted" (78) are entertained. It is possible to "look at it all / Inside out." The solidity of a "statue" is made of an "emblem" (79) foreshadowing the seventies phenomenon of T-shirts with logos.

In the next stanza, the speaker extols his "inability to accept" the "fact" of his lover's absence. He has "power" over his lover, whom he "reflect[s]." In the face of this willful denial of hard and fast reality, "the imagination creates / A claim" virtually to everything. "Factors of accident" assist the imagination to maintain a fantastic "control." "Best to break off / All further choice" (79), says the speaker, who is radicalized around his recognition of an incredible reality. After the "cold collapse" of outmoded reality, we can "water" "into the past with its religious / Messages and burials." With this appreciation of ancient rituals, "A warm and near unpolished entity could begin" (80).

By the seventh stanza, we have clearly moved beyond a "cut-and-dried symposium way of seeing things." However, the speaker must account for the abundance that enables his discourse, his stance, and the economy. There is a "hollow" at the core of the poem's "distribution center." In this hollow are the "ghosts of the streets." Alluding to the Vietnam War, the poem touches on "death in its various forms" and then mentions "the wars abroad" that spoil "the peace / At home." We have nothing to "bear" outside the "surround-ing neighborhood" (80). Wars of expansion are debilitating, and the speaker takes comfort in his powerlessness. The "only world is an inside one" that is "fashioned out of external phenomena." "New kinds of fun" assure us of a "cer-tain future." "Satisfaction," however, can only be "phantom." There is nothing but the "active memorial." "Commas are dropped," and "convention gapes" (81). The poem talks of the outward romanticism of being "all heart and all skin." "Change" is "around us" (82). "Our habits" are confused and "ask us for instructions" (83).

In the nineteenth stanza, "reserves of anxiety and restlessness" become more prominent in the poem. The American "Empire" encounters "hesitation" in its pattern of "possession and possessiveness." There is "so much air of change, but always and nowhere / A cave" (84). By the twenty-fifth stanza "The apotheosis had sunk away." In the twenty-sixth stanza, "The change is more complete than ever before," but it is a "pessimistic lighting up" that is "demanding more than ever to be considered for full / Substance" (86). The poem foresees a return to reality. Curiously, we have learned asceticism from the sixties: "You see, it is / Not wrong to have nothing" (89). Yet this reductivism only facilitates an imaginative life that, in the forty-second stanza, is "consumed" by more ominous future organization in "A surprise dragging the signs / Of no peace after it" (92). Near the end of the poem, the speaker acknowledges his inability to control the love that controls him: "The words sung in the next room are unavoidable" (94).

"Fragment" is Ashbery's most penetrating analysis of the sixties. It is a particularly difficult poem to read when one ignores its periodicity. "The stance," the poem announces to those outside it, "to you / Is a fiction, to me a whole." The poem wrestles between two aspects of sixties expansion. On the one hand, a booming economy makes it possible to denounce an industrial work ethos. "Permissiveness" now has a mainstream currency and no longer "fall[s] back toward recondite ends." "Reality" is "providential." There are "new options" (78), "new kinds of fun" (81), "much air of change" (84), "new experience" (86), and "new passages of being among the correctness / Of familiar patterns" (78). On the other hand, expansion "instantaneously" produces the escalation of an imperialist war. Consumerist "possession" and "possessiveness" create an uncritical "empire." "The grave of authority / Matches wits with upward-spinning lemon spirals" (84).

> Our daily imaginings are swiftly tilted down to
> Death in its various forms. We cannot keep the peace
> At home, and at the same time be winning wars abroad.
>   (80)

"Fragment," like America of the sixties, is never able to reconcile this conflict. However, it manages "to isolate the kernel of / Our imbalance" (82).

The "moment" of the sixties—recalling the crucial introductory phrase of "Fragment" ("a moment's commandment")—produces a sense of unlimited expansion because, metaphorically speaking, the hard-and-fast laws of standards of economics are temporarily suspended. As "A Fragment" puts it, the "day" is "oblong" (78). Limitation is defied, reality is irrelevant, and an exhilarating furlough from it is granted. Indefinite romantic ideals seem more authentic than the eroding realities of industrialism and the cold war.

We associate the sixties with wild expansion. However, the seventies are considered a period of consolidation and codification in which the contradictions of the sixties and reality must be faced. Appropriately, until the midseventies, Ashbery easily can be characterized as an abstract poet whose poems eschew definitive topics. I use the term "abstract" to describe a poem that does not clearly contain reference and subject matter. In this sense, it does not matter whether the topic of an "unabstract" poem is philosophical or unphilosophical and concrete.

Abstraction, in the manner that I use it, and referentiality and subject matter may be considered to be on a spectrum and not opposites that exclude one another. Furthermore, abstraction and topos are perhaps produced more by readings than by texts. Nevertheless, it is my intention here to discuss our tendencies to attribute qualities of abstraction and subject matter when reading the poems that this essay concerns. I am not in these pages preoccupied with whether the site of the dialectic of abstraction and topos is primarily situated within the text or the reader.

I set up the implications of abstraction and the connotations of referentiality and topos as binary oppositions. Abstraction, here, suggests the absence of an agreed-upon reality and an emphasis upon process over product, and subject matter contrastingly suggests a consensus reality and the presence of a set-external reality that is not dependent upon any process or play of language. True, the problematizing of topos is a constant in Ashbery's poetry. However, until the infinitely reproductive mirror play of "Self-Portrait in a Convex Mirror," a definite theme does not provide an obvious focus that can be sustained throughout Ashbery's earlier long poems. Of course, Ashbery's poetry before "Self-Portrait in a Convex Mirror" is not without content. However, the subject matter in almost all of his major poetry before his famed 1974 poem is extremely difficult to trace. (The few exceptions, such as "The Instruction Manual" [SoTr 26–30] are short poems.) Even "Fragment" notably lacks a consistent unifying emblem. Indeed, "Fragment" often alludes to its inability to see a totality outside itself. "Seen from inside all is / Abruptness" (DDS 80). But the subject matter of "Self-Portrait in a Convex Mirror" is ostensibly clearly discernible and visible—in large part helping to account for its popularity. Although "Self-Portrait in a Convex Mirror" is not limited to a consideration of Francesco Parmigianino's *Self-Portrait in a Convex Mirror*, it is nonetheless a meditation upon Parmigianino's painting.

In "Self-Portrait in a Convex Mirror," Parmigianino is trapped within his own mirror creation, which must eventually be destroyed. This is strikingly similar to the manner in which Nixon's espionage systems eventually undo his presidency. I have here examined similarities between Ashbery's Parmigianino and the Richard Nixon of the Watergate affair, as well as the broader cultural context of the midseventies.[9] I argue that just as "Self-Portrait in a Convex Mirror" revives poetic subject matter only to discredit it, the Watergate affair has its roots in the Nixon administration's efforts to exert vast and unchecked presidential powers. Nixon attempts to bypass the "credibility gap" only eventually to magnify and fall prey to it. Nixon is not a villain of history so much as a cultural production that reflects us all. Even if we determine him to be a villain, it still behooves us to understand him in terms of our culture.

Similarly, Ashbery presents his most coherent topos and subsequently undermines it. After all, if the midseventies can be said to codify unaccounted-for aspects of the sixties, the midseventies could then be said to use organizational and surveillance mechanisms to account for what is previously unexplained. However, these organizing instruments of surveillance must themselves be accounted for; as Nixon is undone by his own surveillance mechanisms, so is Parmigianino in Ashbery's poem.

Ashbery's poem about the surveillance tool of the convex mirror initially argues that the human condition is a closed one of self-imprisonment:

> The soul establishes itself.
> But how far can it swim out through the eyes
> And still return safely to its nest? The surface
> Of the mirror being convex, the distance increases
> Significantly; that is enough to make the point
> That the soul is a captive, treated humanely, kept
> In suspension, unable to advance.
>   (SPs 188)

Given this midseventies emphasis on limitation, it is not surprising that the mirror's backing serves as transformative trope. A mirror is, after all, a dynamic antithesis between a transparent window and an opaque "wall." After the round backing of the mirror, which is said to "island" the static scene, is mentioned, it is accounted for and breaks. This displacement of a limiting presence is the ground for "dreams and inspirations on an unassigned / Frequency" (202).

This presence can be likened to the "wall" or barrier aspect of the backing that enables the mirror world of Ashbery's poem. "Dreams and inspirations" suggest the "window" that the poem both refutes and affirms. If we think of referentiality as a kind of wall or horizon of possibility, we can see "Self-Portrait in a Convex Mirror" as a strong precursor of a mideighties poem from Shapiro's *House (Blown Apart)*. (My segue between "Self-Portrait in a

Convex Mirror" and "A Wall" is deliberately textual. The mideighties poems that I treat are a somewhat arbitrary selection, since any mideighties poem will be culturally linked to any midseventies poem. This is not to say that I do not positively value the poems that I discuss as culturally illuminating.)

"A Wall"

I have the right not to represent it.

Though every brick is clear as a doubt
Clear as a tear and a mistranslation
Through the window as through December fourth
The clarity of the facts like light snow
After bad dreams forgotten partly whole
And of the whole a part
One may forget so intently you might write

"I cannot now respond to this abstraction
Unsharcable satire, courtly dream, and so forth
Sorry, not sorry" But try as I shall not to bump
Or bash it or lift a camera to a sill
To penetrate a copy or to think I have invented it

A banal impossibility as night is written
In pages splitting into analogies like walls
I see in this quiet sunlit stylization
Holding forth onto a garden enclosed and yet at times
Open in a melancholy necessary morning:

A wall I neither restored nor could destroy.[10]

The speaker in "A Wall" confronts a wall of agreement and naive realism. Ironically, in this confrontation, the poem finds a topic, ultimately arguing that it is in the resistance to topos that poetry discovers its subject matter.

The poem opens with a strongly reflexive comment that is set off from the rest of the poem as if it were a topic sentence: "I have the right not to represent it." This "right" is apparently derived from the necessities of poetry's means of production. The speaker points out that every "brick" that can be represented is clear as a "doubt" or "mistranslation," even though some may "write" "intently" and call for such "banal" intent and originality by dismissing "abstraction."

Shapiro characterizes reality as one of many "analogies like walls" that are "written / In pages splitting." However, Shapiro's poem is not a simple valorization of the poetic powers—a "quiet sunlit stylization / Holding forth onto a garden enclosed." Instead, Shapiro ends "A Wall" by positing another wall more necessary than the previously described walls of metaphor that can be said to be built of "brick[s] of doubt." The poem concludes with a single line that seems to respond to the poem's demarcated opening line: "I have the right not to represent it." "A wall I neither restored nor could destroy" significantly modifies the impact of the first line of "A Wall." The speaker does not now appear to master what is valuable, although we know this by the speaker's own admission Nonetheless, the poem seems to reach its enabling limits. These limits make possible the poet's apparent "invention." Shapiro's wall functions like Ashbery's backing of the mirror.

However, Shapiro's "Wall" sketches a clearer and more intensely poignant reconciliation than Ashbery's "Self-Portrait in a Convex Mirror" of the overlapping functions of abstraction and realism. Shapiro's poem suggests a period that consciously needs to integrate the necessities of epistemological agreement with the seeming authenticity of the poet's play of linguistic experiences and imaginings.

Shapiro rigorously clips his phrases—each phrase taking on the quality of a light "brick." A paradoxically spiritual materiality is emphasized. The problematic of abstraction and realism is given a place of extreme value. Reality must be met as a tropological limit. "A Wall" exists in, and makes visible, the modes of cultural production in the age of Reagan (who, like Nixon, I do not conceptualize as a favorite bad guy of history but rather a production of our culture), wherein ideology is seen as "reality" and the tropological underpinnings of reality are repressed. Wish fulfillment and surplus spending abound.

Taking a route that can be termed the reverse of the more theoretically inclined Shapiro, David Lehman's "New York City, 1974" mixes poetic abstraction with realism by employing the latter rather than the former as a base.[11] However, this Lehman poem analyzes, practices, and parodies the role of memory in constructing an "objective" reality.

"New York City, 1974" can be said to be a revised memory of "Self-Portrait in a Convex Mirror." Of course, cultural productions tend to revise the cultural productions of preceding eras. The obviousness of this fact sometimes causes us not to apply it.

Ashbery's 1974 poem equates a secretive and powerful, yet declining, New York City of the midseventies with a mirror backing that eventually collapses. In Ashbery's poem, New York depicts a crumbling basis for a reality principle in crisis:

The shadow of the city injects its own
Urgency: . . .

. . . .
. . . New York
Where I am now, which is a logarithm
Of other cities. Our landscape
Is alive with filiations, shuttlings;
Business is carried on by look, gesture,
Hearsay. It is another life to the city,
The backing of the looking glass.
   (SPS 195)

As the third of five poems in the last section of Lehman's most recent book, *Operation Memory* (1990), "New York City, 1974" extends Ashbery's trope.

The volume's title poem concludes both its suite of poems and the book. "Operation, Memory" presents memory as an arduous task.[12] In a Kafkaesque metaphor, the production of our memory of the last twenty years becomes the primary enterprise of that twenty-year period. This enterprise uncannily is depicted as both a military operation and an academic lifestyle. They are combined in a kind of "intelligence work":

  To his separate bed
Each soldier went . . .
  And there I was, in the middle
Of a recession, in the middle of a strange city, between jobs
And apartments and wives. Nobody told me the gun was loaded.

  All my friends had jobs
As professional liars, and most had partners who were good in
bed.
What did I have? Just this feeling of always being in the middle
Of things, and the luck of looking younger than fifty.

At dawn I returned to draft headquarters. I was eighteen
And counting backwards. The interviewer asked one loaded
Question after another, such as why I often read the middle
Of novels, ignoring their beginnings and their ends. When
Had I decided to volunteer for intelligence work?

The speaker often alludes to being a writer and a poet. This metaphoric fusion of the lives of the soldier and the writer responds to the first poem of this sequence: "Vietnam Memorial,"[13] wherein the speaker states that his life had been predicated upon an evasion of fighting in the Vietnam War:

> We who didn't go to Vietnam
> Planned our lives around it just the same.

The poem suggests that life still concerns a complex sense of absence from and presence in the Vietnam War:

> Some numbers never came up.
> We were the lucky ones. The ones who went
> Were forgotten. And I am thinking of them today,
> Thinking of death in Vietnam, and the dead bodies
> That might have been ours.

"Operation Memory," wherein the dubious reality of a life of evasion must be made to cohere, is a logical outcome of, for the speaker, the surrogate basis of the Vietnam War and the post–Vietnam War culture evoked by "Vietnam Memorial."

New York appears in a narrative about the project of remembrance, New York, in "New York City, 1974," as the crossroads of a trip through a void—the midpoint or "backing of the mirror" between the intangible realities of the sixties and the necessary fictions of the eighties. This middle poem in the poetic sequence that concludes *Operation Memory* chronicles a completely open and poetic approach to life:

> Whatever worked: that was the principle
> Behind our cryptic aphorisms, haikus that refused
> To be epigrams.

And yet, in an uncanny allusion to Watergate, Lehman suggests an underpinning that contradicts this kind of operational open-endedness. After all, must there not be some objective standard, some sense of "evidence" that renders interesting an infinite set of particulars:

> If everything is evidence, everything is admissible,
> And my tape recorder proves it.

> I wrote
> Everything down, as though it would otherwise disappear,
> As though everything was meant to end up in a book.

The romps of a group of literary acquaintances in "New York City, 1974" are contextualized by the speaker's comment about himself and a friend: "Neither of us knew what he wanted to do with his life." Ultimately, these strong doubts cannot be separated from poetry and its possibilities, and they are reflected in the ingeniously coherent narrative that Lehman constructs by means of thematically disjunctive poetic sequencing. Lehman's narrative navigates the limits of narration, at times seeming to be stranded yet eventually finding new streams on its beaches.

Lehman, like Shapiro, dynamically uses the ambivalent bifurcation between abstraction and realism that "Self-Portrait in a Convex Mirror" powerfully formulates, and the two younger poets find grounds for the rapprochement of these opposing terms. Indeed, Ashbery's poem itself goes far in explicating and defetishizing the false opposition between the referential and the nonreferential. Shapiro and Lehman react to "Self-Portrait in a Convex Mirror" with rich and startling admixtures of the "real" and the "abstract." Speaking broadly, one might hypothesize that serious art and healthy approaches to living must now integrate the lessons of disjunctive modernism with an awareness that the realistic imperative of recognizability requires abstraction. However, this kind of postmodern poetry, unlike modernism, makes no implicit claim that art is an antenna. For better or worse, modernism has been distributed throughout society, and cultural authority is necessarily in a tenuous position.

There are a multitude of fine mideighties poets who should be represented in this regard. I will discuss only two more of them here by focusing briefly on "And Then There's Us" by Cherríe Moraga and "Minimalist" by Thomas Fink.

Moraga's "And Then There's Us" is a short poetic explanation of its title:

for LaRue and Elvira

Nobody would believe it
to look at us
how our families'
histories
converge.
        Two women on opposite south
        ends of the continent
        working cotton
        for some man

> Nobody would believe it.
> Their backs
> and this country
> collapsing
> to make room for us together.[14]

The poem's speaker addresses two women. She observes that because they look so different, probably racially, that "Nobody would believe" their convergent familial lineage. It is implied that ancestors of the two women whom the speaker addresses are from the pre–Civil War South and prerevolutionary Mexico. The exploitation of their labor, as depicted by a prototypical female ancestor, has paradoxically contributed to the "collapse" of their countries. This collapse engenders an enchanted though actual "room for us together" for the three women.

The construction of race is confronted more frankly and easefully than would have been customary in the midseventies. The race consciousness promoted by "And Then There's Us" is too complicated to be called merely interracial. "Self-Portrait in a Convex Mirror" points toward a "burn[ing] up" of convention[s] for the constructed but "necessary" "roles we have to play." In Moraga, group identification is paradoxically crucial yet acknowledged to be a cultural construct.

Thomas Fink's "Minimalist" is an elegant, syntactically experimental poetic statement upon the many within the one:

> handwriting like blush odor
> you demand stringent marble
>
> think edge—
> square enough empire—
> platform atom limn
>
> again tenant shirks
> contract—
> guess edit perennial—
> unsnared equation predicament
>
> swarm interstices.[15]

The poem's opening couplet sets up an impersonal surface reality that makes one think of the marble of a tombstone. From this wish for the death of the personality and the ego, the absent subject is a "think[ing] edge" that through the construction of a "platform atom," or provisional ego, is able to sketch or "limn" an "empire" for itself that is securely if provisionally "square enough." However, there is an inevitable lapse in the unstated "contract" and this always already "again tenant." The contract must be "perennial[ly]" edited through "guess[es]." This constantly unpredictable "unsnared equation predicament" implies a wild metaphorizing force. The multiplicity of the effects of this force "swarm" the small spaces between our writerly and our mental processes.

The first stanza can be read as a relatively conventional sentence, with the subject "handwriting." The second stanza starts with an imperative that implies the subject "you." The imperative voice dominates the rest of the poem, charging the seemingly unsyntactic poem and equating the second person to "handwriting." In effect, "Minimalist" writes with an implied directness of address. Fink weaves a poem from the exquisite confusions between speaker and addressee in "Self-Portrait in a Convex Mirror."

"Self-Portrait in a Convex Mirror" works aesthetically because it is "true" to its era. This is of course not a truth of naive realism. Its authenticity can rather be attributed to the strength with which it "sounds like" or "makes visible" how culture works. "Self-Portrait in a Convex Mirror" may indeed alternatively be understood as a poet's attempt simultaneously to create and articulate his contemporary voice, pertinence, subject, and self. Those projects inevitably entail a clarification of the cultural moment. "Self-Portrait in a Convex Mirror" clarifies the dynamic tensions of the midseventies, and perhaps of the last quarter of a century, more strongly than any other poem. It is therefore appropriate to consider poets as diverse as Shapiro, Lehman, Moraga, and Fink in the light of Ashbery. Although direct influence is not as likely between Ashbery and Moraga as between Ashbery and the three other younger poets, Moraga subtly uses poetic disjunctions of contexts and line breaks to disseminate her words.

Moraga's speaker, nonetheless, uses a kind of face-to-face conversation with her audience as a powerful tool, and unlike the four other poets discussed, she does not overtly both allude to the poem's self-reflexiveness and shatter its discursive and fictive illusions. These pursuits, and their problematizations, link Ashbery, Shapiro, and Fink, who constantly call the reader's attention to the reading process by writing skillfully nuanced poetries that are balanced between mimesis and antimimesis, thematic representation and sharp disjunction. Such border poetries require more than not making sense. These poets produce a rich language (with a small *l*) poetry that keeps its edge by owning up to an implicit responsiveness to and responsibility for its poetic effects and connotations. They stay close to both a sense of language as a material and language as a promise to represent objects of desire. However, these representations and desires are always adjuncts to what one might consider "good" writing—that is, writing which is ingeniously true to its medium. In this manner, our understandings, feelings, and emotions are trued through poetry. In brief, they dynamically use the ambivalent bifurcation between abstraction and realism that "Self-Portrait in a Convex Mirror" powerfully formulates, and they find grounds for the rapprochement of these opposing terms. Indeed, Ashbery's poem itself goes far in explicating and defetishizing the false opposition between the referential and the nonreferential that some of the more seemingly progressive poets of the seventies and the eighties valorized, wishing to repeat without acknowledgment what Ashbery and others accomplished before the midseventies. Poets like Shapiro, Lehman, Moraga, and Fink, however, react to the poetic and cultural significance of "Self-Portrait in a Convex Mirror" with rich and startling admixtures of the "real" and the "abstract."

NOTES

1. Fredric Jameson, *The Ideologies of Theory*, vol. 2, *Syntax of History* (Minneapolis: University of Minnesota Press, 1988), 205.

2. Fredric Jameson, *The Political Unconscious: Narrative as a Socially Symbolic Act* (Ithaca: Cornell University Press, 1981), 31.

3. Ibid., 10.

4. Louis Althusser, *Lenin and Philosophy*, trans. Ben Brewster (New York: Monthly Review Press, 1971), 42.

5. Ibid., 222–23.

6. Harold Bloom, *Figures of Capable Imagination* (New York: Seabury Press, 1976) 189.

7. Ibid., 187.

8. Jameson, *Political Unconscious*, 13.

9. Stephen Paul Miller, "'Self-Portrait in a Convex Mirror,' the Watergate Affair, and John's Crosshatch Paintings: Surveillance and Reality-Testing in the Mid-Seventies," *boundary* 2 20, no. 2 (Summer 1993): 84–115.

10. David Shapiro, *House (Blown Apart)* (Woodstock, N.Y: Overlook Press, 1988), 14.

11. David Lehman, *Operation Memory* (Princeton: Princeton University Press, 1990) 77–81.

12. Ibid., 85–86.

13. Ibid., 71–72.

14. Cherríe Moraga, *Loving in the War Years, lo que nunca pasó por sus labios* (Boston: South End Press, 1983), 148.

15. Thomas Fink, *Surprise Visit* (New York: Domestic Press, 1993), 12.

BARBARA L. ESTRIN

Re-Versing the Past:
Adrienne Rich's Outrage Against Order

The past is betrayed by the simple fact that the present it was is made absent. It lacks a certain mode, the tone of the quick, the lively, even as it is recalled.

—J. F. Lyotard, "The Survivor"[1]

Citing the consistent failure of any symbolic system to represent women, Judith Butler asks: "If the representations that do exist are normative phantasms, then how are we to reverse or contest the force of those representations?"[2] As a woman and as a writer in *An Atlas of the Difficult World*, Adrienne Rich anticipates Butler's unease and performs precisely the contestation Butler seeks. More self-consciously than Stevens or Lowell, Rich is cognizant of her ambivalent position as representer. In her most recent work, she challenges that position by contesting her own representations, widening the Petrarchan revisionism she began in the 1978 "Twenty-One Love Poems" of *The Dream of a Common Language* to voice both the questions the imagined other, replaced in the poem, might raise and the answers the repressed self, silenced by the poem, might give. Rich enacts the revisionist linguistics Butler proposes by "considering the limits of representation and representability as open to significant rearticulations and transformations" ("Against Proper Objects," 20). It is the openings Rich seeks even as she recognizes that, "like the dyer's hand, [she] is suffused by what [she] works

From *The American Love Lyric after Auschwitz and Hiroshima*, pp. 153–76, 240–42. © 2001 by Barbara L. Estrin.

in."[3] To forge such openings, Rich begins by admitting that poetry is part of the problem. She follows though by recognizing her responsibility not only to identify the expropriations as they occur but to restrategize the forms so that they might flesh out the traditionally muted other.

Rich's subject in *Atlas* is the theory of representation itself. Form appears in the book both as seductive and dangerous, the only means Rich can use and the only prospect she has for articulating her resignifying project. Those revisions involve entering into a previously unthinkable dialogue with the writing self, the poetic form, and even the dead. First Rich imagines the unimaginable and then she gives the unimagined a body, voice, and forum. Unhinging the very signifying structures to which, as poet, she is so powerfully drawn, Rich moves into a country she had never before penetrated so deeply. And it is a risky territory.

While she has received much critical praise for "re-engendering the love poetry sequence" with the 1978 "Twenty-One Love Poems,"[4] in the 1991 *An Atlas of the Difficult World*, Rich confesses how much her own desire for words threatens to make her part of the problem she seeks to solve. In the acknowledgment, Rich takes her poetry into a theoretical domain chronicled neither by those who see her as a militant feminist whose art isn't worth taking seriously nor by those who see her as a formalist poet whose ideology can be theoretically discounted.[5] In *Atlas*, Rich returns once more, as she did in *The Dream of a Common Language*, to Petrarchan poetics. This time, however, she questions whether her earlier deconstructions went far enough. "Twenty-One Love Poems" ends defensively on a note of self-determination: "I choose to walk here. And to draw this circle."[6] In her retrospective reading—and in ours—it remains clear that, in 1978, Rich was still establishing herself as the shaping force of the Petrarchan construct: the poet chooses self, other, and words.[7]

Atlas begins with the assumption that "choice is a very loaded word,"[8] that poetry involves what Butler calls "the melancholic reiteration of a language that one never chose."[9] In *Atlas*, Rich returns to the old forms of representation with a postmodern impulse and exposes the moments of entrapment in the works of her predecessors in order to release the forgotten other. She thereby renegotiates the poetic heritage she had already challenged in "Twenty-One Love Poems." No longer content in 1991 to diagnose suffering "as personal, individual, maybe familial, and at most to be 'shared' with a group specific to the suffering," Rich struggles toward "a vocabulary for pain as communal."[10] The poems in *Atlas* go beyond identity politics into the much more difficult terrain of both imagining again—returning to the original form—and reimagining—superimposing the voice of the repressed on the image of the previously imagined. Dealing with the incommensurable by risking the unspeakable, Rich gives the "other," displaced by the form, a forum in her poems despite the fact that the "other" who speaks will turn around and indict her as a complicitor in the displacement process.

In "Final Notations," "Through Corralitos Under Rolls of Cloud," and "For a Friend in Travail" of *Atlas*, Rich works through the various forms of containment she poetically inherits from generic Petrarchism—of the sonnet, the serial poem, and the *aubade* respectively—to emerge with a vision that includes her own contributions to the process she questions. If it is language that culturally traps us, then what needs to be changed is the language itself. Not only does Rich take issue with her own Petrarchism; she also takes on that of the predecessors whose forms originally seduced her into the other-confining turns of their repressive techniques. When she transforms the Petrarchan poetic in "Final Notations," "Through Corralitos," and "For a Friend," Rich often speaks in the voice of the other who remains repressed in the early, and late, modern male poems her work parallels: Marvell's "Mower's Song"; Stevens's "The Idea of Order at Key West"[11]; and Donne's "Breake of Day." In alluding to those poets who were already reflecting on the power of the desired other (Marvell), the brutality of mere survival (Stevens), and the terror of physical separation (Donne), Rich takes their deconstructions one step further and brings her own work to a deeper exploration of Petrarchism than she had ventured in "Twenty-One Love Poems."

Rich's sense of form as irresistible and claustrophobic is summarized by "Magic Glasses," Edwin Romanzo Elmer's anamorphic cover painting of *Atlas*. There the landscape and the sky are refracted and illuminated again and again, through the foregrounded window pane and magnifying glass, the ciborium-vase at the center, the leafy pattern on the vase and in the blue and brown motif of the marble table. The circles become eggs and the phallic lines at the edge move from square to rectangular, rendering the images both female and male. The distorted images in the magnifying glass and doubled mirrorings in the ciborium neutralize and hence undercut the sexual engenderings they seem to suggest.

The mirrors subtract what the fall landscape completes: the cycle of the seasons that would, by implication, bring on renewal. Since there seems to be no relief, the mirrors also imply that the only thing to be reproduced is the barren landscape that already exists. The clearly defined windows, marking the separation of inner from outer, instead bring the outer inside. The landscape fills the cup and so takes it over. But the ciborium is actually empty, mirroring and revealing the empty self who placed it there. If the inside is the outside, then the self has nothing to offer. If the outside is the inside, then there is no other to satisfy the self. The process of doubling reorganizes the landscape into an empty signifier that the magnifying glass bends out of

shape once again. The magical glasses are black magical glasses, threatening
to render all things merely signs, proliferating in an endless process of dis-
satisfaction. Brittle glass becomes vaporous air as the many containers drift
from the blackness of the window panes to the gray of the horizon into which
everything fades. The blackness seems to creep up and absorb the colors just
as the reversed earth and sky eliminate each other. The painting becomes
anamorphic, as one image struggles against, and then obviates, the other and
both merge into non-differentiated and figure-absorbing space.

The unresolved doubling in the cover painting expresses in visual terms
the poetic of the book where Rich turns the forms she inherits into vehicles
through which she can articulate her own overarching questions. In the process, Rich revives the other overcome by her predecessor's repressions and her
own repressive self. As her poetic magnifying glass mirrors its earlier mirrorings, she threatens to double the exposure. The repressed self appears uncannily, hauntingly, compellingly, to challenge the sign by which it is identified.
Through her magnifications, the other "forgotten" in earlier texts comes to
the surface; the visual presence in turn renders audible "the less legible meanings of sound" (*Collected Poems*, p. 488). Rich's reading of Marvell, Stevens,
and Donne overturns their reading of Petrarch, as the current text "enters a
field of reading as partial provocation, requiring a set of prior texts in order
to gain legibility and initiating a set of appropriations and criticisms that
call into question their fundamental premises" (*Bodies that Matter*, p. 19). The
imbricated "prior text" in all three poems is Petrarchan. When Rich alludes
to Marvell, Stevens, and Donne, she follows their habit of recasting Petrarch
and Petrarch's habit of recasting himself.

Rich's use of prior texts in *Atlas* is a way of getting at prior beings, both
those the poem represents and those it represses. At the center of *Atlas* is the
question that stops the book: "What does it mean to say *I have survived*?" (p.
48). With Lyotard, Rich may be saying that "the survivor always survives a
death, but the death of what life" ("The Survivor," p. 144)? In "Final Notations,"
it is the life of the self overcome by the deadening form Rich personifies; in
"Through Corralitos," it is the life of the buried earlier self and the indifference
of the survivor-murderer to the self who dies. Admitting her vulnerability to the
deadening force in "Final Notations" and culpability for some of the deaths in
"Through Corralitos," Rich negotiates for change in "For a Friend" and thereby
loosens the bind of the forms through which she realizes herself.

First and Last Testament:
"It will become your will" in "Final Notations"

"Final Notations" chronicles the imposition of a form so seductive and so
totalizing that its mere existence makes both a return to self or an attachment

to the other impossible. Representation destroys the representer because the signifier usurps everything. The compulsions of "Final Notations" echo those of the Marvellian text of "The Mower's Song," which in turn reflect those of the Petrarchan text, specifically of *Rime sparse* 23, where, disguised as Mercury, Laura turns Petrarch to stone and declares herself inviolate and unobjectifiable. Marvell invents a Juliana who takes over his profession and mows him down. In 23, Petrarch invents a Laura who is similarly his inventor and similarly his undoer. And that is precisely what the "it" is for the speaker in "Final Notations" where form immobilizes the self in the way that the stone-casting Laura does Petrarch in *Rime sparse* 23.

If Petrarch imagines the woman as imaginer who retaliates by rendering him an object and subsequently by rendering herself unknowable, Rich goes one step further, imagining the "its" desire to permeate everything, not just to privilege dark secrets in an irretrievable locale. While Petrarch's Laura-Mercury indicates the extent to which male forms and their rationales fail to accommodate the woman, Rich's "it" probes even deeper in its destruction of the poet, emerging more compelling than Petrarch's woman. And, while Petrarch instantly turned to stone at Laura-Mercury's command, the victim of "it" experiences a much more drawn out form of torture. For the Laura who actively cuts and speaks and escapes, this "it" "takes," "touches," and "occupies" like a magnetic force that expands with what it extracts. Laura leaves Petrarch cast in stone. Rich's "it" turns the self into "it." As infectious disease, "it" reduces everything, including its discoverer, into a symptom. The moment of contagious takeover is always imminent. That's the poison. The speaker can never get over her vulnerability because she keeps reinfecting herself with what can only be described as a desire for the diseased forms of her repression.

Petrarch invents a Laura-Mercury who challenges his invention; Rich invents an invention, a simulacrum that behaves like Petrarch's evasive Laura-Mercury. In this mechanized world, the deadening impact of the seductive form is indistinguishable from the denying presence of the desired woman who, in turn, bespeaks the "ineluctable absence" of the original self. Slavoj Žižek writes that "the ultimate lesson of virtual reality is the virtualization of the very true reality. By the mirage of 'virtual reality' the true reality itself is posited as a semblance of itself, as a pure symbolic edifice."[12] In the same way, Rich's "it" behaves like the woman in the poem who is an image of the woman in the poet's head. Rich's devouring form equals Marvell's man-eating Juliana, who is another version of Petrarch's poetry-corrupting Laura-Mercury. Rich's unnamed "it" reflects both the poet's desire to control the other it invents and the poet's admission that the invention undoes the inventor, as Laura-Mercury turns Petrarch-Battus to stone, and Juliana threatens Damon when she merely "comes." In naming the other "it," Rich enacts the revenge of the other who, responding to its objectification, refuses to yield. Like the laurel tree, the "it," as a thing not a person, is absolutely unavailable in a form to which the speaker has access.

Nowhere does Rich play with pronouns so unrelentingly as in "Final Notations," where the absorbable "it" is never fully defined and never fully evaded. What is missing from the sonnet is the poetic "I":

> it will not be simple, it will not be long
> it will take little time, it will take all your thought
> it will take all your heart, it will take all your breath
> it will be short, it will not be simple
>
> it will touch through your ribs, it will take all your heart
> it will not be long, it will occupy your thought
> as a city is occupied, as a bed is occupied
> it will take all your flesh, it will not be simple
>
> You are coming into us who cannot withstand you
> you are coming into us who never wanted to withstand you
> You are taking parts of us into places never planned
> You are going far away with pieces of our lives
>
> it will be short, it will take all your breath
> it will not be simple, it will become your will
>   (p. 57)

In "Final Notations" the form engulfs the self in the way that Juliana mows Damon in "The Mower's Song," a poem whose inexorability "Final Notations" follows. Deforming the self, the form ensures that no original being remains. Damon's allusions to Juliana progress chronologically from a history that has already been lived to a malignancy that is about to erupt, a narrative thread that becomes an emotional threat:

> When Juliana came and She
> What I do to the Grass, does to my Thoughts and Me.[13]

Damon's past is replaced by Juliana's presence: she takes over his being. His beginning lies with the fatal "when" of Juliana's initiation into his life just as his end will result from the imminent danger of her being about-to-arrive. The past is never over for Damon. It keeps happening again. The fatal moment (when Juliana came) is the cause of his present dissolution (because Juliana never goes away). She becomes his Mower, doing to him what he did to the grass and what Laura-Mercury did to Petrarch-Battus. In her presence, he is objectified as grass to her will. She walks all over him.

When Rich adopts Marvell's menacing tone and renames the fatally attractive woman as the fatally compelling form, she too splits the poem to link the memory of desire to the anticipation of death. And, if death climaxes with a war simile, love begins with a sex symbol, the bed as the place for birth (accouchement) and conception (engendering):

> It will occupy your thought
> as a city is occupied, as a bed is occupied

As Petrarchan other, Juliana emerges indistinguishable from Damon's self. But if Damon demonizes Juliana in a rather simple exchange of Petrarchan other for Petrarchan self, Rich's demon is much more complex. In the overlap of "it will not be simple" as occupier of the poem's beginning, middle, and end, Rich indicates that becoming the other (as Damon does) embattles sexuality and leaves the battle of the sexes unresolved. War (as a city is occupied by an invading army) and sex (as a bed is occupied by a beloved partner) are totalizing and equal. Like Stevens's couch, Rich's bed is both the place of the sexually desired other and the seat of the creatively fecund mother. But, in vacillating between a military zone and an erotic site, her similes not only heighten the connections between infantile and sexual desire. They make the connection between love and war clear.

With the thrice repeated, "it will not be simple," Rich outlines the three-fold nature of the takeover that dissolves the collective memory of historical experience ("as a city is occupied"), involves the present feeling of collective loss ("you are taking parts of us"), and commands the future occupation of a new task ("it will become your will"). "It" is consuming (like love) and fragmenting (like death). In the end, the complexity devastates: as desire (will), it is an all-inclusive obsession; as legacy (will), it remains all that is left behind for future generations: "It will become your will." With the doubled "will," Rich bequeathes her compulsions to her successors. If Marvell speaks to the heraldry of death in the familiar meadow, Rich anticipates new forms ("you are taking parts of us into places never planned"). Those new places lie beyond the limits of conventional representation.

In the octet, the "I" preaches to an implied "you" as a teacher preparing a child for a difficult lesson but, in the crucial third stanza, the "I," joining with her fellow pupils, speaks directly to the intruder, describing the invasion as it occurs: "you are coming into us … you are taking parts of us … you

are going far away." As current actions that signify a debilitating and desta-
bilizing process, "entering, taking, and leaving" contemporize the devasta-
tion. The anticipated threat comes now. Like a television reporter caught in a
media event as it unfolds, the narrator incredulously witnesses the imminent
takeover. Only the reporter is also the victim in the narrative she relates.
The vulnerability she describes is her own: it is, as the "we" indicates, "ours."
The "I" is trapped by the picture she describes. The scenario demands total
surrender—"we cannot withstand you"—and represents a desired end—"we
never wanted to withstand you." Unable to defend the self, "we" are broken
from the start. Unable to perpetuate the self, "we" are retrospectively phrased
in terms of a negative desire. Thus, the "you" effaces the past—"you are going
far away with pieces of our lives"—and changes the future—"you are taking
parts of us into places never planned." In this case, the self is overridden by
the fragmentation, as the desired other becomes the invading army and the
love poem is overcome by the war poem. As other, the "will" threatens the self
even though, as self, the "will" expresses its desire. That sense of unauthor-
ized ownership (as a city is occupied) violates the assurance of reproductive
enterprise (as a bed is occupied) to make the assumed form of renewal the
actual source of annihilation. The speaker is *pre-occupied*. "Final Notations"
suggests that sublimation not only requites the desiring body; it replaces it:
"it will become your will."

In "Final Notations," form dominates everything. Caught in the signifying web, the self is immobilized by a desire which, in its capacity to take over
the self, replaces the woman Petrarch and Marvell demonize. The form is all.
"Final Notations" also chronicles the connection between poetry and politics.
Love poems may lead to bed-time stories. But the mechanism is the same as
that of war-time stories. The totalizing form of their trap is interchangeable:
"as a city is occupied . . . as a bed is occupied." Rich argues that the impulse
behind the love poem is a death drive, a preoccupation present in the poetic
from the start. But she also incriminates the self as occupant of the form that
is so compelling. "Through Corralitos" speaks on behalf of the self forgotten
by the compulsions Rich indicts in "Final Notations." There, the self replaced
by the sublimating poem continues uncannily to exist. That spectral other
gathers strength as "Through Corralitos" progresses and the deformed self is
imagined in all its ghastly emanations.

Outraging the "I": "Through Corralitos Under Rolls of Cloud"
In "Through Corralitos," Rich revives yet another Laura implicated in the
Rime sparse: the Laura-Medusa of 366 who rises to utter her revenge against
the surviving Perseus. The series opens, however, on the traditional terrain of Petrarchism and the laurelized landscape of trees and fruits. Rich

prepares for her devastating attack on the poet-Perseus-self by first writing about the typical victim in the poetic construct, Laura-Daphne:

> Through Corralitos under rolls of cloud
> between winter-stiff, ranged apple-trees
> each netted in transparent air,
> thin sinking light, heartsick within and filmed
> in heartsickness around you, gelatin cocoon
> invisible yet impervious—to the hawk
> steering against the cloudbank, to the clear
> oranges burning at the rancher's gate
> rosetree, agave, stiff beauties holding fast
> with or without your passion,
> the pruners freeing up the boughs
> in the unsearched faith these strange stiff shapes will bear.
>   (p. 46)

The "ranged apple trees . . . oranges burning at the rancher's gate . . . rose tree . . . agave" are, like Petrarch's laurels in the *Rime sparse*, former Daphnes "holding fast." They are arranged by pruning man whose mutilating purpose is paradoxically to propagate. He lays the trees bare so that they will in turn "bear" fruit as testimony to the patriarchy. If the denied sexuality of the poetic Daphne annuls female reproductivity, these Daphnes have already given in to the demands of their pursuers. As previously mutilated Daphnes, the "stiff beauties holding fast" catch the oxymoronic sense of movement (fast-paced) that goes nowhere certain (holding-back) so that the pattern perpetuates patriarchal imperatives in its logical impossibilities and parodies Petrarchan denials in its fruitful inevitabilities. The "stiff beauties holding fast" are pinned down from the very beginning, locked in place by the economic desire of the "pruners" who cut them to size so that they will propagate more fully. Rich's "stiff trees" yield to the rancher's reality, as they fulfill his lust for patriarchal fruition. The ranchers use the doctrine of Petrarchan sublimation economically, turning the body of the violated woman into the medium for financial gain just as the poet redacts the traditional laurel into the vehicle for literary fame.

Rich's trees are peculiarly bookish, already laurelized. The narrative follows a camera motion—"heartsick within and filmed in heartsickness around you"—that records no emotion. The landscape seems psychological ("heartsickness without you") but is hostile to the pathetic fallacy ("with or without your passion"). That movement toward stillness and death (winter stiff) and stillness awaiting movement and birth (gelatin cocoon) encapsulates the self-canceling process of the poem. One season inevitably overrides the other. The feminine resistance to masculine power values that Daphne represents in the Petrarchan ethos is subsumed by the deliberate obviation of female initiative in the patriarchal ranch Rich images.

Paralleling the shift in the landscape from one that seems sympathetic ("filmed in heartsickness around you") to one that persists indifferently ("with or without your passion") is the strange relationship of the narrator to the "you" throughout all of "Through Corralitos": at first sympathetic, then malignant, then sympathetic again and, finally, indifferent. Withdrawing from the "you" in poems I and II, the narrator rubs salt into the wound of the resistant and dying self. In poems III and IV, she shifts gears and speaks on behalf of the "you" injured by her initial commentary, her acidity sharpened into the venom of Medusa, this time directed against the survivor. Such shifts also work against the reading audience that is first included in the sympathy, as the "I" speaks for an implied "you"; and then is implicated in the villainy, as the "I" asks accusatory questions of the reading "you."

At first, in poem I, the narrator seems to include the "you" in her assessment, arguing that the world resonates with "your" pain. By the end of poem I, she maintains, contrarily, that, the world wags on without "you" too. That shift is recorded through the changing meaning of the thrice repeated "stiff" ("winter stiff . . . stiff beauties . . . strange stiff"). Transforming the agency of the tree from victim, to survivor, to ghost, Rich plays on *stiff*: as seasonal (and therefore temporary) state; as the constant condition of self-preserving womanhood; and, finally, as a dead body in a bizarre *film noir*. Each of the meanings of stiff depends on its modifier. "Winter stiff" depicts a self frozen by its position in time; "stiff beauties" are frigid in their unresponsiveness and defiant in their refusal to yield to passion; "strange stiffs" are psychological corpses that haunt the living. Those reversals follow a three-part split in the narration from sympathetic, through anti-poetic, through spectral that prepares for the split in the second poem, where the speaker describes a simple feeling, recovery after sickness, that separates the "you" from its past ("uncertain who she is or will be without you," p. 47) as, in the first poem, she had severed the "you" from the landscape ("with or without your passion," p. 46). With the "strange stiffs," Rich enters the nether world as her critique moves from an examination of patriarchy to an indictment of the surviving self, who turns out to be no different in her indifference from the ranchers.

In the guise of the spectral "stiff," she challenges the notion of survival after the horrors twentieth-century life produced. Bringing the political into the poetic, Rich takes off from a prose thought found in a 1984 essay and brought to fruition in her work of the nineties, "Notes Toward a Politics of Location":

The growing urgency of an anti-nuclear, anti-militarist,
movement must be a feminist movement, must be a socialist
movement, must be an anti-racist, anti-imperialist movement.
That it's not enough to fear for the people we know, our own
kind, ourselves.[14]

In the prose passage, Rich calmly arrives at an assessment of political movements based on identity politics to say "it's not enough." "Through Corralitos" questions the sufficiency of "mere" survival by progressively changing
its levels of intensity and complexity. First there is the simple recovery after
illness in poem II; then there is the question of community survival in
poems III and IV Finally, there is the question of self-survival in poem V.
Can the poet who sacrifices a self for the poem subsequently recall the self
who died? Or does her recovery in the poem place her so far out of touch
with her earlier self that return is impossible? The voice of the earlier self
cannot even be fathomed. In poem II, the "you" recovers callously; in poems
III and IV, the callous recovery is named. But in poem V, recovery itself
seems impossible. Medusa torments the surviving Perseus. The repressed
self haunts the forgetter.

First, the body's survival is presented by the narrator as a stab-in-the-
back to the dead:

this other who herself barely came back,
whose breath was fog to your mist, whose stubborn shadow
covered you as you lay freezing,
    (p. 47)

The embryonic and initially protective other ("whose breath was fog to your
mist, whose stubborn shadow / covered you") is dismissed, as the body—in
its drive to survive—seems utterly indifferent to its earlier comforter. In the
narrator's indictment, the ritualized motion of survival surfaces as an act
of deliberate cruelty to the dead. The subtle rhyme between the "barely" of
poem II and the "bearing" of poem I links the future survivor to the fruitful
trees. As the "strange stiff" shapes are estranged from the "stiff beauties," so
the "other" who "barely came back" feels no remorse for her dead self. The
field of difference between life and death is hardly there as the field of difference between *bearing* fruit and holding fast seemed *barely* there in poem
I. Yet it makes all the difference. The shadow self is the Medusa who, in
poems III and IV, takes over the central voice.

In poem III, the narrator begins by attacking the surviving "you" for not
realizing herself except in contrast to the other she left behind:

> what do you know
> of the survivor when you know her
> only in opposition to the lost?
>   (p. 48)

She then complicates the question by arguing that the presumed survivor
only escapes by a narrow-minded reading of the self:

> What does it mean to say *I have survived*
> until you take the mirrors and turn them outward
> and read your own face in their outraged light?
>   (p. 48)

Light—the objectively illuminating source that focuses indiscriminately
on whatever catches it—becomes the subjectively speaking mirror that
turns the focus on the guilty originator. The shadow this time becomes
the inquisitor. In "Through Corralitos," the mirror finally produces a
point of view—outraged light—through which the survivor reads her own
face to learn that she survives over her own dead body, at the expense of
her dead body. When Rich's outraged mirror speaks, it turns the survivor
into a Claudius who kills his brother, a Perseus who beheads Medusa. The
outraged light in the mirror speaks on behalf of the double, the other who
is victimized by what the survivor determines. To read the image from the
point of view of the outraged light in the mirror is to see the originating
self as repressive and to read survival as a victimization of the represented
other. The light and sound gradually merge so the mirror (a source of light)
becomes a point of view (the voice of Outrage) reflecting a disembodied
person that finally becomes an embodied voice, a speaker in the poem
punctuated (as in a Ben Jonson play) as a humor. The voice brings the
Lyotardan forgotten to life again.

Finally, the voice of Outrage emerges as a full-blooded character in the
play, having progressed from the third poem, where it is a reflective visual
mirror, to the fourth poem, where it is the subjective auditory point of view.
The named Outrage asks questions that traditional discourse—and even the
radical feminist rhetoric of Rich's earlier poetry—cannot bring itself to ask.
As in "Final Notations," the "I" and the "you" join together in the face of a
common enemy. But that union lasts only until Outrage breaks through the
glass and speaks on her own behalf:

> Outrage: who dare claim protection for their own
> amid such unprotection? What kind of prayer

is that? To what kind of god? What kind of wish?
(p. 49)

Outrage's questions point to the contrast between the vastness—the utter ruthlessness—of the "such" as measured against the vulnerability—the extreme defenselessness—of "unprotection." Guarding the victimized in their fragility, she also points an accusatory finger at people who do nothing but protect "their own." The chiasmic relationship between Outrage's identification of the marginialized and denouncement of the repressors renders her simultaneously defendant and prosecutor. She facilitates the revival of those repressed in the past even as she represents the gathering force of those who previously had no voice of their own.

Rich's device—the setting apart of lines of the poem to be spoken by a feeling that emerges a fleshed out character in the poem—is part of her conspiracy to turn on safe assumptions. In the fourth poem, those safe assumptions have a poetic history in the *locus amoenus* the narrator uses to define the sense of security she shatters in three stages: (1) through the myths of Diana and Actaeon; (2) after the death of Narcissus on behalf of Echo; and finally (3) through the voice of Outrage who speaks of the original Medusan violation as another version of the story of Actaeon and Diana and of the interiorization of Echo by Narcissus. The narrator describes Outrage:

> That light of outrage is the light of history
> springing upon us when we're least prepared,
> thinking maybe a little glade of time
> leaf-thick and with clear water
> is ours, is promised us, for all we've hacked
> and tracked our way through: to this:
> (p. 49)

She draws two mythological circles, one menacing and the other comforting, and then contracts them so that their dark end precedes their innocent beginnings. The glade is first Diana's pool, the safe harbor invaded by Actaeon, "springing upon us when we're least prepared," and then the false/safe feeling such places encourage ("thinking maybe a little glade of time . . . is ours"). Then it is Narcissus's pool, with its mirror of clear water, and the place of death, leaf thick, with its already growing and entangling narcissi. Time past—"hacked / and tracked" our way through—and time present—the point of final epiphany—coalesce in the "this." Like Stevens's Narcissus confronted with what he "did not expect,"[15] Rich's Narcissus is already ensnared by his own desire. In the landscape of repression and revenge, there is no clear picture. Blurred from the start, the mirror is "leaf-thick," assuming the foliage of Narcissus's metamorphosis.

In the safety of the imagined enclave, the poem becomes a duet of politeness:

> What will it be? Your wish or mine? your
> prayers or my wish then: that those we love
> be well, whatever that means, to be well.
> (p. 49)

With the casualness of conversation, the prayer and the wish occupy the scene of the glade, as the "I" and the "we" join together at the wishing-well, throwing platitudes at each other. The wishing-well is the well-wisher. Time becomes place. Place becomes person. Noun (wishing-well) merges with verb (well-wishing). Everything is an image that turns into a mirage. If the water has no margin, the glade evaporates. The end is an image without a body: Narcissus in the water; Medusa on the shield. The glade and pool become the scene where Outrage speaks. The false safety, of Diana, Narcissus, and Perseus, emerges the harsh reality of Medusa, Echo and pointed accusation.

In response to the shallow conversation of hollow embodiment, Outrage speaks. The source of light in III turns into the voice of thunder in IV. Breaking all bounds, Outrage fleshes itself out in shattering words:

> who dare claim protection for their own
> amid such unprotection?
> (p. 49)

The speech not only unsettles the goddess Diana for whom the nymphs claim protection in the Actaeon myth, it also deconstructs the representation of Diana as female goddess whose vengeance for the shattered glade bifurcates the world into hunted and victims. Similarly, Medusa, whose presence in the poem conflates warrior and enemy, demonstrates that there are no shields. But more than that, it dismisses the territorial claim of the enclave. Inside the mirror is Echo who, in the end, voices her revenge by turning Narcissus into her. Rich's questions resonate from the myth to the twentieth century. After Auschwitz and Hiroshima, how can there be a protected place "amid such unprotection"? How can we draw a ring around "our own" when such circles leave the "unprotected" outside? And what of the very idea of "our own" and the exclusionary reality that brands those not "our own" vermin? If Outrage shatters boundaries to speak her question, she also questions the boundary-making impulse, which is hierarchical and hegemonic, on behalf of the avenging victim. The made-up word "unprotection" (which suggests total vulnerability), like the made-up body "Outrage" (which represents unbridled anger), reiterates that time differences vanish as mythic violations bring on contemporary horrors. Crashing through the protected enclave of the glade, the unsponsored Medusa undermines the accepted forms of social difference and the binary differences of literary forms to disrupt all conventions.

Finally, the tiny wishing well emerges, in poem V, the whole ocean in the "boom of surf . . . the undertow . . . the reef" that undo safety. The narrator assumes Medusa's revenge and cancels survival:

> She who died on that bed sees it her way:
> She who went under peers through the translucent shell
> cupping her death and sees her other well,
> through a long lens, in silvered outline, well
> she sees her other and she cannot tell
> why when the boom of surf struck at them both
> she felt the undertow and heard the bell,
> thought death would be their twinning, till the swell
> smashed her against the reef, her other still
> fighting the pull, struggling somewhere away
> further and further, calling her all the while:
> she who went under summons her other still.
>   (p. 50)

The poem recalls both the bed of poem II, where the primacy of the "she" who died is asserted as memory, and the glade of poem IV, where the assumptions of those who survived are undone as possibility. "Well" is repeated as adverb (seeing well) and adjective (well other) until finally, it becomes a noun (like the watery wishing-well of poem IV). As the water becomes a mirror, the dead self sees her double—well enough—and finds her whole—well again: Perseus as triumphant and callous warrior.

The sub-marine periscope becomes the super-terrestial telescope as the victim sights the survivor through the Earth's distance. Outlined in silver, the well "she" assumes the remoteness of a star. The rhyme of well with swell and bell again mingles sight and sound as the waves "tell" and the telling waves surface as inevitable death knells. The end is inexorable in the mistaken thought—"death would be their twinning"—and unfinal. "She who went under summons her other still." The opening sense of movement without body in the personless participles of "Corralitos I" climaxes in the closing frame of body without movement: "she who went under summons her other [to] still[ness]" ("Corralitos, V"). If the *light* of Outrage scatters the obsessive image of one other, it also shatters the poetical belief in artistic mastery.

The *voice* of Outrage reflected in poems III–V seems an answer to the calm complacency of Stevens's "rage for order" in the "Idea of Order at Key West." Rich's poem functions as a postmodernist rebuttal of Stevens's modernist triumph:

> Ramon Fernandez, tell me, if you know,
> Why when the singing ended and we turned
> Toward the town, tell why the glassy lights,
> The lights in the fishing boats at anchor there,
> As the night descended, tilting in the air,
> Mastered the night and portioned out the sea,
> Fixing emblazoned zones and fiery poles,
> Arranging, deepening, enchanting night.
>
> Oh! Blessed rage for order, pale Ramon,
> The maker's rage to order words of the sea,
> Words of the fragrant portals, dimly-starred,
> And of ourselves and of our origins,
> In ghostlier demarcations, keener sounds.
> (*Collected Poems*, p. 130)

In Stevens, the singing woman inspires the feeling that men can conquer the mysteries of nature, and ominous night, through the mastery of art, and glassy lights. Stevens's oxymoron—"rage for order"—exceeds the natural cancellations of the ebbing and flowing sea and the waxing and waning night. The hierarchy of poetry, with its "ghostlier demarcations" and "keener sounds," outdoes the dominion of origins in the sea and the prophecies of doom in the skies. All "things" are annulled by the rage, as they are sucked back into the "*idea* of order." The rage for order of Stevens's poetic insists that the body of art precedes the world's body in nature. In the beginning was the word.

When Rich turns to the light of Outrage, her victim has no words. While the Stevens of "Idea" never questions why the singing woman stopped, the Rich of "Through Corralitos" speaks on behalf of the silent woman until, finally, she acknowledges the impulse to repress the inspiring other that haunts all poetic distillations. In Stevens's "Idea," the woman disappears as she is replaced by her song. In "Through Corralitos," the woman refuses to disappear. Stevens invites Ramon Fernandez to tell, as he is *already* telling, why art seems to master nature. Rich's "she" "cannot tell" why the "she" [who went under] "summons her other still," why death invokes silence, not words. In Rich's poem, Medusa turns the surviving Perseus to the stillness of stone. In Stevens, the call to language continues as an infinite incantation to fluidity. The woman's song stirs the poet who, in turn, challenges Ramon Fernandez to the words that might, at some future time, answer his questions. Male poet calls to his successor across the continents to continue the male quest. Rich's "she" breaks the connection. Her "she" is condemned to silence. Isolated, the dead "she" can only summon her other to a similar death.

The repeated phrase—"her other still"—frames life in terms of a battle against death—"fighting the pull, struggling somewhere away." Finally, everything is constricted by the unremitting pull of death calling the other [to the] "still[ness of immobility]." We know that the surviving other fights the pull of death and struggles "further and further" as the "she" who died is left (in remoteness) far behind. But what remains ambiguous is the subject of "calling her all the while":

> her other still
> fighting the pull, struggling somewhere away
> further and further, calling her all the while:
> she who went under summons her other still.
>   (p. 50)

Does the survivor "fight, struggle, and call" or is it the dead "she" who continues to recall her live self while the "other" struggles and fights somewhere away out of earshot? Do the living recall the dead or are the dead silenced because, unheard, they are forgotten?

Is the "she" who survives, like the nurturing Demeter to the overcome Persephone, or the poet Orpheus to the stung Eurydice, the subject of the calling? The myths of Demeter and Orpheus center on the active desire of those who survive to keep seasonally or poetically "calling" for the missing child and wife. Demeter and Orpheus never give up on the dead. Their myths are commemorative and poetic. Does the call here reverse the myth with Eurydice pulling Orpheus back to the underworld again, Persephone beckoning her mother to "still" life, and Medusa turning Perseus to the "stillness" of stone? Or, like the Elusinean mysteries and Athena-Medusa-Perseus, does the calling suggest that other and self are the same? In the end, the call for a response results in silence. The call to movement ends in paralysis. If the "she" who died summons the survivor, then the myths are reversed. It is the dead who pull the survivors to them and, hence, recall what the living repress. Thus the dead deaden the living because there is no surviving if living means denying the existence of the selves who "went under." The clear demarcations are muddied. In poem IV, space converges as the protective enclave is haunted by those it excluded. In poem V, time collapses as the survivor is haunted by the self it repressed.

What has Rich imagined here in this "pas de deux" that questions the survival of the chosen people; the beloved other; the living self? The command to stillness brings on the silence of the end of the poem even as the light of Outrage disorders the stratifications structuring the beginning of the poem. And, where Stevens ends with the "blessed rage for order" that confirms the melodious song, Rich's poem is haunted by the harsh voice of Outrage. In that echo, she negates Stevens's "ghostlier demarcations" that outline origins of difference somewhere in the past and the "keener sounds" that speak to destinies of power somewhere in the future. Rich renders the "idea" of order obsolete. Stevens's "ghostlier demarcations" merely reiterate the long history of repression. The demarcating mechanism ties the "keener sounds" to the violative impulse at the beginning. Where Stevens ends in the oxymoronic "rage for order" that preserves the male hierarchies of Petrarchan form, Rich's Outrage breaks the form and pushes out the center to reveal the Medusa as form shatterer. In Stevens's "Idea of Order," the woman disappears as the male poets toss her inspirational resources between them, in a game of catch-up that finally abjects her completely. Deprived of the consolations of kind, Rich's self is left in the terminations of stillness. The other "stills" the self away from the sentimentalization of poetry and the idea of its redeeming power. Unlike Ramon Fernandez whom Stevens commands to "tell," the dead self "cannot tell" herself apart from the living self who, nevertheless, moves further and further away. Her recovery is signified by her refusal to listen. The self who survives is one dimensional. Her "stillness" in persistence speaks to a hollowness reflected in an essential indifference to the calling. Like Elmer's ciborium, the form is an empty shell whose distillations speak of the *ghastliness* of demarcations.

"Through Corralitos" chronicles the history of the dead "she" by bearing witness to what Lyotard calls the immemorial, "that which can neither be remembered (represented to consciousness) nor consigned to oblivion."[16] The shattering question—"who dare claim protection"—points toward the "unprotection"—the silence—that implicates a culture that denies the repressed other a narrational place. While the Stevens of "The Idea of Order at Key West" glories in the culture he inherits, Rich insists that that very culture may have played a role in the unspeakable events of the century. When Memory speaks in "Eastern War Time," the poem that precedes "Corralitos," it turns the mirror on the survivor to say that no poem can "do right" by the dead:

Memory says: Want to do right? Don't count on me.
I'm a canal in Europe where bodies are floating
I'm a mass grave
   (p. 44)

I am standing here in your poem unsatisfied
Lifting my smoky mirror
   (p. 44)

Like the mirror in "Through Corralitos," Memory returns in infinite regression to the fires of the past. But it is a history of violation. And, like the amassing ocean in "Through Corralitos," the mass grave in "Eastern War Time" makes "doing right" in the poem somehow massively wrong. Lifting the "smoky mirror" to reveal an emptiness at the origin, Memory turns form into a deformation. In Stevens, the "blessedness" of the oxymoron "rage for order" produces an art that justifies the necessary repressions. In Rich, the voice of Outrage commands the Medusan stillness that ends poetic distillation. What survives is ultimately turned to stone. If the self merely assimilates the other, the future is condemned to repeat the past in the way that Perseus mirrors Medusa. And, if the future repeats the past, then what Lyotard calls the process of "appearance" and "disappearance" simply allows for replacement: the well self takes over for the victim; the healed society forgets the past; the poem sublimates the life. Memory cannot be relied on because the forgotten never had a narrative place. In "Through Corralitos," Outrage protests the dehumanizing, deindividualizing, massive lunge toward survival that folds (and so suppresses) the other into the self. Her unanswerable questions smash mirrors to "contest" the force of the representations Rich uses and to destabilize the traditional sites of poetic usurpation. In "Eastern War Time," as in "Through Corralitos," time and space converge. The mass graves of Europe spill over from the continental canals of the forties to flood the room of the nineties poem.

Travailing after Outrage: "For a Friend"
In "For a Friend in Travail," Rich asks questions which can be answered. Focusing directly on the other and rearticulating the *aubade* tradition, Rich encourages a friend to "tell" her suffering.[17] In "Corralitos," the other is silenced and distant, overcome by the waves. In "For a Friend," the other seems right there in her self-consciousness:

What are you going through? she said, is the great question.

Philosopher of oppression, theorist
of the victories of force.

We write from the marrow of our bones. What she did not
ask, or tell: how victims save their own lives.

That crawl along the ledge, then the ravelling span of fibre strung
from one side to the other, I've dreamed that too
Waking, not sure we made it. Relief, appallment, of waking.
Consciousness. O, no. To sleep again
O to sleep without dreaming.

How day breaks, when it breaks, how clear and light the moon
melting into moon-colored air
moist and sweet, here on the western edge.
Love for the world, and we are part of it.
How the poppies break from their sealed envelopes
she did not tell.

What are you going through, there on the other edge?
   (p. 51)

The lady in Donne's *aubade*, "Breake of Day," accuses the man of having a "businesse" that takes him away from her.[18] In "For a Friend," Rich's "I" makes the other's business her own. Unlike Donne's lady who dreads the death day brings, the "I" of "For a Friend" speaks of daylight as a precursor to night, "moist and sweet." After the difficult night, difference is at once shattering— "how day breaks"—and nothing—"how the moon melts into moon-colored air." In "Through Corralitos," the terrible end of the myth circles round to the innocent beginning so that death triumphs. In its three repetitions, the "break" of Rich's *aubade* calms the separation anxiety of Donne's "Breake of Day" because its harshness is softened by the melting moon and absorbed by the moony air. Already colored sympathetically, the air *breaks*, and thereby softens, the fall. Nothing is final. Here, Rich draws *this circle*, as she did in "Twenty-One Love Poems," to say something else: "in this round world the corners are imagined." The difference of difference is less significant than being "part of it." In *extremis*, the precarious western ledge (the dark night of the soul) merges with the saving eastern edge (the bright light of waking). To break the "sealed envelope" may not be to tell. It may be to listen. The poppy heralds a red-lettered day. The poet who meets a friend in "travail" facilitates a birth into the other, not a separation (as in "Twenty-One Love Poems") but a joining. Unsealing the envelope and penetrating beyond the sound barrier are acts that also open the self up to the other's expressiveness: "what are you going through?" Victims save their own lives by keeping the narrative thread alive: the "ravelling span of fibre strung."

In the responding letter, the other "tells." The self listens. Like a hand reaching across an abyss, the question forms a connection to the other that spans the difference to open the possibility for dialogue. That connection suggests that the envelope can spontaneously open to reveal new life inside rather than to shatter the life outside. The allusion to dream and sleep again, like Hamlet's "consummation / devoutly to be wished" (3.1. 63–64)[19] speaks to the death-wish—the appallment—in day's pale light, the "death-drive" that connects the postmodern to the early modern and Rich's *aubade* to Donne's "Breake of Day."

The moon-colored sky is both comforting and draining: yet another replication of an already known pallor. Rich's "appallment" condenses Hamlet's "pale cast of thought." But her "consciousness," a heroic waking to the other, is not quite Hamlet's conscience, a cowardly quaking in the self. The "undiscovered country" that gives Hamlet pause is the other-discovered country language bridges in Rich's poem when it unseals the edges. For Hamlet, the question centers on the self in isolation. For Rich, it moves the self into the community: "what are you going through?" If Hamlet's alternatives in the "To be or not to be" speech are indistinguishable from each other, Rich's *what* is answerable. It provides a safety net where language can soften into meaning. Like daylight fusing with moon-colored air and like Lowell's crocus in "The Day" (*Day by Day*, p. 53), the poppies "break" from their sealed envelopes to open up meltingly and to begin the quiet discourse that comes after the voice of Outrage. The question casts the extending rope, dangling a poetic line that heals the self, angling a political line that imagines the other. Like Donne's "inward narrow crooked lanes / [that] Do purge sea waters fretful salt away" ("The Triple Foole," p. 52), the question—"what are you going through?"—intimates that the difficult tunnel has the light of articulated language at the end. Asking the question presupposes an answer, one not yet formulated but still possible.

* * *

In "Final Notations," Rich echoes the Marvell of "Damon the Mower" to demonstrate how language and its necessary formulae overtake self and its presumed independence. When the self projects itself as other, the other, in turn, endangers the self "it will become your will." In "Through Corralitos," Rich argues that language and what she calls mere "containment" (*Points of Departure*, p. 7) confine both the depicted other and the depicting self. But, in "For a Friend," she goes beyond the breaking point and over the edge to speak, as Donne appears to in "A Valediction: Forbidding Mourning," against "the breach." Her line, "the ravelling span of fibre strung / from one side to the other," seems at first glance to be an equivalent of Donne's "an expansion / Like gold to ayery thinnesse beat" (p. 63). But, while Donne's solid gold fades into vaporous thinness, Rich's ravelling span weaves itself back again, forming a solid bridge to the saving "ledge." Rich speaks beyond the inevitably of the chasm and in the hope of an "expansion" that commemorates the possibility of return. Her language spans the distance between self and other to "see how words come down to us and how we can go on with them" (Montenegro, *Points of Departure*, p. 7). The present tense of "what are you going through" has a future end in sight. The travail of death pain fuses with the travail (in its obsolete sense) of birth pain and thereby becomes the means to a rebirth in a place "where the end of suffering will begin."[20]

In providing the substance for an answer by phrasing the question in answerable terms, the inquisitor of "For a Friend" also assures the future of narrative. "Final Notations" dictates the last word. "For a Friend" assumes another story, one contained within the letter of the sealed envelope. Through the encirclements of internal rhyme, that letter moves away from the abyss of self to turn the corner from the "outer edge" and to find poetic footing in the containing—hence saving—inner ledge. The reified "you" in "For a Friend" goes beyond the invented other of "Twenty-One Love Poems" to focus on something not yet drawn there: the future possibility of an other who escapes Petrarchism's other-denying forms, an Eve with a life of her own. That Laura-Eve is palpably present, as she is in those rare moments in *Rime sparse* 181, 188, 237, and 354, where the woman seems to return the poet's desire with a desire of her own. The overwhelming difficulty in *Atlas* is the horror of the past that remains "unsatisfied / lifting [its] smoky mirror" (p. 44). In "Through Corralitos," the mirror reflects "outward/in outrage" to point toward "such unprotection" (p. 49). In "For a Friend," the victim is given a voice and a body, though the answer to the question—"what are you going through?"—is not yet given. In *Atlas*, Rich "opens" the way to what will be her continuing "transformation" and "rearticulation" ("Against Proper Objects," 20) of the forms she inherits. In her next book, the 1995 *Dark Fields of the Republic*, Rich "goes on" despite her sense that "this life of continuing is for the sane mad / and the bravest monsters" (*Dark Fields*, p. 71) to stretch the boundaries and the oxymoron still further. Entering the interspace of the oxymoronic sensibility she inherits from her Petrarchan predecessors, she moves inside and outside of the margins to accommodate the form to the other in the self and the selfhood of those others expropriated by the repressions she so "monstrously" and "bravely" identifies in *Atlas*.

NOTES

1. "The Survivor," tr. Robert Harvey and Mark S. Roberts, *Toward the Post-Modern*, ed. Robert Harvey and Mark S. Roberts (Atlantic Highlands, New Jersey: Humanities Press, 1995), p. 162.

2. "Against Proper Objects," *differences*, 6. 2 & 3 (1994): 20. Future references are cited in the text.

3. "Inscriptions," *Dark Fields of the Republic* (New York: Norton, 1995), p. 71. In a note to *Dark Fields*, Rich writes:

> I had written "suffused," later began looking up the line I was quoting from memory: was it Coleridge? Keats? Shakespeare? My friend Barbara Gelpi confirmed it was Shakespeare, in his Sonnet 111: *Thence comes it that my name receives a brand / And almost thence my nature is subdued / To what it works in, like the dyer's hand.* I have kept "suffused" here because to feel suffused by the materials that one has perforce to work in is not necessarily to be subdued, though some might think so. (pp. 78–79)

4. Jane Hedley, "'Old Songs with New Words': The Achievement of Rich's 'Twenty-One Love Poems,'" *Genre* 23 (1990): 351. Refer to Alice Templeton, "The Dream and the Dialogue: Rich's Feminist Poems and Gadamer's Hermeneutics," *Tulsa Studies in Women's Literature* 7 (1988): 295. Hedley and Templeton anticipate Kevin McQuirk in "Philoctetes Radicalized: 'Twenty-one Love Poems' and the Lyric Career of Adrienne Rich," *Contemporary Literature* 34 (1993): 61–87 as well as Thomas Byers, "Adrienne Rich: Vision as Rewriting," *World, Self, Poem*, ed. Leonard Trawick (Kent, Ohio: Kent State University Press, 1990), pp. 144–52 and Lorrie Smith, "Dialogue and the political Imagination in Denise Levertov and Adrienne Rich," *World, Self, Poem*, pp. 155–62.

5. For a summary of the poetic dismissals, see Craig Werner, *Adrienne Rich: The Poet and Her Critics* (Chicago and London: American Library Association, 1988), pp. 37–41. Gayle Rubin and Judith Butler object to Rich's theory but see it only in terms of where Rich was at an earlier stage in her career. "Sexual Traffic," *differences* 6.2 & 3 (1994): 74–76.

6. *The Dream of a Common Language* (New York: Norton, 1978), p. 36.

7. Sandra Runzio writes that "Although the word 'choice' does not appear until Poem XV, 'choice' as a premise lingers in virtually all of the poems [of 'Twenty-One Love Poems']," See "Intimacy, Complicity, and the Imagination: Adrienne Rich's 'Twenty-One Love Poems,'" *Genders*, 16 (1993): 71.

8. See Rich's interview with David Montenegro, *Points of Departure: International Writers on Writing and Politics* (Ann Arbor: University of Michigan Press, 1991), p. 7.

9. *Bodies that Matter: On the Discursive Limits of Sex* (New York: Routledge, 1993), p. 242.

10. "Defy the Space that Separates," *The Nation* 263. 10 (1996): 34.

11. For a discussion of the pivotal connections between Rich and "The Idea of Order at Key West" that cites *What is Found There*, see Jane Hedley, "Re-forming the Cradle: Adrienne Rich's 'Transcendental Etude,'" *Genre* 28.3 (1995): 348–350. On other connections between Rich and Stevens, refer to Jacqueline Brogan "'I can't

be still': Or Adrienne Rich and the Refusal to Gild the Fields of Guilt," *Women's Studies* 27.4 (1998): 311–30 as well as "Wrestling with Those 'Rotted Names': Wallace Stevens' and Adrienne Rich's 'Revolutionary Poetics,'" *The Wallace Stevens Journal* 25.1 (2001): 19–39.

12. Slavoj Žižek, *Tarrying with the Negative* (Durham: Duke University Press, 1994), p. 44.

13. Andrew Marvell, *Poems and Letters, Third Edition*, ed. H. M. Marguliouth, rev. Pierre Leguois, and E. E. Duncan Jones (Oxford: Oxford University Press, 1971), p. 48.

14. *Blood, Bread and Poetry* (New York: Norton, 1986), p. 225.

15. "Three Academic Pieces," *The Necessary Angel: Essays on Reality and the Imagination* (New York: Knopf, 1951), p. 79.

16. Bill Readings, *Introducing Lyotard* (London: Routledge, 1991), p. xxx.

17. For a sustained discussion of the way in which Rich writes of, and communicates, pain in her poetry, see "The 'Possible Poet': Pain, Form and the Embodied Poetics of Adrienne Rich in Wallace Stevens's Wake," *The Wallace Stevens Journal* 25. 1 (2001): 40–51. There, Cynthia Hogue writes that "as a feminist, Rich asserts, inserts, a suffering woman's body into the Canonical body of Western poetry surely in some sense as an audacious revision . . . of the blazon," 44.

18. *The Elegies and Songs and Sonnets*, ed. Helen Gardner (Oxford: Oxford University Press, 1965), p. 36.

19. *Hamlet*, ed. Harold Jenkins (New York: Routledge, 1982), p. 278.

20. Nadine Gordimer, *Burgher's Daughter* (New York, 1979), p. 356.

ROGER GILBERT

Contemporary American Poetry

The story of the first half of the twentieth century in American poetry is largely a story of individual poets: Frost, Stevens, Pound, Williams, H. D., Moore, Eliot, Crane. By comparison the second half of the century looks muddy and crowded. While a few postwar poets have achieved demi-canonical stature, there still seems to be little agreement about which individuals or groups have mattered most in the last fifty years. This means that doing justice to the richness and variety of the period requires something other than the major-poet paradigm that has governed most accounts of the first half of the century. No half-dozen or dozen figures can be taken as 'representative' of the full range of contemporary American poetry. I propose instead to use three complementary frames of reference, each of which provides a slightly different perspective on the period and its achievements. The frames I have in mind are decades, generations and poetic schools. All of these ways of dividing up the period contain an element of the arbitrary, but by looking at contemporary American poetry through each one in turn I hope to construct a more rounded picture than any of them can give by itself.

Decades

The 1950s began under the sway of the New Criticism and its criteria for poetic excellence; the early work of Randall Jarrell, John Berryman, Elizabeth

From *A Companion to Twentieth-Century Poetry*, edited by Neil Roberts, pp. 559–70. © 2001 by Blackwell Publishers Ltd.

Bishop, Robert Lowell, Richard Wilbur, Karl Shapiro and Howard Nemerov all fell into the New Critical mode. This kind of tightly wrought poem continued to be written well into the fifties, but the dominant tendency of that decade was towards a loosening of the formal and stylistic criteria the New Criticism had established. That loosening took several forms. Poems began to open themselves to a broader, more miscellaneous range of detail; a certain randomness began to replace the controlled coherence of the New Critical style. Syntactically this shift manifested itself as a tendency towards parataxis, loose concatenations of words and clauses rather than the logically subordinated grammar of the New Critical poem. More broadly it showed itself in a preference for structures based on juxtaposition and accumulation like lists and narratives, rather than the more syllogistic organization typical of forties poems. Poems in the fifties no longer centred themselves on a single metaphor that rigorously determined all its details. Instead they often favoured metonymic associations between images and ideas, connections based on accidental features of proximity, contiguity or succession. Tidy containment gave way to unruly sprawl, most prominently in Allen Ginsberg's *Howl* (1956), with its long Whitmanesque lines and wildly associative inventories.

These stylistic changes reflected a more basic shift from a conception of the poem as a self-contained artefact to an idea of the poem as a rendering of experience in all its temporal flux and variety. This experiential aesthetic led to an increasing intimacy of tone and subject matter. Where New Critical poems tended to sound somewhat aloof and impersonal, poems in the fifties spoke in a variety of personal registers from conversational candour to urgent self-revelation. And where New Critical poems often focused on cultural and historical subjects with no direct connection to the speaker's life, poems in the fifties frequently dealt with personal circumstances and occasions in great detail. The fifties were of course when the so-called Confessional mode emerged in the openly autobiographical work of poets like W. D. Snodgrass and Robert Lowell. But many poets in the fifties not directly associated with the Confessional style also wrote poems grounded in the particulars of their own private experience.

Much has been said about the supposed split between academic and avant-garde poets in this period—between the 'raw' and the 'cooked', to use the terms put forward by Lowell. But while it's true that distinct camps and coteries existed, as reflected most famously in the rival anthologies *New Poets of England and America* (1957) and *The New American Poetry* (1960), the dominant fifties style cut across those factional divisions. The most significant and influential works of the period from both academic and avant-garde circles shared a desire to accommodate a larger, more diverse range of fact and experience than had been possible under New Critical norms. Books like

Theodore Roethke's *Praise to the End* (1951), Charles Olson's *Maximus Poems / 1–10* (1953), Elizabeth Bishop's *A Cold Spring* (1955), Robert Lowell's *Life Studies* (1959), W. D. Snodgrass's *Heart's Needle* (1959), Gwendolyn Brooks's *The Bean Eaters* (1960), Randall Jarrell's *The Woman at the Washington Zoo* (1960), Kenneth Koch's *Thank You* (1962) and Frank O'Hara's *Lunch Poems* (1964, but written mainly in the fifties), despite their manifest differences of style and subject, all reflect the general widening and loosening of manner that transformed American poetry in the fifties.

The 1960s saw a shift from this densely detailed, experiential style to a starker, more visionary mode that often seemed to leave the realm of experience behind in its push towards the ineffable. The expansive parataxis of the fifties gave way to a hushed and elliptical style; lines, sentences and poems all grew shorter, as though striving for a condition beyond language. The influence of modern European and Latin American poetry showed itself in a preference for isolated, dreamlike images that resisted narrative or thematic articulations. Robert Bly was the most influential spokesman for this new style; his 1963 essay 'A Wrong Turning in American Poetry' attacked the empirical cast of fifties poems and called for a freer, less rational kind of imagery. The work of Bly and his friends James Wright, Galway Kinnell and Louis Simpson exemplified what came to be called the Deep Image style, loosely grounded in Jungian psychology. The style might be characterized as a marriage of Poundian Imagism with European and Latin American Surrealism; the emphasis is at once on the presentation of sharply defined images and on the exploration of unconscious associations and resonances.

Much work in the sixties shared in the general movement away from empirical fact and towards various modes of the unconscious and the ineffable. Sylvia Plath's *Ariel* (1965), perhaps the decade's most famous book of poems, clearly partakes of this visionary tendency despite its superficial link to Confessional poetics. Other volumes that typify the sixties style include Bly's *Silence in the Snowy Fields* (1962), Wright's *The Branch Will Not Break* (1963), Simpson's *At the End of the Open Road* (1963), Denise Levertov's *O Taste and See* (1964), Adrienne Rich's *Necessities of Life* (1966), Kinnell's *Body Rags* (1967), W. S. Merwin's *The Lice* (1967), Gary Snyder's *The Back Country* (1967), Robert Duncan's *Bending the Bow* (1968) and Mark Strand's *Reasons for Moving* (1968). Many of these volumes also share the conjunction of anti-rational poetics and oppositional politics that the critic Paul Breslin has described under the rubric 'the psycho-political muse'. The Vietnam war in particular inspired an apocalyptic strain of vision quite distinct from earlier, more realistic modes of war poetry.

One of the effects of the general shift from empirical representation to ineffable vision was a marked change in the vocabulary of contemporary poetry. The proper names and concrete nouns that swelled the lines of fifties poems gave way to a more restricted set of words evoking dream rather than reality: light, dark, water, stone, field, sky, star, bone, and so on. Generic terms replaced particulars; poets tended to write of animals, birds and trees rather than squirrels, jays and sycamores. A kind of purifying of poetic language seemed to be at work, as though poets wished to cleanse their medium of the contaminating effects of history, culture, even nature. Such purification eventually runs up against hard limits; many critics began to complain of the monotony that resulted from the continual recycling of the same handful of elemental words. By the early seventies the stark, stripped-down style of much sixties poetry, which initially seemed daring and fresh, had come to seem mannered and artificial.

In the 1970s the reaction against the sixties style took the form of a return to what the critic and poet Robert Pinsky called 'prose virtues'. Pinsky's influential book *The Situation of Poetry* (1976) criticized what he took to be the extreme nominalism of sixties poetry, which led in his analysis to a thoroughgoing distrust of language as a medium for thought and representation. Rather than limiting itself to shadowy evocations of the silence beyond speech, Pinsky argued that contemporary poetry should avail itself of all the resources of language, including generalization, description and narrative. Pinsky's umbrella term for the qualities he felt needed to be readmitted to poetry was 'discursiveness', and the term is a useful one for characterizing the larger tendencies of seventies poetry. If poets in the sixties appeared to be pushing poetry as far from prose as possible, establishing a special vocabulary and syntax wholly distinct from ordinary usage, poets in the seventies seemed intent on reclaiming much of the idiom of prose as a legitimate part of poetry's domain.

The discursive style of the seventies had as one of its hallmarks a more elaborate syntax, devoted not to the proliferation of factual detail, as in the fifties, but to the complexities of abstract thought. The short declarative sentences favoured by poets in the sixties were replaced by longer sentences full of qualifications, parentheses, semicolons and subordinate clauses. Lines became longer as well in order to accommodate this more expository, discursive syntax. Many poems in the seventies openly modelled themselves on prose forms like the letter, the essay and the journal. Perhaps the book that most fully established this new style was John Ashbery's much-honoured *Self-Portrait in a Convex Mirror* (1975), whose title poem drew on the language of art history, philosophy and cultural criticism. Other books in the vein included A. R. Ammons's *Sphere* (1974), James Merrill's *Divine Comedies* (1976), Richard Hugo's *31 Letters and 13 Dreams* (1977), C. K. Williams's *With Ignorance* (1977), Adrienne Rich's *The Dream of a Common Language* (1978), Robert

Hass's *Praise* (1979), Pinsky's *An Explanation of America* (1979) and Douglas Case's *The Revisionist* (1981). Even the late work of older poets like Elizabeth Bishop, Robert Lowell and Robert Hayden reflected the influence of the discursive mode; Lowell's *History* (1973), Bishop's *Geography III* (1976) and Hayden's *American Journal* (1978) all contain a higher proportion of prose idiom and discursive elaboration than their previous books.

The 1980s saw a turn from the rational continuity of the discursive style to a more splintered, disjunctive idiom that emphasized the mind's inability to make satisfactory connections and generalizations. Like the fifties, the eighties were characterized by highly visible rifts between different poetic factions: those working in traditional forms, those in the revitalized avant-garde, and those writing in the autobiographical free verse codified by creative-writing workshops. Again, however, the period style cut across these lines. Formalists, experimentalists and workshop poets alike began producing poems heavy with information, fragments of cultural, social, political and physical data without obvious interconnections. While this style shared the paratactic looseness of the fifties style, it lacked the experiential ground that unified most fifties poems, the sense that however random a poem's particulars might seem they all originated in the poet's own experience. Instead this style reflected the precipitous growth of computer and media technologies, which triggered an enormous increase in the availability of raw information without providing ways of sorting and assembling it into coherent wholes. One analogy sometimes invoked for this style was channel-surfing, the restless wandering among unrelated images and narratives made possible by the proliferation of cable TV channels.

Many eighties poems laid special emphasis on the ironic dissonance between political and ethical questions on the one hand and aesthetic and sensual pleasures on the other. Images of suffering and exploitation were often set beside images of consumption and enjoyment with little or no commentary, as though the mere contrast spoke for itself. The result was a poetry of troubled yet vague conscience, passively reflecting the contradictions and disjunctions of its time. Some books in this mode include Albert Goldbarth's *Arts and Sciences* (1986), Alice Fulton's *Palladium* (1986), Jane Miller's *American Odalisque* (1987), Leslie Scalapino's *Way* (1988), Ron Silliman's *What* (1988), Donald Hall's *The One Day* (1988), Bob Perelman's *Face Value* (1988), Robert Hass's *Human Wishes* (1989), Frederick Seidel's *These Days* (1989), Paul Hoover's *The Novel* (1990) and Robert Pinsky's *The Want Bone* (1990). For all their formal differences, these books share a densely informational texture in which clauses, lines and sentences become atomized 'bits' crowded together without apparent logical or narrative design. Vikram Seth's surprisingly successful verse-novel *The Golden Gate* (1986), written in Pushkin's rhymed sonnet stanzas, displays a similarly high density of information and a comparable irony about the clashing values of American culture, albeit with a light patina of plot and character to hold the work together.

In the 1990s the flattened, fragmented, quintessentially 'postmodern' poetics of the eighties modulated towards a new lyricism that brought with it a return to spiritual and even religious themes. Words that had become nearly taboo in the ironic eighties began to reappear in poems and even book titles: soul, God, sky, angel, saint, spirit. The religious beliefs betokened by this vocabulary were hardly orthodox, and while they may have shared something with the various spiritual practices known under the rubric 'the New Age', they tended to be darker and more uncertain in their sense of cosmic authority. In fact a number of nineties poets could be described as Gnostic in their evocation of a hostile universe ruled by an alien God. Others offered glimpses of a more benevolent divinity, but with little faith in its accessibility through human institutions.

Stylistically this turn to religious or transcendental concerns showed itself in a variety of ways. The relentless contemporaneity of reference that marked much eighties poetry did not recede completely, but was balanced by more archaic elements. Poems in the nineties became more allusive, evoking or expounding older texts and voices as though to authorize their own spiritual exploration. Augustine, Dante, Traherne, Dickinson, Emily Brontë and Wittgenstein were only a few of the tutelary figures summoned up by poets in the nineties. Classical myth, once scorned by contemporary poets as a throwback to the dusty erudition of Pound and Eliot, now reappeared, albeit in sleekly updated forms. Syntax became more porous and elliptical than it had been in the eighties, less freighted with information and more open to the ineffable. Yet the disjunctiveness of the eighties mode persisted; few nineties poets wrote with the kind of discursive clarity and coherence prevalent in the seventies. Nor did the nineties witness a return to the elemental, 'pure' diction of sixties poetry; vocabulary in the nineties remained diverse, with heterogeneous words and idioms often placed in sharp counterpoint. Examples of this style include Li-Young Lee's *The City in Which I Love You* (1990), Jorie Graham's *Region of Unlikeness* (1991), Allen Grossman's *The Ether Dome* (1991), Thylias Moss's *Rainbow Remnants in a Rock Bottom Ghetto Sky* (1991), Sandra McPherson's *The God of Indeterminacy* (1993), Brenda Hillman's *Bright Existence* (1993), Ann Lauterbach's *And For Example* (1994), Carolyn Forche's *The Angel of History* (1994), Rita Dove's *Mother Love* (1995), Anne Carson's *Glass, Irony and God* (1995), Susan Stewart's *The Forest* (1995), Lucie Brock-Broido's *The Master Letters* (1995), Michael Palmer's *At Passages* (1995), Reginald Shepherd's *Angel, Interrupted* (1996), Larissa Szporluk's *Dark Sky Question* (1998) and Kathleen Peirce's *The Oval Hour* (1999). Once again these books differ in many ways, but they share a longing for the sublime, whether conceived as light or dark, that pulls them away from the thick realm of information inhabited by much eighties poetry.

Generations

The generation of poets born between 1905 and 1920 is the first that can legitimately be regarded as 'contemporary', though most of its key figures are long dead, many of them prematurely: Theodore Roethke, Delmore Schwartz, Randall Jarrell, John Berryman, Charles Olson, Robert Lowell, Muriel Rukeyser, Elizabeth Bishop. (The most prominent survivors are Stanley Kunitz, Gwendolyn Brooks and Ruth Stone, all of whom have remained remarkably active well into their seventies and eighties.) These are poets who struggled in the shadow of the senior modernists, most of whom were alive and productive for much of the younger poets' own careers. Their primary innovation was to adapt the techniques of modernism, with its aesthetic of impersonality, to a more directly autobiographical kind of poetry. As the first generation of American poets to grow up in the age of Freud, they returned obsessively in their poetry to familial and especially parental themes and conflicts, often refracted through childhood memory. Indeed their most visible legacy may simply be the claiming of family life in all its ambivalence as a subject for poetry.

With a few exceptions the careers of these poets seemed to share a general trajectory from early success to later disappointment, a movement that was often exacerbated by various forms of self-destructive behaviour. While individual temperament certainly played a part in these tendencies, it must be noted that this generation occupied a difficult transitional phase in the cultural status of the American poet. Older modernists like Frost, Sandburg and Eliot had revived the image of the public poet, a figure lauded in print and lionized at lectures and readings. Like most of their generation they remained largely outside the academy, supporting themselves primarily through extra- or para-literary endeavours. Lowell's generation, by contrast, lived within yet often on the fringes of the university, not holding tenured jobs for the most part but moving nomadically from one post to another. At the same time the spectacle of the modernist titans seems to have bred in many of these younger poets an urgent sense of competitiveness. Olson, Berryman, Roethke and Lowell in particular all apparently felt themselves to be vying for the title of 'top bard', and this aggressive drive for pre-eminence both fuelled and in certain respects disfigured their work. Lacking both the amateur status of the modernists and the professional security of younger poets fully ensconced in the academy, many of these poets found themselves assuming the role of literary celebrities, rewarded not for their expertise in the classroom but for their enactment of various public ideas of poethood. The career of Dylan Thomas, who spent much of his later life in America, established the pattern for this generation, both in its achievements and its disasters.

The next generation of poets, those born between 1920 and 1935, is an extraordinarily rich one. For the most part these poets did not suffer from the personal and professional tribulations that afflicted the previous generation. Perhaps because they came of age when the great modernists were already fading from the scene, they also seem to have felt less burdened by their legacy. Under the influence of New Critical doctrines many of these poets began their careers writing tightly controlled formal verse, but then abruptly shifted to a more 'open' or 'naked' style in the sixties; these included James Wright, W. S. Merwin, Robert Bly, Galway Kinnell, Donald Hall, Anne Sexton, Adrienne Rich, Sylvia Plath, and to a lesser degree John Ashbery and James Merrill. Others, like Allen Ginsberg, A. R. Ammons, Frank O'Hara, Robert Creeley and Amiri Baraka, worked in open form more or less continuously. By and large this was a privileged and well-educated cohort; many of them attended Ivy League schools like Harvard, Princeton and Columbia, and several made their debuts in the pages of the prestigious Yale Younger Poets Series, then judged by W. H. Auden, who along with William Carlos Williams served as the group's unofficial mentor. Today this generation continues to be a dominant presence in American poetry, producing important works, receiving major awards, and occupying the country's most prestigious academic positions.

Perhaps one reason the poets of this generation have exhibited such remarkable staying power is that they did not all emerge at once. A few, like Ginsberg and Snodgrass, made their greatest impressions in the fifties; others, like Plath, Wright, Creeley, Merwin and Bly, received more attention in the sixties; while still others, like Ammons, Ashbery, Merrill and Rich, did not have their full impact until the seventies. This staggering of recognition allowed more members to find an audience for themselves, thus mitigating the kind of competitive jockeying the previous generation had seen. There seems to have been a tacit agreement among these poets to share the shrinking amount of cultural capital granted American poetry in the period, rather than fighting over who would receive the greatest rewards. This freed them to explore a wide variety of styles and modes, from traditional form to radical experiment, from aesthetic meditation to political address, from personal narrative to nebulous myth. As a result many of these poets were able to forge highly original and distinctive voices. Indeed not since the first-generation modernists had a group of American poets sounded so different from one another and so like themselves; one need only read a line or two by Ammons, Ginsberg, Merrill, Rich, Ashbery, Merwin, Plath or Creeley to recognize its authorship.

In some respects the next generation of poets, those born between 1935 and 1950, are in a position analogous to the Lowell generation, working in the shadow of the high modernists. But while the continued prominence of their elders has certainly slowed their own reception, this younger generation has also benefited enormously from the increasing professionalization of American poetry. The first generation of poets largely shaped by graduate creative-writing programmes, almost all of them have moved into teaching positions in such programmes. In addition to paying respectable salaries, these creative-writing programmes also support a vast network of journals, readings, prizes, grants and fellowships, a system sometimes cynically referred to as 'Po Biz'. But while this institutional system has provided them with greater cultural and financial stability than earlier generations had enjoyed, it has also fostered higher degrees of conformity and factionalism. Perhaps inspired by their critical colleagues, poets of this generation have tended to align themselves with particular ideologies or styles and then proselytized on their behalf to their students. The result has been a general decline in originality, and a tendency for popular styles to reproduce themselves with little variation. It may also be, as Donald Hall has suggested, that this generation suffers from a diminishment of poetic ambition, and that a desire for professional advancement has replaced the hunger for immortality that once drove poets, reducing the overall amount of risk-taking, genuine innovation and thematic scope in their work. It's possible, of course, that a few members of this generation will yet emerge as major figures. Certainly many of them are tremendously gifted, but so far there is no Seamus Heaney among them.

It's too early to make any firm assessment of the next and for all practical purposes last generation of twentieth-century American poets, those born between 1950 and 1965. But there are hopeful signs of a new catholicity and adventurousness in many of them. This spirit shows itself partly in a willingness to combine or synthesize styles and techniques that had been considered incompatible by their predecessors. Thus traditional lyricism and avant-garde disjunctiveness have begun to mingle in interesting ways in the work of some younger poets. A desire to address broader political and metaphysical themes has also begun to make itself felt. For the most part these poets are as much products of the workshop system as their immediate predecessors, subject to the same pressures and disincentives. Yet they may well prove more successful at resisting the lure of professionalism. This generation will only be coming into full maturity during the first years of the new millennium, and if history is a guide major literary innovations tend to occur at such times. Whether the American poets now in their thirties and forties will manage, as Yeats did, to remake themselves as poets of a new century or will simply preserve the language of the century they were born in remains to be seen, but there is cause for optimism.

Schools

Finally, it's worth paying some attention to the various 'schools' and other affiliations of poets that have flourished in contemporary American poetry. These need to be treated with a certain scepticism; often they prove to be critical artefacts rather than strongly grounded movements promoted by the poets themselves. Nonetheless they have exerted considerable influence in the presentation and reception of contemporary poetry. I shall only briefly mention those schools most dominant from 1950 to 1970, several of which are treated separately in this volume. The Confessional poets were never particularly receptive to the label bestowed on them by the critic M. L. Rosenthal; their relations with one another were more social than polemical. The Black Mountain school, by contrast, were active correspondents and pedagogues who spent much time and energy articulating and defending their poetic principles. The Beat poets also developed some fairly programmatic ideas about their work, though their statements are generally less weighty and theoretical than those of the Black Mountain group. The New York school, led by Frank O'Hara, John Ashbery and Kenneth Koch, tended to be much more playful in their poetics, often mocking the manifesto-like rhetoric of other schools. These last three groups were largely established and codified by Donald Allen's anthology *The New American Poetry*, which organized its contributors into sections based on aesthetic affiliation and included a thick appendix of poetic statements. In the 1960s the Deep Image group emerged under the leadership of Robert Bly, whose influential journal *The Sixties* provided a vehicle for the dissemination of their poems and poetics. In the same decade a group of politically outspoken African-American poets associated with the Black Arts movement formed, whose members included Amiri Baraka, Sonia Sanchez, Audre Lorde, June Jordan and Don L. Lee. Finally we can identify a *de facto* school that might be dubbed the 'university wits'; this company included Richard Wilbur, Anthony Hecht, Daryl Hine, John Hollander and Richard Howard, all poets of exceptional elegance, erudition and urbanity.

As these older groups have gone into various stages of ossification, new poetic schools and consortiums have continued to spring up in the last thirty years. The most polemically focused and organized of these newer groups are undoubtedly the Language school and the New Formalists, representing extremes of avant-gardism and traditionalism respectively. Despite their radical differences in aesthetic orientation, there are some surprising symmetries between these groups. Both consider themselves marginal in relation to what they regard as the hegemony of mainstream poetry (which the Language poets like to call 'official verse culture'). Both have produced copious treatises on behalf of their poetics, with the Language poets arguing that conventional syntax, traditional verse form, and linear narrative all transmit conservative ideologies, and the New Formalists claiming that the dominance of free verse represents an elitist withdrawal from poetry's potentially vast popular audience. Both movements are led by a small group of vocal propagandists: the Language school by Charles Bernstein, Ron Silliman and Bob Perelman, the New Formalists by Timothy Steele, Frederick Turner and Dana Gioia. Despite their claims to marginality, both these groups are well-represented in magazines and anthologies, and their members hold tenured positions at a number of major universities. Indeed it's clear that the considerable attention their work has received owes a great deal to its group packaging and the polemics that accompany it.

The hegemonic mainstream targeted by both the Language and New Formalist poets is most often identified with graduate creative-writing programmes, which many accuse of breeding dull uniformity and joyless professionalism. In fact American creative-writing programmes are by no means homogeneous; many have distinct characters of their own. But it's also true that their proliferation has helped create a kind of insider culture modelled on other academic fields; this can be seen in the proliferation of acronyms like MFA (Master of Fine Arts), AWP (Associated Writing Programs) and APR (*American Poetry Review*, the most visible outlet for mainstream poetry), which constitute a kind of professional code. The process of 'workshopping' poems can indeed have the effect of eradicating eccentricities and imposing a kind of shared decorum; poems produced in or influenced by writing workshops tend to favour first-person narrative and meditation in a relatively subdued style. But again it should be noted that not all programmes are equivalent. To mention only two, poets trained at the Iowa Writer's Workshop, under the guidance of faculty like Donald Justice, Marvin Bell and Gerald Stern, generally practise varying blends of the Confessional and Deep Image styles (though recently there are signs of change under the influence of the younger and more experimental poet Jorie Graham); while Stanford, thanks to the enduring influence of the poet-critic Yvor Winters, has produced a number of poets working in a more discursive and intellectual vein, like Robert Pinsky, Robert Hass, James McMichael and John Matthias.

When we look beyond academia, the most significant development in American poetry of the last two decades has been the emergence of a vibrant performance culture. The most popular manifestations of this culture are the events known as 'poetry slams', which combine poetry reading and sports contest. Selected audience members typically rate a series of poets on a scale of one to ten, based on the quality of their poems and the skill with which they perform them. Obviously such a procedure tends to reward crowd-pleasers, and a group of poets has grown up who specialize in this kind of work, with a heavy emphasis on humour, rhythm and theatrics. The influence of rap lyrics is plainly audible in much of this poetry, as is that of stand-up comedy. But the true begetters of this mode are the Beats, who gave raucous readings in coffee-houses and bars during the 1950s, often with jazz accompaniment. In the eighties and nineties the atmosphere of those events was recreated in new venues like the Nuyorican Poets' Cafe, the unofficial centre of performance-poetry culture in New York.

This performance culture has tended to be quite ethnically diverse; Latino and African-American poets in particular have been drawn to the performance scene, perhaps because of their rich vernacular traditions. In the mainstream poetry world there has also been a dramatic upsurge in the number of minority poets publishing and teaching. While they are sometimes gathered into ethnically specific anthologies—African American, Asian American, Latino, Native American, etc.—they also form a broader coalition, too diverse to be called a school, that usually goes under the banner of multi-cultural poetry. Such poetry tends to be autobiographical and often explores personal and family history as it intersects with broader ethnic narratives; Rita Dove's *Thomas and Beulah* (1986) is a particularly celebrated example of this mode. Many gay and lesbian poets also focus on the relation between individual experience and group identity, and they too are sometimes treated as a distinct poetic community, whose significant voices include Frank Bidart, Mark Doty, Marilyn Hacker, Paul Monette and Minnie Bruce Pratt. Region is another category that distinguishes particular groups of poets, most notably those from the South, many of whom retain a distinct vision and style linked to the long tradition of Southern literature; notable members of this group include Robert Penn Warren and James Dickey in the older generations, Dave Smith, Robert Morgan, Andrew Hudgins and Rodney Jones in the younger. Finally we can identify a loose conglomeration of committed or activist poets, mainly on the left, who define their work primarily in terms of its political engagement and efficacy. This is by no means a small or specialized group, embracing as it does the work of mainstream poets like Adrienne Rich, Allen Ginsberg, Carolyn Forche and Philip Levine, as well as important minority poets like Amiri Baraka and Gwendolyn Brooks. The last two decades have seen renewed interest in the openly political poetry of the 1930s and 1960s; many young poets in particular seem eager to revive aspects of that tradition.

Ultimately, of course, our sense of the significant patterns and tendencies of late twentieth-century American poetry will depend on the shape and direction of twenty-first-century American poetry. Whether this period will be known for its plethora of competing schools and styles or as the crucible of a new poetic synthesis must for now remain uncertain. The story of contemporary poetry cannot be fully told while it is contemporary.

Bibliography

Altieri, Charles (1979). *Enlarging the Temple: New Directions in American Poetry During the 1960s*. Lewisburg: Bucknell University Press.

Altieri, Charles (1984). *Self and Sensibility in Contemporary American Poetry*. Cambridge: Cambridge University Press.

Bloom, Harold (1976). *Figures of Capable Imagination*. New York: Seabury Press.

Bly, Robert (1991), *American Poetry: Wildness and Domesticity*. New York: Harper and Row.

Breslin, James (1984). *From Modern to Contemporary: American Poetry, 1945–1965*. Chicago: University of Chicago Press.

Breslin, Paul (1987). *The Psycho-Political Muse: American Poetry Since the Fifties*. Chicago: University of Chicago Press.

Damon, Maria (1993). *The Dark End of the Street: Margins in American Vanguard Poetry*. Minneapolis: University of Minnesota Press.

Feierstein, Frederick (1989). *Expansive Poetry: Essays on the New Narrative and the New Formalism*. Santa Cruz, CA: Story Line Press.

Holden, Jonathan (1986). *Style and Authenticity in Postmodern Poetry*. Columbia: University of Missouri Press.

Kaladjian, Walter (1989). *Languages of Liberation: The Social Text in Contemporary American Poetry*. New York: Columbia University Press.

Longenbach, James (1997). *Modern Poetry After Modernism*. New York: Oxford University Press.

Molesworth, Charles (1979). *The Fierce Embrace: A Study of Contemporary American Poetry*. Columbia: University of Missouri Press.

Nelson, Cary (1981). *Our Last First Poets: Vision and History in Contemporary American Poetry*. Urbana: University of Illinois Press.

Perelman, Bob (1996). *The Marginalization of Poetry: Language Writing and Literary History*. Princeton, NJ: Princeton University Press.

Perkins, David (1987). *A History of Modern Poetry, Volume Two*. Cambridge, MA: Harvard University Press.

Perloff, Marjorie (1991). *Radical Artifice: Writing Poetry in the Age of Media*. Chicago: University of Chicago Press.

Pinsky, Robert (1976). *The Situation of Poetry: Contemporary Poetry and Its Traditions*. Princeton, NJ: Princeton University Press.

Rasula, Jed (1996). *The American Poetry Wax Museum: Reality Effects, 1940–1990*. Urbana, IL: National Council of Teachers of English.

Shetley, Vernon (1993). *After the Death of Poetry: Poet and Audience in Contemporary America*. Durham, NC: Duke University Press

Spiegelman, Willard (1989). *The Didactic Muse: Scenes of Instruction in Contemporary American Poetry*. Princeton, NJ: Princeton University Press.

Stein, Kevin (1996). *Private Poets, Public Acts: Public and Private History in Contemporary American Poetry*. Athens: Ohio University Press.

Vendler, Helen (1995). *Soul Says: On Recent Poetry*. Cambridge, MA: Harvard University Press.

Von Hallberg, Robert (1985). *American Poetry and Culture, 1945–1980*. Cambridge, MA: Harvard University Press.
Williamson, Alan (1984). *Introspection and Contemporary Poetry*. Cambridge, MA: Harvard University Press.

ANTHONY HECHT

Treasure Box

1.

In our bicentennial year, Charles Simic and Mark Strand, two poets of
kindred excellences and temperaments, published an anthology entitled
Another Republic and devoted to seventeen European and Latin American
poets whose work was (and still largely remains) outside the orbit and canon
of this nation's taste and habit of mind. The seventeen included Vasko Popa,
Yannis Ritsos, Fernando Pessoa, Miroslav Holub, Zbigniew Herbert, Paul
Celan, and Johannes Bobrowski, along with a few more familiar Nobel lau-
reates-to-be. The editors lumped their poets into two general batches, the
"mythological," a group that included Henri Michaux, Francis Ponge, Julio
Cortázar, Italo Calvino, and Octavio Paz, and another group, the "historical," devoted to Yehudah Amichai, Paul Celan, Zbigniew Herbert, Czeslaw
Milosz, and Yannis Ritsos, while acknowledging that some of the poets fall
between the two stools, or partake of both categories, while resisting identification with either one. They furthermore define the "mythological" strain
by deriving it from sources in Surrealism.

Surrealism has never really enjoyed much favor in North America, a fact
Octavio Paz has explained this way:

> The French tradition and the English tradition in this epoch are
> at opposite poles to each other. French poetry is more radical,

From *The New York Review of Books* 48, no. 16 (October 18, 2001). © 2001 by NYREV.

more total. In an absolute and exemplary way it has assumed the
heritage of European Romanticism, a romanticism which begins
with William Blake and the German romantics like Novalis, and
via Baudelaire and the Symbolists culminates in twentieth-century
French poetry, notably Surrealism. It is a poetry where the world
becomes writing and language becomes the double of the world.[1]

Furthermore, our sense of Surrealism, at least when it figures in poetry, is
of something facile, lazy, and aimless except in its ambition to surprise by a
violation of logic, taste, and rigor. Bad Surrealism can grow tiresome very
easily, and one does not feel encouraged to continue reading a poem such as
Charles Henri Ford's "He Cut His Finger on Eternity," which begins:

> *What grouchy war-tanks intend to shred*
> *or crouch the road's middle to stop my copy?*
> *I'll ride roughshod as an anniversary*
> *down the great coiled gap of your ear.*

If we have no good native Surrealists, we can at least boast of a few
fine imported ones, of which Charles Simic is certainly one of the best.
"Imported," however, is the wrong term for someone who was a refugee,
a DP (Displaced Person) who was born in Belgrade in 1938 and left when
he was fifteen. The poetry Simic writes is not simply better than bad Surrealism; it is what we instantly recognize as a responsible mode of writing,
a poetry that, for all its unexpected turns, startling juxtapositions, dream
sequences, mysteries, will be found, upon careful consideration, to make
a deep and striking kind of sense. It is utterly without Dali pretensions or
Dada postures. It makes no appeal to the unconscious for the liberty to write
nonsense. In Simic's art especially we must attune our ear to a voice usually softspoken, often tender, not infrequently jolly, the sort of lover of food
who has been instructed in starvation. No single poem of his can be said to
represent the whole range of his gifts, or the variety of his comedic sense,
so often tinged with grief, or laced with that special brand of the sardonic,
ironic humor characteristic of Corbière or Laforgue. Yet I think that in a
poem of his called "Views from a Train" something essential of his poetic
intelligence makes itself beautifully audible:

> *Then there's aesthetic paradox*
> *Which notes that someone else's tragedy*
> *Often strikes the casual viewer*
> *With the feeling of happiness.*

There was the sight of squatters' shacks,
Naked children and lean dogs running
On what looked like a town dump,
The smallest one hopping after them on crutches.
All of a sudden we were in a tunnel.
The wheels ground our thoughts,
Back and forth as if they were gravel.
Before long we found ourselves on a beach,
The water blue, the sky cloudless.
Seaside villas, palm trees, white sand;
A woman in a red bikini waved to us
As if she knew each one of us
Individually and was sorry to see us
Heading so quickly into another tunnel.

This is neither simple allegory nor dream, but a fused vision embracing both. The first four lines initially seem to recall La Rochefoucauld's bitter acknowledgment, "In the misfortunes of our best friends we often find something that is not displeasing." But the poet gives depth to what passes in the *Maxims* for ruthless candor and lacerating exposure. The "aesthetic paradox" connects the brutal pleasure in another's pain with Aristotle's *Poetics* and the classic demonstration of how an audience, by a double act of identification and distancing, can find artistic and poetic pleasure in viewing deep torment and agony.

The next four lines seem to be offered as illustration to the generalization of the opening. They served to remind me precisely of a photograph by Henri Cartier-Bresson, in which a group of boys, viewed through the hole in a wall undoubtedly made by a bomb, appear to be taunting and attacking one of their number who is on crutches. The picture is titled simply "Seville, 1933." It may well be quite unknown to the poet, but he is the survivor of bombings by the American Air Force, occupation by the Nazis, and further occupation by the Communists, in a war-ravaged and desperately poor country, so he knew, both from close up as well as distanced by time and travel, the situation depicted in the photograph.

"All of a sudden we were in a tunnel." The lines that immediately follow blot out all the external world for a brief interval, as we return to our inwardness, not only as we slip in and out of sleep but as our very thoughts negotiate between external and internal experience. The woman waves to us from a privileged setting of seaside villas with palms and white sand. Our view of her is as fleeting as was the view of the naked children and lean dogs. Tragedy, we are being reminded, is not a presentation of pure agony, but of the change of state from good fortune to misfortune. The poem presents both in what seems like the wrong order. But the order doesn't matter, since we are "heading so quickly into another tunnel." It may be we ourselves who are the tragic figures in this poem, for we do nothing, we are simply passive viewers, while the children, the dogs, and the woman lead lives of which we catch only a glimpse. In the manner of other Simic poems, there are no neat and easy conclusions to be drawn, yet the poem is full of strange revelation, darkness and brilliance, sadness and luxury.

The luxury is, for the most part, a rare ingredient in Simic's poetry, where it is more than likely to appear as some simple but satisfying food. What this poet is particularly gifted at revealing is the derivation of joys and pleasures from the most unlikely, and even forbidding, sources, as here in a poem called "Unmade Beds":

> *They like shady rooms,*
> *Peeling wallpaper,*
> *Cracks on the ceiling,*
> *Flies on the pillow.*
> *If you are tempted to lie down,*
> *Don't be surprised,*
> *You won't mind the dirty sheets,*
> *The rasp of rusty springs*
> *As you make yourself comfy.*
> *The room is a darkened movie theater*
> *Where a grainy,*
> *Black-and-white film is being shown.*
> *A blur of disrobed bodies*
> *In the moment of sweet indolence*
> *That follows lovemaking,*
> *When the meanest of hearts*
> *Comes to believe*
> *Happiness can last forever.*

The last six lines compose a "sentence" without a main verb. It is purely descriptive, a blurred, grainy vision of a movie, itself a vision, of something fleeting that is nevertheless both wonderful and durable. Of course, being an old black-and-white film, this can be pure delusion, and not very persuasive at that. Is all our happiness mere delusion? Is that film like the shadow-play on the walls of Plato's cave? And if it is no more, isn't it still to be cherished, being all we have? If we find ourselves in a fleabag hotel room, is this an adequate symbol for our normal existence? Is it folly or heroism to be able to rise above the sordors of this world? The elements of Simic's remarkable life, to which I will turn shortly, may suggest what answers he might give to such questions. Certainly that hotel room, soiled as it is, nevertheless is much to be preferred to Sartre's in *Huis Clos*. Another poem, "Firecracker Time," starts off with some of the same mixed ingredients:

> *I was drumming on my bald head with a pencil,*
> *Making a list of my sins. Well, not exactly.*
> *I was in bed smoking a cigar and studying*
> *The news photo of a Jesus lookalike*
> *Who won a pie-eating contest in Texas.*
> *Is there some unsuspected dignity to this foolishness?*
> *I inquired of the newly painted ceiling.*

There are sixty-eight poems in *Night Picnic*, none of them long, most of them fitting on a single page. But it's not easy to convey the fine variety this collection so generously presents. Here, for example, is a poem that itself revels in variety:

THE ALTAR

> *The plastic statue of the Virgin*
> On top of a bedroom dresser
> With a blackened mirror
> From a bad-dream grooming salon.
> Two pebbles from the grave of a rock star,
> A small, grinning windup monkey,
> A bronze Egyptian coin
> And a red movie-ticket stub.
> A splotch of sunlight on the framed
> Communion photograph of a boy
> With the eyes of someone
> Who will drown in a lake real soon.
> An altar dignifying the god of chance.
> What is beautiful, it cautions,
> Is found accidentally and not sought after.
> What is beautiful is easily lost.

The heterogeneous simplicity of these assembled items brings to mind certain photographic interiors by Eugène Atget or Walker Evans, pictures full of deep feeling, eloquent of frugal and damaged lives that nevertheless cling to small tokens of hope. And I can think of no poem that so powerfully conveys the raging, frenzied lusting of pubescent boys as does "The Cemetery":

> *Dark nights, there were lovers*
> *To stake out among the tombstones.*
> *If the moon slid out of the clouds,*
> *We saw more while ducking out of sight,*
> *A mound of dirt beside a dug grave.*
> *Oh God! the mound cried out.*
> *There were ghosts about*
> *And rats feasting on the white cake*
> *Someone had brought that day,*
> *With flies unzipped we lay close,*
> *Straining to hear the hot, muffled words*
> *That came quicker and quicker,*
> *Back then when we still could*
> *Bite our tongues and draw blood.*

Such a poem cannot fairly be labeled "surrealist," and yet it has about it a pungency of pain, fear, sex, and death blended into an extraordinary brew of life that is far from the literal world of commonplace experience. The distinct miscellaneousness that crops up in so many Simic poems does not lend itself to the confident summing-up that Emerson so cheerfully posits in "The American Scholar":

> What would we really know the meaning of? The meal in the fir-kin; the milk in the pan; the ballad in the street; the news of the boat; the glance of the eye; the form and the gait of the body;—show me the ultimate reason of these matters;—show me the sublime presence of the highest spiritual cause lurking, as always it does lurk, in these suburbs and extremities of nature; let me see every trifle bristling with the polarity that ranges it instantly on an eternal law; and the shop, the plough, and the leger, referred to the like cause by which light undulates and poets sing;—and the world lies no longer a dull miscellany and lumber room, but has form and order; there is no trifle; there is no puzzle; but one design unites and animates the farthest pinnacle and the lowest trench.

While it is true that Simic lives, writes, and teaches in New Hampshire, he does not share the New England Transcendentalist's serene assurance of ultimate coherence. It may be that the determining difference between the

two poets is to be found in the fact that Simic's childhood was spent in a
war zone, a condition that tends to discourage an easy credence in universal
laws. When Simic resorts to poetic apostrophe, which he permits himself to
do only rarely, it is with abundant irony, as in "Book Lice," which begins,

> *Dust-covered Gideon Bibles*
> *In musty drawers of slummy motels,*
> *Is what they love to dine on.*
> *O eternities, moments divine!*
> *Munching on pages edged in gold*

—and which continues toward an anguished, grotesque, and altogether
unforeseen ending. Simic's hard-bitten distrust of the facile reconciliation
of disparities is finely expressed in "Bible Lesson":

> *There's another, better world*
> *Of divine love and benevolence,*
> *A mere breath away*
> *From this grubby vacant lot*
> *With its exposed sewer pipe,*
> *Rats hatching plots in broad daylight,*
> *Young boys in leather jackets*
> *Showing each other their knives.*
> *"A necessary evil, my dear child,"*
> *The old woman told me with a sigh,*
> *Taking another sip of her sherry.*
> *For birds warbling back and forth*
> *In their gold cage in the parlor,*
> *She had a teary-eyed reverence.*
> *"Angelic," she called them,*
> *May she roast in a trash fire*
> *The homeless warm their hands over,*
> *While beyond the flimsiest partition*
> *The blessed ones stroll in a garden,*
> *Their voices tuned to a whisper*
> *As they dab their eyes*
> *With the hems of their white robes*
> *And opine in their tactful way*
> *On the news of long freight trains*
> *Hauling men and women*
> *Deeper into the century's darkness.*

And yet it strikes a reader with considerable force that the word "happiness" figures in Simic's poems with uncommon and notable frequency—sometimes humbly, to be sure, as when he writes of "That mutt with ribs showing / . . . His tail on the verge of happiness"—but by my estimate more often and more unselfconsciously than in the work of any other poet I can think of. It is clearly a feeling about which he has much to say.

2.

It has been a matter of some importance for a number of writers deliberately to deflect the public's interest in their personal lives, and to insist that it is only their work that really counts. They may claim that their work, carefully read, becomes self-portraiture; or that they have extinguished their personality through their art, which has its own aesthetic interest wholly distinct from their personalities. Eliot forbade any biography to be written about him (a bidding that has been frequently disregarded); Auden requested that all his letters be burned (a wish that has not been widely honored).

This distinctive shyness is in part a way of pointing to, and affirming the significance of, the finished *oeuvres*, as contrasted, perhaps, with their as yet unfinished, and possibly disorderly, lives. For art can be polished to a fare-thee-well, while life is not always shapely or subject to complete control. To an intermediary who sought to arrange a newspaper interview with A.E. Housman, the poet responded,

> Tell him that the wish to include a glimpse of my personality in a literary article is low, unworthy, and American. Tell him that some men are more interesting than their books but my book is more interesting than its man. Tell him that Frank Harris found me rude and Wilfrid Blunt found me dull. Tell him anything else that you think will put him off.

There have indeed been men whose lives eclipse the public's interest in their works (Dylan Thomas, Byron, Wilde, Pound, Cellini), while there have indisputably also been those, like Wallace Stevens, whose lives have been comparatively colorless, or who, like Eliot and Auden, feel that their private lives are none of the public's damn business.

Charles Simic is unusual in that the events of his life, both large and small, continue to interest him enormously without for a moment seeming to compete with the no less interesting but altogether different and distinctive realm of his poems. He has previously published a number of memoirs under the titles of *Wonderful Words, Silent Truth* (1990), *The Unemployed Fortune-Teller* (1994), and *Orphan Factory* (1997), all published by the University of

Michigan Press. He has made use of details from these accounts, sometimes revising them slightly, in the course of composing *A Fly in the Soup*, an eloquent, candid, and touching account of the life he shared, off and on, with his parents in Yugoslavia and America, an account that is, by turns, deeply moving and hilarious.

There is very little posturing in these pages. Simic avoids all bids for sympathy, and is able, with remarkable courage, to present himself in moments of childhood heedlessness, in a critical and unfavorable light. Even before he got to the United States he acquired lifelong American tastes for jazz, films, and food, about which he can be enthusiastic:

> Some years back I found myself in Genoa at an elegant reception in Palazzo Doria talking with the Communist mayor. "I love American food," he blurted out to me after I mentioned enjoying the local cuisine. I asked him what he had in mind. "I love potato chips," he told me. I had to agree, potato chips were pretty good.

As an apt epigraph for this book, Simic quotes Raymond Chandler: "Don't tell me the plot . . . I'm just a bit-player." And given the violent international dimension of the tale he has to tell, his choice of this quotation is self-effacing, witty, and characteristic of this book throughout, not least in its distinctive Americanness. It recalls not only *noir* fiction and film, but that special American film idiom in which the grandeurs of Shakespearean vision, with all the world a stage, with one man in his time playing many parts, "his acts being seven ages," are set aside and we have instead the Hollywood caste and cast system, with superstars and walk-ons, and with a high likelihood of a something less than conclusive plot.

When Charles Simic was three years old, in April 1941, the building across the street from where he lived was hit by a bomb at five in the morning:

> The number of dead for that day in April in what was called by the Germans "Operation Punishment" ranges between five thousand and seventeen thousand, the largest number of civilian deaths in a single day in the first twenty months of war. The city was attacked by four hundred bombers and over two hundred fighter planes on a Palm Sunday when visitors from the countryside swelled the capital's population.

Three years later, on Easter Sunday, April 16, 1944, "The British and the Americans started bombing Belgrade . . . , heavy bombers 'conducting strikes against Luftwaffe and aviation targets' with 'approximately 397 tons of bombs.'"

By this time he was all of six. He recalls that

> Belgrade was a city of the wounded. One saw people on crutches on every corner . . .
>
> Once, chased by a friend, I rounded the corner of my street at top speed and collided with one of these invalids, spilling his soup on the sidewalk. I won't forget the look he gave me. "Oh child," he said softly. I was too stunned to speak. I didn't even have the sense to pick up his crutch. I watched him do it himself with great difficulty . . .
>
> Here's another early memory: a baby carriage pushed by a humpbacked old woman, her son sitting in it, both legs amputated.
>
> She was haggling with the greengrocer when the carriage got away from her. The street was steep, so it rolled downhill with the cripple waving his crutch as if urging it on faster and faster; his mother screaming for help, and everyone else was laughing as if they were watching a funny movie . . . Keystone cops about to go over a cliff . . .
>
> They laughed because they knew it would end well in the movies. They were surprised when it didn't in life.

What deeply impresses a reader of Simic's memoirs is his strong hold on humanity, which is completely divorced from any taint of sentimentality. Even as a child he had acquired an uncommon fortitude, humor, and balance. In the midst of chaos and calamity he is poised and good-natured, and is able to find a redeeming comedy in the most unlikely places:

> When my grandfather was dying from diabetes, when he had already one leg cut off at the knee and they were threatening to do the same to the other, his old buddy Savo Lozanic used to pay him a visit every morning to keep him company. The two would reminisce about this and that and even have a few laughs.
>
> One morning my grandmother had to leave him alone in the house, as she had to attend the funeral of a relative. That's what gave him the idea. He hopped out of bed and into the kitchen, where he found candles and matches. He got back into the bed, somehow placed one candle above his head and the other at his feet, and lit them. Finally, he pulled the sheet over his face and began to wait.

When his friend knocked, there was no answer. The door being unlocked, he went in, calling out from time to time. The kitchen was empty. A fat gray cat slept on the dining room table. When he entered the bedroom and saw the bed with the sheet and lit candles, he let out a wail and then broke into sobs as he groped for a chair to sit down.

"Shut up, Savo," my grandfather said sternly from under his sheet. "Can't you see I'm just practicing."

Simic writes well of his parents, though he shows a clear preference for his father. Both parents were cultivated, his mother having done graduate work in music in Paris, his father having become an engineer, and young Charles discovering serious reading—Dickens, Dostoevsky, Mann, Serbian ballads and folk poems—in their library when he was ten. His mother tended to look down upon her husband's family as somewhat coarser and inferior to her own, and this, together with the fact that she was not a good cook, may have swayed her older son in his partiality. For young Simic, then and still, seemed to favor the more disreputable members of his family. Of one of his mother's aunts, he writes,

> Nana was the black sheep in the family. It was whispered that she cheated on her old husband, was spending his money recklessly, and used bad language. That's what I loved about her. This elegant, good-looking woman would swear often and shamelessly.

He feels the same affection for a blacksmith great-grandfather:

> I liked the stories about this great-grandfather of mine, one of them especially! How he had not been paying taxes for some time and how one day the cops came in force to arrest him. He pleaded with them not to take him away and make his children orphans. He even had a suggestion. What if they were to give him a part-time job at the police station, make him a deputy or something, so he could earn some extra money and pay his taxes?
>
> Well, the cops, being local fellows and knowing [this great-grandfather], took pity on him. At the police station the arrangements were made. He was issued a rifle and was even given a small advance on his pay for other purchases related to his new duties. There were tears of gratitude on his part, everyone was moved, and after many handshakes [he] left. He made his way straight to the tavern, where he stayed for three days raising hell. When he was thoroughly out of his mind, he made the waiters carry four tables

outside at gunpoint. Then he ordered that the tables should be stacked one on top of the other, with a chair and a bottle of booze at the very top. There he climbed, drunk as he was. A crowd had gathered by then. There were Gypsies, too, fiddling and banging on their tambourines. When he started shooting his rifle and shouting that no Simic was ever going to be a stupid cop, the police showed up. They beat the daylights out of him and threw him in jail.

Like other kids his age, young Simic trafficked in gunpowder. This was obtained from unexploded shells, bullets lying about in the streets. The nose of the bullet was inserted into a kitchen spigot and pried away from the shell casing. The gunpowder was traded for valuables like comic books, toys, above all cans of food. Extraction of the gunpowder was obviously a delicate operation. "One day a kid on our block lost both his hands." Yet in the midst of all this, the poet assures us, "I was happy," and we believe him, even though we learn that his father was arrested by the Gestapo, released, and after making his way to Italy, rearrested by the German army, who accused him of being a spy. They put him in a prison in Milan, from which he was released by American forces. He subsequently made his way to the States, his wife and two children following by graduated stages, stopping in Paris for about a year, where they lived frugally and were rarely able to eat at a restaurant. "We didn't have much money," observes Charles, now about fifteen, "and my mother was a type of person who didn't care what she ate."

It was a gloomy, damp, and lonely interval, during which he befriended a few boys his own age:

> These French boys I hung around with were very nice. They came from poor families. Now that they were doing badly in school, they knew their lives would be hard. They had absolutely no illusions about that. In the meantime, they had the street smarts, the humor and appetite for adventure, that reminded me of the friends I had left behind in Belgrade . . .

—and that remind the reader of the author himself. Although he has become a highly sophisticated and well-educated man, it is still these non- or anti-academic virtues that most please him, and please us in him.

What is important in this book is not its narrative thrust or chronological development. It reads like a child's box of jumbled treasures, made the more wonderful by the oddness of their assortment. But since what is most important about Charles Simic is his poetry, I will home in now on what he has to say on this topic:

The book that made all the difference to my idea of poetry was an anthology of contemporary Latin American verse that I bought on Eighth Street. Published by New Directions in 1942 and long out of print by the time I bought my copy, it introduced me to the poems of Jorge Luis Borges, Pablo Neruda, Jorge Carrera Andrade, Drummond de Andrade, Nicholas Guillen, Vincente Huidobro, Jorge de Lima, César Vallejo, Octavio Paz, and so many others. After that anthology, the poetry I read in literary magazines struck me as pretty timid. Nowhere in the *Sewanee Review* or the *Hudson Review* could I find poems like "Biography for the Use of the Birds" or "Liturgy of My Legs" or this one by the Haitian poet Emile Roumer, "The Peasant Declares His Love":

High-yellow of my heart, with breasts like tangerines,
you taste better to me than eggplant stuffed with crabs,
you are the tripe in my pepper pot,
the dumpling in my peas, my tea of aromatic herbs.
You're the corned beef whose customhouse is my heart,
my mush with syrup that trickles down the throat.
You're a steaming dish, mushroom cooked with rice,
crisp potato fried, and little fresh fish fried brown . . .
My hankering for love follows wherever you go.
Your bum is a gorgeous basket brimming with fruits and meats.

It is perfectly understandable that this poem should have met with sympathy and delight in Simic. He will later tell us, "If I were to write about the happiest days of my life, many of them would have to do with food and wine and a table full of friends." Lest anyone think this a trifling matter, Simic will note, on the same page, "I have to admit, I remember better what I've eaten than what I've thought. My memory is especially vivid about those far-off days from 1944 to 1949 in Yugoslavia, when we were mostly starving."

Neither should we be surprised to find, in *Night Picnic*, this fine poem:

SWEET TOOTH

Take her to the pastry shop on Lexington.
Let her sample cream puffs at the counter,
The peach tarts on the street.
If topping or filling spurts down her chin,
Or even better, down her cleavage,
Lick it off before it dribbles down her dress.

With people going by, some pretending
Not to see you, while others stall,
Blinking as if the sun was in their eyes
Or they've left their glasses at home.
The uniformed schoolgirls, holding hands
In pairs, on their way to the park,
Are turning their heads, too, and so are
The red-faced men humping sides of beef
Out a freezer truck into a fancy butcher shop
While she continues to choke on an éclair,
Stopping momentarily with a mouthful
To wince at a brand-new stain on her skirt,
Which you've had no time to attend to,
Giving all your devotion to the one higher up.

"When I started writing poetry in 1955," Simic tells us in *The Unemployed Fortune-Teller*, "all the girls I wanted to show my poems to were American. I was stuck. It was never possible for me to write in my native language." And his beginnings as a poet were not always met with sympathy and understanding:

> "Your poems are just crazy images strung arbitrarily together," my pals complained, and I'd argue back: "Haven't you heard about surrealism and free association?" Bob Burleigh, my best friend, had a degree in English from the University of Chicago and possessed all the critical tools to do a close analysis of any poem. His verdict was: "Your poems don't mean anything."

"Another time," he recalls,

> I was drinking red wine, chain-smoking, and writing, long past midnight. Suddenly the poem took off, the words just flowing, in my head a merry-go-round of the most brilliant similes and metaphors. This is it! I was convinced there had never been such a moment of inspiration in the whole history of literature. I reread what I'd written and had to quit my desk and walk around the room, I got so excited. No sooner was I finished with one poem than I started another even more incredible one. Toward daybreak, paying no attention to my neighbor's furious banging on the wall, I typed them out with my two fingers and finally passed out exhausted on the bed. In the morning I dragged myself to work, dead tired but happy.

> When evening came, I sat down to savor what I wrote the night before, a glass of wine in my hand. The poems were terrible! Incoherent babble, surrealist drivel! How could I have written such crap? I was stunned, depressed, and totally confused.

He learns a lesson about his art while listening to the jazz saxophonist Sonny Rollins:

> It was great. The lesson I learned was: cultivate controlled anarchy. I found Rollins, Charlie Parker, and Thelonious Monk far better models of what an artist could be than most poets. The same was true of the painters. Going to jazz clubs and galleries made me realize that there was a lot more poetry in America than one could find in the quarterlies.

And near the end of this lively and heartening book of memoirs, Simic is able to articulate his own artistic credo or *ars poetica*:

> The task of poetry, perhaps, is to salvage a trace of the authentic from the wreckage of religious, philosophical, and political systems.
>
> Next, one wants to write a poem so well crafted that it would do honor to the tradition of Emily Dickinson, Ezra Pound, and Wallace Stevens, to name only a few masters.
>
> At the same time, one hopes to rewrite that tradition, subvert it, turn it upside down, and make some living space for oneself.
>
> At the same time, one wants to entertain the reader with outrageous metaphors, flights of imagination, and heartbreaking pronouncements.
>
> At the same time, one has, for the most part, no idea of what one is doing. Words make love on the page like flies in the summer heat, and the poem is as much the result of chance as it is of intention. Probably more so.

"The god of chance" of whom he has written—see "The Altar," above—has looked with a very special favor upon Charles Simic, and he is fully aware of this, and manifestly grateful.

NOTE

1. Quoted by Paul Auster in the introduction to his *Random House Book of Twentieth-Century French Poetry* (1982), p. xxxi.

LINDA GREGERSON

The Sower Against Gardens

The gods, that mortal beauty chase,
Still in a tree did end their race.

—Andrew Marvell

Louise Glück is one of those enviable poets whose powers and distinction emerged early and were early recognized. Her work has been justly admired and justly influential, as only work of the very first order can be: work that is so impeccably itself that it alters the landscape in which others write while at the same time discouraging (and dooming) the ordinary homage of direct imitation. In 1992 Glück published a sixth book and in 1996 a seventh, which, in their sustained engagement with inherited fable and inherited form, in their simultaneously witty and deadly serious subversions, constitute a deepening so remarkable that it amounts to a new departure. These books are unlike one another in any number of outward dispositions, but they share a common intellectual purchase; they are two poles of a single project.

1. Like Me
The Wild Iris makes its entrance late in the life of a tradition and its self-wrought woes: the moral and aesthetic dilemmas of sentimental projection, the metaphysical dilemma of solitude (if the others with whom I am in

From *Kenyon Review* 23, no. 1 (Winter 2001): 115–33. © 2001 by *Kenyon Review*.

dialogue are merely the projections of self, I am alone in the world, and, worse, the world has been lost on me). The poet plants herself in a garden and dares its other Creator to join her. The poet construes her garden to be an anthropomorphic thicket and a series of moral exempla. The poet ventriloquizes all the voices—floral, human, transcendent—in a family quarrel about love and sustenance. With equal portions of bravura and self-deprecation, wit, and rue, *The Wild Iris* mindfully renders its dilemmas by means of an interwoven series of dramatic monologues. These have, some of them, been published separately (they are poems of great individual beauty), but they are not separable: the book is a single meditation that far exceeds its individual parts.

The monologues are of three sorts: (1) those spoken by a human persona to God, or to that which holds the place of God, (2) those spoken by the botanical inhabitants of the garden cultivated by the human persona, and (3) those spoken by divinity. The poems addressed to God take their titles and their rhetorical premise from the Christian canonical hours (here reduced from seven to two), which mark the daily cycles of prayer. The poems spoken by flowers, groundcover, and one flowering tree take their color and argument from the circumstances of individual species (annuals vs. perennials, shade plants vs. sun plants, single blossoms vs. multiple): excluded from voicing are only those vegetable denizens identified with human "use" or consumption. The God-voiced poems take their titles from the saturating conditions of nature: weather, season, the qualities of wind or light. The poet is clearly aware that her central device, the affective identification that characterizes so large a portion of nature poetry in English, has sometimes borne the stigma of "fallacy," so she incorporates a preemptive ironist:

> The sun shines; by the mailbox, leaves
> Of the divided birch tree folded, pleated like fins.
> Underneath, hollow stems of the white daffodils,
>   Ice Wings, Cantatrice; dark
> leaves of the wild violet. Noah says
> depressives hate the spring, imbalance
> between the inner and the outer world. I make
> another case—being depressed, yes, but in a sense passionately
> attached to the living tree, my body
> actually curled in the split trunk, almost at peace,
>   in the evening rain
> almost able to feel
> sap frothing and rising: Noah says this is
> an error of depressives, identifying

with a tree. Whereas the happy heart
wanders the garden like a falling leaf, a figure for
the part, not the whole.
   ("Matins" 2)

If we are paying attention, we can discern the season before Noah names
it: daffodils are a spring flower; the leaves of the birch tree are as yet unfolded.
But the foreboding that attaches to the season is entirely inexplicit until
Noah is made to comment upon it and, commenting, to deflate it. "Entirely"
is perhaps misleading. In situ, in the full *Wild Iris*, some portion of foreboding inevitably infects this poem by way of the poem that immediately
precedes it. In that previous poem, which is also the title poem, the awaken-
ing rendered in the voice of an iris is a transition of stirring beauty ("from
the center of my life came / a great fountain, deep blue / shadows on azure
seawater") and intractable pain ("It is terrible to survive / as consciousness /
buried in the dark earth"). But that which is metaphysical in "The Wild Iris"
and mythic in the mind of the "Matins" speaker (notice her partial invoca-
tion of Daphne) is in Noah's breezy analysis a thing considerably more banal.
Instead of ontology, the garden's resident ironist discerns psychology; instead
of tragic insight, the symptomatic "presentation" of temperament or disease.
This witty, transient pathologizing of point of view produces a marvelous
mobility of tone, a mobility manifest in local instances of Glück's earlier work
but never so richly developed as in the present volume. And never so stra-
tegically important. By anticipating and incorporating the skeptical reader,
by fashioning the poetic sequence as a dialogue with disbelief, the speaker
procures considerable license for her extravagant impersonations of violets, of
witchgrass, of Eve in the Garden, nay, of God. We find early on that we will
grant this speaker any number of investigations-by-means-of-likeness. And
why? Because we like her.

God and the flowers speak with the voice of the human; the human
writer has no other voice to give them. The flowers sense, or describe sensation, in unabashedly human terms: "I feel it / glinting through the leaves,"
says the shaded vine, "like someone hitting the side of a glass with a metal
spoon" ("Lamium" 5). They measure aptitude by contrast or analogy with
human aptitude: "[T]hings / that can't move," says the rooted tree, "learn
to see; I do not need / to chase you through / the garden" ("The Hawthorne
Tree" 10), "I am not like you," says the rose, "I have only / my body for a voice"
("The White Rose" 47). God speaks in the voice of an earthly parent who has
reached the end of his tether: "How can I help you when you all want / different things" ("Midsummer" 34); "Do you suppose I care / if you speak to one
another?" ("April" 20). God explains himself by analogy and contradistinction

to the human: "I am not like you in this, / I have no release in another body" ("End of Summer" 40). God, like his creatures, assumes the simplifying contours of the familial: "You were like very young children, / always waiting for a story. . . . / I was tired of telling stories" ("Retreating Light" 50).

But likeness marks an irreparable chasm as well:

> So I gave you the pencil and paper.
> I gave you pens made of reeds
> I had gathered myself, afternoons in the dense meadows.
> I told you, write your own story.
>
>   . . .
>
> Then I realized you couldn't think
> with any real boldness or passion:
> you hadn't had your own lives yet,
> your own tragedies.
> So I gave you lives, I gave you tragedies,
> because apparently tools alone weren't enough.
>
> You will never know how deeply
> it pleases me to see you sitting there
> like independent beings . . .
>   ("Retreating Light" 50)

That "like" is ice to the heart. Those who achieve authentic independence require no "like."

Shadowing this book is the troubling possibility, indeed, the certain knowledge, that its analogies are false or partial. "Whatever you hoped," says God in the voice of the wind, "you will not find yourselves in the garden, / among the growing plants. / Your lives are not circular like theirs" ("Retreating Wind" 15). Worse yet from the poet's perspective, her analogies may be forced: "[I]f this were not a poem but / an actual garden," one skeptical interlocutor opines, "then / the red rose would be required to resemble nothing else, neither / another flower nor / the shadowy heart" ("Song" 27). Our Renaissance forebears had a term for the clothing of divinity in earthly garments: they called this process "accommodation." Because we are weak, because we cannot behold divinity face to face, God "accommodates" himself to our limits, agreeing to be known by elements available to human sense. These measures, however, are imperfect and interim:

I've submitted to your preferences, observing patiently
the things you love, speaking

through vehicles only, in
details of earth, as you prefer,

tendrils
of blue clematis, light

of early evening—
you would never accept

a voice like mine, indifferent
to the objects you busily name,

your mouths
small circles of awe—

And all this time
I indulged your limitation . . .
    ("Clear Morning" 7)

Glück's couplets do not in any straightforward sense coincide with the divisions of dialogue, but they do, subtly, remind us that accommodation is a two-part contract. God's patience is not infinite: "I cannot go on / restricting myself to images // because you think it is your right / to dispute my meaning" ("Clear Morning" 8). In order to grant his creatures an interim meeting place, the Creator agrees to interim diminishment. But this delicate contract breaks down the minute it is presumed upon:

You were not intended
to be unique. You were
my embodiment, all diversity

not what you think you see
searching the bright sky over the field,
your incidental souls
fixed like telescopes on some
enlargement of yourselves—
    ("Midsummer" 34–35)

Do not flatter yourselves, the Creator warns. Despite what you imagine, what I allow you for a time to imagine, I am not like you.

2. We

And you are plural. You are mere repetitive examples, as the crowd beneath your feet can witness:

> Not I, you idiot, not self, but we, we—waves
> of sky blue like
> a critique of heaven: why
> do you treasure your voice
> when to be one thing
> is to be next to nothing?
> Why do you look up? To hear
> an echo like the voice
> of god? . . .
>   ("Scilla" 14)

The plural pronoun is a reproach to vanity, and in *The Wild Iris* it issues not only from below but from above as well, and in the harsher second person:

> You wanted to be born: I let you be born.
> When has my grief ever gotten
> in the way of your pleasure?
>
> Plunging ahead . . .
> as though you were some new thing, wanting
> to express yourselves . . .
>
> never thinking
> this would cost you anything,
> never imagining the sound of my voice
> as anything but part of you—
>   ("End of Winter" 10)

The accusatory mode is one the human persona can adopt as well. "[H]ow can I live / in colonies, as you prefer," she asks, "if you impose / a quarantine of affliction, dividing me / from healthy members of / my own tribe" ("Matins" 26). This counter-complaint, with its foundational recourse to a singular self, is all the more credible for missing the point.

But the leverage inherent in the first-person plural has not been entirely lost on the human speaker: she too can manipulate the moral advantage in numbers when she will: "Unreachable father, when we were first / exiled from heaven, you made / a replica, a place in one sense / different from heaven, being / designed to teach a lesson" ("Matins" 3). In one sense, the speaker's imperturbable assumptions about didactic function are simply another manifestation of self-regard: the garden cannot simply be; the garden must mean; it was made for me. And though the speaker describes an affliction shared with others, or one particular other, of her kind, the shared aptitude appears to be for solitude: "Left alone, / we exhausted each other" ("Matins" 3). What lifts these passages above the common run of vanity is the ground of knowing they describe: "We never thought of you / whom we were learning to worship. / We merely knew it wasn't human nature to love / only what returns love" ("Matins" 3). In *The Wild Iris* as in its dominant line of lyric forebears, unrequited longing is the constitutive feature of consciousness. The garden is a sign because it is redolent with absence. The sharers in the garden come to know themselves by knowing that something is missing; their very failure to sustain one another is part of the message.

Given all this absence, what may we infer about the Maker? He has absconded. His voice is "the persistent echoing / in all sound that means good-bye, good-bye— / the one continuous line / that binds us to each other" ("End of Winter" 10–11). The "we" that includes deity is a "we" shot through with departure, so in his leaving, the deity has left us one another, another "we." And how have we made use of this solace?

No one's despair is like my despair—

You have no place in this garden
thinking such things, producing
the tiresome outward signs; the man
pointedly weeding an entire forest,
the woman limping, refusing to change clothes
or wash her hair.

Do you suppose I care
if you speak to one another?
But I mean you to know
I expected better of two creatures
who were given minds: if not
that you would actually care for each other

at least that you would understand
grief is distributed
between you, among all your kind, for me
to know you, as deep blue
marks the wild scilla, white
the wood violet.
   ("April" 20)

The irritable reaching after uniqueness ("No one's despair is like my despair") has taken its toll on human community. Despair has become for the couple in the garden a competitive pastime. But behind the orthodox proposition that despair is a species of pride, self-made and self-sustained, lies a yet more chilling possibility: what if we are on to the truth in spite of ourselves? What if grief is indeed our only claim to distinction? When the biblical faithful are forced to consider that their ends may not be coincident with the ends of the Creator, they have generally contrived to find this difference reassuring: God knows better; God makes us suffer for our own good. But what if God doesn't know better at all? Or what if his knowing doesn't have much to do with us? What if, except for our suffering, God could not tell us apart?

The distributed personae of *The Wild Iris* think through to the other side of this all-but-unthinkable proposition from time to time, think beyond the obvious panic such a proposition induces, and address deity as another of the vulnerable species of creation:

  —I am ashamed
at what I thought you were,
distant from us, regarding us
as an experiment . . .
  . . . Dear friend,
dear trembling partner, what
surprises you most in what you feel,
earth's radiance or your own delight?
  ("Matins" 31)

This is not the voice of first, or naive, intimacy, not the voice of the child who takes for granted that the parent is near, but the voice of willed, or revisionist, intimacy, the voice of the adult who has wearied of blame. It is a voice that may be adopted not only by the privileged species for whom the garden was created but also, and with equal eloquence, by the garden's humblest residents:

Because in our world
something is always hidden,
small and white,
small and what you call
pure, we do not grieve
as you grieve, dear
suffering master; you
are no more lost
than we are, under
the hawthorn tree, the hawthorn holding
balanced trays of pearls: what
has brought you among us
who would teach you, though
you kneel and weep,
clasping your great hands,
in all your greatness knowing
nothing of the soul's nature,
which is never to die: poor sad god,
either you never have one
or you never lose one.
    ("Violets" 21)

Nowhere in this limpid book does its triangular logic emerge with greater resonance. The human addresses God for the most part; the flowers and God address the human. And sometimes, to the flowers, the human appears in the guise of God, as flawed as the God to whom humans turn. But where is the human in "Violets"? Between "our world" and "your great hands," the human may be present, for once, chiefly by omission. And the posited soul: how is it that the violets know it? Do they have a soul? Does God? Does one have to have a soul in order to know the nature of the soul? Or does one know the nature of the soul only from the outside, only by being without one? Are we to imagine that the poor sad god in the garden grieves at being without a soul? Or does he grieve because he is unable to be rid of the soul? The only point on which the violets appear to speak unambiguously, a point quite devastating enough, is that grieving will not *make* a soul.

We three then: the two in dialogue and the one just beyond the bounds of dialogue, in whom the dialogue is grounded. The triangular manipulation of presence is as old as the lyric itself. He who sits beside you, writes Sappho. She that hath you, Shakespeare writes. Jealousy stands for but also masks a more frightening possibility. "Much / has passed between us," writes Glück; "or / was it always only / on the one side?" ("Matins" 13).

3. Reciprocal

The spectral possibility that gives lyric its urgency is not that the beloved isn't listening, but that the beloved doesn't exist. Prayer takes place at the edge of a similar abyss:

> Once I believed in you; I planted a fig tree.
> Here, in Vermont, country
> of no summer. It was a test: if the tree lived,
> it would mean you existed.
>
> By this logic, you do not exist. Or you exist
> exclusively in warmer climates,
> in fervent Sicily and Mexico and California,
> where are grown the unimaginable
>
> apricot and fragile peach. Perhaps
> they see your face in Sicily; here, we barely see
> the hem of your garment. I have to discipline myself
> to share with John and Noah the tomato crop.
>   ("Vespers" 36)

The poet's logic here is that of clever blackmail. God won't show? Perhaps he can be taunted into breaking cover. The speaker plants a fig tree, or the story of a fig tree, as a dare. When the fig tree predictably dies, the dare modulates to witty demotion. Are you not here, Father? Perhaps you are somewhere else? Or perhaps you are littler than we thought. To propose that God might "exist exclusively in warmer climates" is to bait a withholding deity: it goes without saying that God can be no God unless he is every-where at once. Or does it? Perhaps the absurdity cuts both ways. Perhaps comedic gesture throws into relief the deep peculiarity of an all-or-nothing system that is premised on "jealousy." A jealous God gets the jealous chil-dren ("I have to discipline myself," etc.) he deserves.

> If there is justice in some other world, those
> like myself, whom nature forces
> into lives of abstinence, should get
> the lion's share of all things, all
> objects of hunger, greed being
> praise of you. And no one praises
> more intensely than I, with more
> painfully checked desire, or more deserves

to sit at your right hand, if it exists, partaking
of the perishable, the immortal fig,
which does not travel.
   ("Vespers" 36)

Gospel has promised that the poor shall possess the kingdom of heaven,
and the poet wants her share, "the lion's share," of this compensatory promo-
tion. Far from admitting greed as grounds for penance, she brazenly advances
greed as the badge of special comprehension and thus of special desert. If
God has bounty to dispense, then perhaps, like other patrons, he may be
bribed. Praise is the coinage of patronage, whose darker side is "if." "If there is
justice in some other world": the conditional clause says justice in the present
world has fallen short. "If it exists": the conditional clause insinuates that part
of the power, and part of the power to judge, resides with the believer. If the
Father, in order to exist, requires our faith as we require his bounty, we may
have found the key to reciprocal consent. But lest the contract prove too dry,
the poet does not stop here, does not pause too long to congratulate herself
for unmasking the circular structure of vested interest. She returns instead to
the object that passes between the master and the lovers in the garden, that
makes the longing palpable, or nearly so: the promised, the withheld, the
here-and-absent fig.
   For the lover is a gardener too:

In your extended absence, you permit me
use of earth, anticipating
some return on investment.
   ("Vespers" 37)

This gardener glances obliquely at the parable of the talents (see Matthew
25; see Milton's 19th sonnet). It is a useful parable, invoking spiritual and
mercenary economies in unseemly proximity. Unseemliness prompts resistance, a common heuristic device. It also prompts reproach:

   I must report
failure in my assignment, principally
regarding the tomato plants.
   ("Vespers" 37)

Adopting the disconsonant diction of spreadsheet and quarterly report, the
gardener achieves a wicked deadpan, fair warning that she does not intend
to shoulder the failure alone:

> I think I should not be encouraged to grow
> tomatoes. Or, if I am, you should withhold
> the heavy rains, the cold nights that come
> so often here, while other regions get
> twelve weeks of summer.
>   ("Vespers" 37)

The multiplying indecorums now include domestic comedy. The disgruntled
dependent resourcefully finds that she is not to blame after all, that someone
else has caused her fault, someone whose crime is the misapportionment of
original love. And then, apparent concession: "All this / belongs to you." But
the concession is quickly withdrawn:

>   . . . All this
> belongs to you: on the other hand,
> I planted the seeds, I watched the first shoots
> like wings tearing the soil, and it was my heart
> broken by the blight, the black spot so quickly
> multiplying in the rows. I doubt
> you have a heart, in our understanding of
> that term. You who do not discriminate
> between the dead and the living, who are, in consequence,
> immune to foreshadowing, you may not know
> how much terror we bear, the spotted leaf,
> the red leaves of the maple falling
> even in August, in early darkness: I am responsible
> for these vines.
>   ("Vespers" 37)

The hilarious, instantaneous taking back of that which was fleetingly
granted—God's proprietary interest in creation—begins in petulance: mine,
says the poet; the suffering is mine. But petulance expands to a counter-
charge—you have no heart—that bit by bit accumulates plausibility. God's
loftier perspective, his comprehensive vision, begins to look like insuffi-
ciency. For comprehensiveness is by its very nature incapable of something
too, incapable of "foreshadowing," of temporal habitation, of partialness and
partiality, the realms of feeling possessed by those who are subject to time.
Unfolding these realms, the human voice becomes tutelary, makes concession to the newly contemplated incapacities of deity: "You may not know."

    And then the inventory of terror: the spotted leaf, the falling leaf, the
early darkness. And, signaled by the colon, the syllogistic revelation: I am the

only one left to be responsible. The line is not merely syllogistic, of course. Spoken within the parameters of apostrophic address, and spoken to one who might have been assumed to be responsible himself, it is a reprimand: unlike you, I take my responsibilities to heart. The reprimand is also a piece of gamesmanship, another in the series of rhetorical moves designed to flush God out. By what standard may we judge its success? God has not, we must confess, been coerced into unambiguous manifestation. On the other hand, the game has not quite stalled. For even as the speaker makes her sinuous case for self, something beyond the self—a "we" who bear the terror, the vines—has claimed the self's attention. This may be small. It is certainly strategic. But even in the momentary, the strategic assumption of responsibility, the self accrues a new degree of moral dignity. This moment may be as close as God will come.

In poem after poem, *The Wild Iris* delineates a reciprocal drawing out of spirit. This is not to say it is a sanguine book:

> Sometimes a man or woman forces his despair
> on another person, which is called
> baring the heart, alternatively, baring the soul—
> meaning for this moment they acquired souls—
> ("Love in Moonlight" 19)

Moonlight is reflected light, light "taken from another source," and love in this light a kind of violent seizing, or theft. The God who may or may not exist may take his logic from moonlight or love or, failing that, from parables. "You are perhaps training me to be / responsive to the slightest brightening," the poet ventures. "Or, like the poets, / are you stimulated by despair?" ("Vespers" 43). The poet takes a walk at sunset in the company of her despair. And in helpless arousal or deliberate grace, in one of two contrary modes, the God she refuses to look for appears:

> As you anticipated,
> I did not look up. So you came down to me:
> at my feet, not the wax
> leaves of the wild blueberry but your fiery self, a whole
> pasture of fire, and beyond, the red sun neither falling
>   nor rising—
> I was not a child: I could take advantage of illusions.
>   ("Vespers" 43)

This final resolution might be epigraph to the entire book of the garden.

4. Domestic

The domestic comedy that offers counterpoint to metaphysical debate in *The Wild Iris* assumes center stage in *Meadowlands*, the book of poems Glück published four years later. In this new book, the garden has given way to landscape of a different sort: the grasslands behind a childhood home on Long Island or surrounding the home of a twenty-year marriage in Vermont, the grasslands long buried beneath a football stadium in industrial New Jersey. Glück's subject has long been the zero sum game of the nuclear family (even when she grants a place to grandparents, aunts, and a sister's children, they are merely the reiterative instances of nuclear entrapment). The wit and the paradox, the razor-edge renderings of human motivation and human stalemate have been in place for decades. But now they are fresher, deeper than ever before. What has moved the project forward so dramatically is a structural insight: the deployment of inherited patterns (devotional hours, growing season, garden epic, voyage epic, scripts for different voices) on a book-length scale. Like *The Wild Iris*, *Meadowlands* has been constructed as a single argument, internally cross-referenced, dramatically unified. Its story is the breakdown of a marriage, and its template is Homeric.

What has the marriage in *Meadowlands* to do with the story of Odysseus and Penelope? Its time span is roughly twenty years, divided into two decade-long segments, one of them "happy." Its measure is roughly the span of a young son's growing into manhood, and judgment, and ironic commentary. Its outward incidents are driven by a husband's appetite for adventure. Its deeper momentum derives from the tension between excursus and domesticity. But the template yields rich results precisely because its fit is only approximate.

> Little soul, little perpetually undressed one,
> do now as I bid you, climb
> the shelf-like branches of the spruce tree;
> wait at the top, attentive, like
> a sentry or look-out. He will be home soon;
> it behooves you to be
> generous. You have not been completely
> perfect either, with your troublesome body
> you have done things you shouldn't
> discuss in poems. Therefore
> call out to him over the open water, over the bright water
> with your dark song, with your grasping,
> unnatural song—passionate,
> like Maria Callas. Who

wouldn't want you? Whose most demonic appetite
could you possibly fail to answer? Soon
he will return from wherever he goes in the meantime,
suntanned from his time away, wanting
his grilled chicken. Ah, you must greet him,
you must shake the boughs of the tree
to get his attention,
but carefully, carefully, lest
his beautiful face be marred
by too many falling needles.
  ("Penelope's Song" 3)

If the second Homeric epic has held enduring appeal for female narra-
tors, this surely has something to do with Penelope's leveraged position in a
complex economy of desire. The human heroines of the *Iliad* are essentially
single-function figures, the bearers of prophecy, grief, beauty, and fidelity in a
world whose primary contests—erotic, political, martial—are waged by men.
But Penelope's position is sustained by ambiguities as rich as those that sustain Achilles. She weaves a shroud for a patriarch who is not yet dead; she
rules a royal household, albeit in a compromised and declining state, during
the prolonged absence of her husband and the minority of her son; she entertains a populous band of suitors whose extended address makes her uniquely
immune to the erosions of age. Penelope has every reason to delay, and the
reader has every reason to lodge in her vicinity. Her cup is never empty, her
position ever summary: wife, mother, queen, perpetual subject of desire. If the
quality of that desire is somewhat clouded by a husband's waywardness and
the suitors' greed and boorishness, its breadth and duration are nevertheless
the stuff of fantasy. Finally, crucially, Penelope's composite position makes her
a center of consciousness, something to which not even the paragon Helen
may aspire.

"[B]ut carefully, carefully, lest / his beautiful face be marred / by too
many falling needles." The poet wears her mythic trappings lightly when it
suits her: the frank anachronisms of Maria Callas and grilled chicken are fair
indicators. The falling needles of a pine tree may be a poem's only oblique
allusion to the heroine's clothworking artistry, which signifies retirement (the
upstairs loom) and an aptitude for aggression (some damage to the hero's
face). The framework of *Meadowlands* will open to admit any number of
irreverent intrusions from late in the second millennium: a dishwasher, a
purple bathing suit, the neighbors' klezmer band, a resolute vernacular. Nor
are the book's mythic templates exclusively Homeric: one poem draws its
title and its premise (the ordinary miracle of marriage) from the wedding at

Cana, one is addressed to the serpent of Genesis, several make of birds and beasts and flowering plants a built-to-purpose parable. Narrative foundations are overlapping and distillate: the wife divides her perspective among several alter egos, several island wives, including her chief rival, Circe. The husband's reiterated departure seems sometimes to be his departure from the modern marriage, sometimes the infidelities that prepare for that departure, sometimes Odysseus' departure for Troy, sometimes his serial departures on the homeward trip to Ithaca, sometimes the shadowy final departure rehearsed in epic continuations like the *Inferno* or the lost *Telegonia*.[1]

The great advantage of broad outline is its suppleness, its freedom from clutter.

> The Greeks are sitting on the beach
> wondering what to do when the war ends. No one
> wants to go home, back
> to that bony island, everyone wants a little more
> of what there is in Troy, more
> life on the edge, that sense of every day as being
> packed with surprises. But how to explain this
> to the ones at home to whom
> fighting a war is a plausible
> excuse for absence, whereas
> exploring one's capacity for diversion
> is not.
> ("Parable of the Hostages" 14)

This freedom from clutter is a rhetorical talent shared by Telemachus, whose earlier incarnation was as Noah in *The Wild Iris*. Telemachus has learned that ironists need never be out of work:

> When I was a child looking
> at my parents' lives, you know
> what I thought? I thought
> heartbreaking. Now I think
> heartbreaking, but also
> insane. Also
> very funny.
> ("Telemachus' Detachment" 13)

The domestic quarrel, with its soul-destroying pettiness and convolution, would seem to be inimical to lyric poetry. One of the great technical

triumphs of *Meadowlands* is to have found a form in which the soul destroy-
ing can be transmuted to the spirit-reviving. The genius is not just in the leaving out, though elision is its indispensable method, but also in the undressed,
unwashed leaving in:

> Speak to me, aching heart: what
> ridiculous errand are you inventing for yourself
> weeping in the dark garage
> with your sack of garbage: it is not your job
> to take out the garbage, it is your job
> to empty the dishwasher. You are showing off again . . .
>   ("Midnight" 26)

But Glück's finest formal innovation in this volume is reserved for the
structure of domestic dialogue. She tracks the wild non sequitur, the sidestep
and the feint, the ambush, the afterthought, the timed delay. As in Penelope's
weaving, the thread that seemed to have been dropped resurfaces, having
meanwhile lent its tensile continuity to the underside of the narrative.

> How could the Giants name
> that place the Meadowlands? It has
> about as much in common with a pasture
> as would the inside of an oven.
>
> New Jersey
> was rural. They want you
> to remember that.
>
> Simms
> was not a thug. LT
> was not a thug.
>
> What I think is we should
> look at our surroundings
> realistically, for what they are
> in the present.
>
> That's what
> I tell you about the house.
> No giant
> would talk the way you talk.

You'd be a nicer person
if you were a fan of something.
When you do that with your mouth
you look like your mother.

You know what they are?
Kings among men.

    So what king
    fired Simms?
("Meadowlands 3" 34)

Ten such dialogue poems appear in the course of *Meadowlands*, eleven if one counts, and one should, the epigraph. All are distinguished by the same minimalist annotation—the woman speaking in indented stanzas, the man flush left and by a handful of recurrent themes. Once the convention and the leitmotifs have established themselves, the poet is free to begin and end in heady, hilarious medias res: three bare lines and a single speaker in "Meadowlands 2," another single speaker in "Void." No matter that the partner in speech is silent for the moment: these poems are cast as rejoinders and thus take part in a two-part song. Their workings are in situ, inseparable from the tonal and semantic resource of the book. Given the theme of the book, of course, this indissolubility of the whole achieves no little poignance. And greatly to its credit, it achieves delight. The reader is granted the pleasures of an initiate, one who knows the players without a scorecard, and the pleasures of an exuberant pace. No small prize to rescue from the ashes.

5. One

    Let's play choosing music. Favorite form.

Opera.

    Favorite work.

Figaro. No. Figaro and Tannhauser. Now
it's your turn: sing one for me.
    (Epigraph to *Meadowlands* ix)

Mozart's is a comic opera of marriage. Wagner's is a tragic romance, in which the hero philanders and the heroine dies of a broken heart. Sing one, says the hero: make the one tradition comprehensive. Do the different voices, and make them add up to a whole. Sing for me: make me miss you when I am gone.

"[A] figure for / the part," said Noah in an earlier book. "[N]ot," he said, "the whole" ("Matins" 2). But his subject was the happy heart. Part of the wit that unites these books is their tracing of great epic themes—Milton's in the first instance, Homer's in the second—to their origins in the domestic. By means of this tracing they continue the logic already inherent in their lofty predecessors. But the latter-day garden and the meadowlands share another logic too, a logic more specific to the lyric. They posit conversation in a fertile world: my part, yours, the whole making more than the sum of its parts. And always they hear the conversation breaking down, the answer reduced to echo, the several voices to one. "The beloved doesn't / need to live," says the weaver in equal parts grimness and joy. "The beloved / lives in the head" ("Ithaca" 12).

NOTE

1. The *Telegonia* (sixth century B.C.) takes its name from Telegonus, son of Odysseus and Circe. On the structural kinship and durable erotic powers of rival women, this lost epic was apparently superb: its plot is said to have included the ultimate marriage of Circe to Telemachus and Penelope to Telegonus, two mothers to two sons. Odysseus had by this time succumbed.

WORKS CITED

Glück, Louise. *Meadowlands*. Hopewell, NJ: Ecco Press. 1996.
———. *The Wild Iris*. Hopewell, NJ: Ecco Press, 1992.

DAVID BROMWICH

Self-Deception and Self-Knowledge in John Hollander's Poetry

John Hollander said once in praise of W. H. Auden that he had an ear that was like a moral sense. Of course, nothing could ever be a moral sense, not even moral judgment is, but if you have to pick a bodily organ to make the metaphor, the ear is a provocative choice. All the more so in view of Lord Shaftesbury's original epigram, which specifies a different location: "Shou'd One, who had the Countenance of a Gentleman, ask me, 'Why I wou'd avoid being nasty, when nobody was present.' In the first place I shou'd be fully satisfy'd that he himself was a very nasty Gentleman who cou'd ask this Question; and that it wou'd be a hard matter for me to make him ever conceive what true Cleanliness was. However, I might, notwithstanding this, be contented to give him a slight Answer, and say, "Twas because I had a Nose.'" Compared to such simplicity of command, the moral ear is subtle, almost secretive—a double agent in the field of aesthetic experience. It has been said that poets in their elegies are often mourning for themselves. We don't notice as easily how poets in their compliments are often describing themselves—or themselves under ideal conditions. Nor is this an instance merely of wishful projection. To declare to others and even, much of the time, to ourselves what we would be known as, is so difficult a task that all but the best and worst eventually have to resort to code.

From *Southwest Review* 86, nos. 2/3 (2001): 246–53. © 2001 by *Southwest Review*.

John Hollander is a poet whose ear is sometimes like a moral sense. But, to catch the way this works, one has to understand moral in close relation to mores, and in relation to manners or "small morals." The sense is also affiliated with morale—the poise by which a character seems unexchangeably to accept a style that suits it. Morale is the portrait painter's greatest subject, and the poems that I will speak of all have an element of portrait painting.

Helicon was the mountain in Boetia from which sprang the fountains of the muses, and the characters in the poem "Helicon" are the young Hollander and Allen Ginsberg "in their unguessing days," when they were students at Columbia, both aspiring poets but neither of them yet known for the work that would make them imaginatively distinct. The action of the poem is a fraternal adventure, a trip to St. Luke's to donate blood; and an allegorical conceit is lightly hung on this journey—the unasked giving of blood seeming the analogue and inverse of the gift by the muses of an inspiration that can't be taken on board in number, weight, and measure. Also just above the surface of the plot is a memory—evoked in some lines I will not quote—of a practical joke the poet once played at the university's public fountains: filling them with powdered detergent and concentrated essence of grape to counterfeit a scene of religious miracle-making, the only thing in nature as strange, if it is in nature, as the inspiration given by the muses.

One more piece of context is relevant to the tone and shading of the poem, which together make such an exuberant and delicate achievement. Hollander and Ginsberg had been close friends. It wouldn't be true to say that either was the ascendant mind, but Ginsberg was a very different figure then from the celebrity who emerged in the late fifties and sixties; and of the two he seems to have been the more consciously advanced: the poems he was writing around that time have been published under the title *The Gates of Wrath*—their style is a blend of Marvell, Blake, and Hart Crane. So "Helicon" looks back at an early moment of a friendship. But in the years between Ginsberg had published *Howl*, and Hollander reviewed it with dismissive confidence and scorn, the abrupt and unqualified manner of one making sure not to sound as if he ever could have been the author's friend. I've heard John Hollander speak of Allen Ginsberg, critically and affectionately, yet he never mentioned that review and has never chosen to reprint it; and I suspect in some part of himself, looking back, he thought the review misjudged. We find our way to a semblance of self-knowledge "having been steered there only by the heart's mistakes / In the treasonable night," as Hollander says in "West End Blues," the poem that follows "Helicon" in *Visions from the Ramble*. The double portrait of "Helicon" is a penance for a small treason of the affections, and it offers the revival of a memory, one of the rare gifts friendship alone can give.

Allen said, *I am searching for the true cadence.* Gray
Stony light had flashed over Morningside Drive since noon,
Mixing high in the east with a gray smoky darkness,
Blackened steel trusses of Hell-Gate faintly etched into it,
Gray visionary gleam, revealing the clarity of
Harlem's grid, like a glimpse of a future city below:
When the fat of the land shall have fallen into the dripping pan,
The grill will still be struck with brown crusts, clinging to
Its bars, and neither in the fire nor out of it.
So is it coming about. But in my unguessing days
Allen said, *They still give you five dollars a pint at St. Luke's,*
No kickback to the intern, either.

The voices of proverb and prophecy mingle, in these opening lines, with a colloquial speech in possession of worldly wisdom and in search of a way of truth. The Dantesque evocations that follow in the poem's central scene are insistent enough to give the poem a traditional continuity, but without the mood music of epic allusion as one comes to know it in a poem like *Four Quartets.* If anything, the gravity of the diction is faithful to a nearer model, the American realist prose of the forties, and that is part of its enchantment.

Inquiries and directions. Many dim rooms, and the shades
Of patient ghosts in the wards, caught in the privileged
Glimpses that the hurrying visitor always gets;
Turnings; errors; wanderings; while Allen chattered on:
I mean someday to cry out against the cities, but first
I must find the true cadence. We finally emerged
Into a dismal chamber, bare and dusty, where, suddenly,
Sunlight broke over a brown prospect of whirling clouds
And deepening smoke to plummet down, down to the depths
Of the darkness, where, recessed in a tiny glory of light
A barely visible man made his way in a boat
Along an amber chasm closing in smoke above him—
Two huge paintings by Thomas Cole opened, like airshaft
Windows, on darkening hearts, there by the blood bank.

Cole's paintings of life's journey make an appropriate (ponderous, earnest, impressive) frame for the mock-epic journey the poem itself recounts with an unmocking dignity. The meter is a touch of craft that completes the effect—a meter shared by other poems in *Visions from the Ramble*, yet it has a special rightness here. It is loosely accentual, six or seven beats to the line, and has a look and feel close to Blake's fourteener, an invention that certainly belonged to Ginsberg's idea of the "true cadence."

The poem comes to its ending easily, anecdotally, when the plasma bottle is full.

> Then rest; then five dollars. Then Allen
> Urged us out onto the street. The wind sang around the corner,
> Blowing in from the sound and a siren screeched away
> Up Amsterdam Avenue. *Now you have a chocolate malted*
> *And then you're fine*, he said, and the wind blew his hair like
>   feathers,
> And we both dissolved into nineteen forty-eight, to be whirled
> Away into the wildwood of time, I to leave the city
> For the disorganized plain, spectre of the long drink
> Taken of me that afternoon. *Turning a guy*
> *On*, said Allen last year to the hip psychiatrists
> Down in Atlantic City, *that's the most intimate thing*
> *You can ever do to him*. Perhaps. I have bled since
> To many cadences, if not to the constant tune
> Of the heart's yielding and now I know how hard it is
> To turn the drops that leaky faucets make in unquiet
> Nights, the discrete tugs of love in its final scene,
> Into a stream, whether thicker or thinner than blood, and I know
> That opening up at all is harder than meeting a measure:
> With night coming on like a death, a ruby of blood is a treasure.

Turning a guy on—to drugs, that is—another medical procedure but with a pomp of put-on solemnity absent in the scene remembered here: the phrase and the version of community it sells are an unconscious parody of the companionship the poem has recalled. A guy, by definition, is anyone, the sort of anyone you can benefit without having much feeling for. The falseness of that promise is taken up quickly and held: "Perhaps." Opening up in poetry or friendship is not a matter of turning the drip of the faucet into a steady stream. Intimacy, like imagination, happens by accident and oddly. So the last couplet pulls together the allegory with a metaphysical compactness: blood and wine, spontaneous expression and gush, true cadence and the talking and listening of friends—all treasured up now in a ruby of blood, a memory caught in one of those privileged glimpses the unhurrying visitor to his own life may sometimes get.

There are inspired glimpses of self-knowledge in the sequence of 1976, *Reflections on Espionage*, whose contents are the messages of a spy operating under the code-name Cupcake. This seemed to me, when I first read it, and still does seem one of Hollander's most characteristic poems and at the same time his most unusual. The self of the artist and operative Cupcake utterly vanishes into a sense of fellowship with all who share "the work"—the work of poetry and spying, which throughout the book are metaphors for each other. His termination and disappearance are a consequence of madness and incapacity, but they are also a necessary effect of an enterprise that finally dwarfs individuals, as Shelley in the *Defence of Poetry* and Eliot in "Tradition and the Individual Talent" in different ways suggested that poetry must do. By contrast, the ideal cherished by Cupcake, that one might so submerge oneself as to be lost, but lost with a purpose in a collective and impersonal and redemptive project—this is a delusion, which nevertheless draws strength from the vivid idea of a corps or guild or game or circus greater than any of its participants, to which one uniquely belongs. The hero of *Reflections on Espionage* contrives, from his partial wisdom, a delirious hope of being freed from self-consciousness, as if the work could offer a foolproof way to achieve two goals at once: a truth one has pieced together oneself and a truth one can stand and know from outside. This is the dream of every born decipherer. And yet, maybe one has to be afflicted with such enthusiasm in order to maintain a generous disposition toward non-utilitarian work of any kind. This seems to be Cupcake's drift of thought when he speaks of a poet or spy named Ember.

> He has grown astonishingly beautiful
> In the past few years as the high quality
> Of the work he does for us has become more
> Apparent. Is it something in his cover—
> Something that builds character where only a
> Personality is called for? Or has he
> Secretly revealed himself to take drink of
> A sweet and demanding source. That would be bad:
> He would be found out all too quickly. But he
> Looks too well—it is as if the work itself
> Were nourishing him now. How he has risen
> From the old ashes of himself! I recall
> His former crabbed privacies, his sad, fussy
> Insistence on obscure French restaurants at
> Noon for passing messages, the bizarre keys
> For ciphers he would invent. Now he seems an
> Illumination of the ordinary.

Here what might be envy is sublimated into a feeling more akin to wonder: "as if the work itself / Were nourishing him now." Cupcake for his part, having coded and organized himself to a final opacity, is finally consumed by the work. A happier fate is assigned to the hero of "The Mad Potter"—a touching lyric that belongs, though distantly, to the group of poems I have been describing. He pours himself into all his works and finds nothing but himself. It is not clear how madness in such a setting differs from dedication to a calling. Perhaps the only difference is the mad potter's loss of awareness of a world from which he was called.

A work of art that is genuinely interested in (to borrow a favorite phrase of Hollander's) "the matter of art" will be interested in self-deception. This is the part of self-knowledge that stands receptive to construal by the eye and ear—the visible shadow of a recessive object that can never sculpt itself into legible form. I conclude with another autobiographical poem, "Early Birds," from Hollander's most recent book, *Figurehead*. This fragmentary anecdote of a vaudeville performer, George Moran, in his after-years in Los Angeles, makes a natural pair with "Helicon," though I don't know if the poet conceived of it that way. The title refers to an old comedian once known for a bit about the early bird and the worm, and to the boy John age 17 in California alone that summer, in flight from a fear he still doesn't fully understand.

>   I see
> The 17 year old boy I was
> Adrift one languid summer in
> L.A., working from time to time
> As an incompetent soda-jerk,
> Or pearl-diver, equally
> Bumbling, at the Pig 'n' Whistle
> Downtown (residues of morning
> Oatmeal and of barley soup—
> Those were the messiest to clean)
> Or not working, the while living at
> The Hotel Barbara at Sixth
> And Alvarado—then a shabby,
> Peaceful, not unrighteous spot.

These solitaries, old and young, idle away the evening hours in talk and in listening: that is the heart of the poem. The rest is a mission entrusted by the old man to the young—to get in touch with his daughter in New York, whom he hasn't heard from in years—a mission that the poet tells us, on his return to a gregarious life, he found plausible reasons disguised as obstacles to prevent his carrying out. Two years later Moran died, at 67, and writing the poem Hollander is 67.

> And for the unproselytizing
> Sect of the Rememberers—
> I, the boy then, some of you—
> All our various vaudevilles are
> Giving way to faster brighter
> Dumber slower stuff, and even
> Stories told of them perform their
> Dimming time-steps as they slowly
> Shuffle off to Buffalo.

Faster, brighter, dumber, slower stuff—a totally characteristic phrase, and is it not marvelous how we know what he means? Dumber and slower because of the way it is faster and brighter. What has gone out of American popular culture is much of the wit, much of the humor, much of the sentiment. What has come in is cleverness and knowingness—understood not as the obnoxious traits of an elite, but as universally desirable and deployable. Billy Crystal and Eddie Murphy, and Burns and Allen: what to say of the difference of style, when it is a difference also of morale, the way the ear takes in the words? The newer pair are so much faster, brighter, dumber, slower; and they are so because they don't have to listen. I think of George Burns (let him stand for any resilient poet, spy, or comedian) pausing as he admires, in the last words Gracie said, a most peculiar inference or non sequitur or circuitous but irrefutable QED. It leaves Burns only pleasantly stunned, and where a normal man would sputter and bluster he keeps his cool and holds his cigar. But this is a way of listening—a suspended and ever-resumable relation with the world and the mayhem of its attempt to recruit one for its ends. In reading and thinking about some of Hollander's poems, we feel we are on the scene as a gifted contemporary performs the work of listening that is another name for self-knowledge and for sanity.

WILLARD SPIEGELMAN

Jorie Graham's "New Way of Looking"

In the richly laconic aphorisms that make up the "Adagia" in Wallace Stevens's *Opus Posthumous*, we come upon two that might serve as points of entry into the alluring, stern, fiercely defiant sensibility of Jorie Graham:

> The thing seen becomes the thing unseen.
> The opposite is, or seems to be, impossible.
> . . . .
> Description is an element, like air or water.[1]

Like all good epigrams, these nuggets provoke questions more than they provide answers. "Becomes" means "complements" as well as "turns into"; Stevens, sympathetic student of Emerson and Baudelaire, intuits a constant symbolic relationship between the natural world and the world of the spirit. Even more ambiguous than the meanings of "becoming" are its processes. When the visible turns into the invisible, it logically disappears from sight: It evaporates, escapes notice. But we must qualify the tentative second half of Steven's pronouncement: things *previously* unseen can heave into view, making themselves visible before finally vanishing. Angels and all otherworldly emissaries come and go at will. For his part, the poet demands a disciplined attendance on the "thing seen," with a hope of capturing or rendering its

From *How Poets See the World: The Art of Description in Contemporary Poetry*, pp. 173–200. © 2005 by Oxford University Press.

essence through an act of accurate observation in order to put himself in touch with the circulating currents of the invisible. The act of "description" becomes a significant element, although not the only one, in his task. Stevens chooses his elements cunningly: not earth and fire, the two most capable of being seen, but air and water, the first invisible, the second translucent. One might as well try to catch the wind as try to describe anything.

The frustrations inherent in such efforts mark the continuing explorations by the one contemporary poet who is most drawn to the visible world and distrustful of it in equal measure. If the major tradition of poetic description has meant keeping one's eye steadily on one's subject (the line that runs from Wordsworth through Hopkins down to such diverse lookers-on or lookers-at as A. R. Ammons, Gary Snyder, and Charles Tomlinson), then Jorie Graham has alighted upon a new vantage point, one that refuses to look evenly and patiently, and that makes its maneuvers by nervously cross-cutting from one item, gesture, scene, or thought, to another. For all her intensity, Graham is not really an intimate poet. It is hard to get to know her, just as it is sometimes hard to know what one of her poems is literally "about." Her difficulty has everything to do with how she looks at the world and then renders her vision in her poems. Description is a central element in her work, but like air and water, it is a medium often invisible or dark.

Where John Ashbery has fashioned a poetry that moves seamlessly along a flow chart, recording all sensations at all frequencies and in as many tones, moods, or layers of diction as possible, Graham proceeds by interruption and asides, with a flickering glance that makes (in another nod to Stevens) the visible a little hard to see. Even her syntax differs from that of Ashbery, whose long sentences are structurally sound, although the references may be opaque (the form remains intact, but the subject disappears from view), as well as from that of Amy Clampitt, whose old-fashioned Miltonic, sinuously baroque tendrils reproduce, microcosmically, a plentiful world of flora and fauna. In a famous letter to Thomas Poole, Coleridge once observed that the use of parentheses signaled the very drama of thought, which showed the thought growing and ramifying and made of the words on the page a living process rather than a *hortus siccus*, a vibrantly Gothic (i.e., English) rather than a deadeningly classic (i.e., French) style.[2] Graham's drama of thought is jagged, unreticulated, looking more often like blips on a computer screen than branches gracefully arching away from a central stem. Especially in her most recent books the parenthetical remarks, visible lacunae, syntactic interruptions, experiments with phrasing and lineation, and the pull of the line against that of the sentence all lead to one inevitable conclusion: that what she calls, in the title of one poem, "The Dream of the Unified Field" (*Materialism*, and repeated as the title of her 1995 Pulitzer Prize–winning anthology of her own work) must remain a dream only, never a fact, whether in the provinces of painting and physics, or within the human psyche, or in the universe of the seen and the unseen. Buckminster Fuller's observation—"Unity is plural and at minimum two"—has special resonance for Graham, as her rival tendencies, to unify and to diversify or shatter, have political, philosophical, and, above all, aesthetic causes and consequences in her poetry.

Graham courts the unexpected. Some later poems demonstrate satisfying closure just as some earlier ones do not. Her poems move mysteriously, using—indeed, enacting—description as part of their quest for adequate form. Making the visible a little hard to see begins with her covers. On the dust jackets of eight of her volumes are reproductions of paintings, all of which call into question the nature of seeing. *Erosion*, with a photograph of the poet on the cover, is the exception, but even here the picture extends *beyond* its overlaid framing lines. The Mark Rothko painting on *Hybrids of Plants and of Ghosts* insists on the ways one shade of color blurs into another. The half picture of a naked woman by an open window on *The End of Beauty* divides Eric Fischl's painting and tantalizes us with a frame (the dimensions of the cover) imposed upon an abbreviated image. A version of Mantegna's *Christ Descending into Limbo* on the cover of *Materialism* depicts a swirling, caped figure seen from behind, with leg and hair the only visible body parts. Figures from a fresco by Giotto are seen in profile at the bottom of *Swarm*; five people in clear profile stand out from the undifferentiated others who melt into the background or the left-hand border. *Never* reproduces a small portion of Vermeer's *The Astronomer*, showing two hands, one globe, and a window. The symbolism is clear: a miniaturized world confronted not by a complete human being but only by his grasping, measuring hands.

Most telling of all is Francis Bacon's *Study of a Figure in a Landscape* on the cover of *Region of Unlikeness*, where the blurred outlines of human likeness dissolve into the surround of a field. What Graham calls "the great *thereness* of being" in this volume ("Untitled," 17) suggests that reality, essence, and identity exist at a remove, and that the attempt to capture them is inevitably doomed. Magritte's painting of Pascal's coat on the cover of *The Errancy* is complete, but the coat itself is tattered and ripped, exposing the city and sky behind and beneath it. In all these cases, you *can* judge a book by its cover: the illustrations refuse to come into focus, into a neat box or frame, and even when the illustration is complete, as are the Rothko and Magritte pictures, it poses questions of representation. The exception (i.e., a completed picture without explicit irony) proves the rule: *The Dream of the Unified Field* reproduces Bartolo di Fredi's *The Creation of Eve*. Adam's wished-for unification involves sleep and then the birth of Eve by an act of separation from his own body. Like Adam, Graham dreams of a unity that can occur only through fracture. Her poems, like the covers of her books, assay figural description and landscape painting but refuse completion. It is as though Graham wishes she were Poussin, inserting human figures in a pastoral landscape, but is prohibited from doing so. All paradises are, if not lost, at least inaccessible.

In *Materialism* Graham announces with uncharacteristic nostalgia her longing for an old-fashioned Romantic organicism:

> . . . Reader,
> wind blowing through these lines I wish were branches,
> searchlight in daylight, trying as I
> am trying
> to find a filament of the real like some twist of
> handwriting glowing in the middle
> distance—somewhere up here, in the air—
>   ("Young Maples in Wind")[3]

She wants to find a filament of the real, but she also tries to create one in the twist of her handwriting. A poem like this invites instructive comparison with the work of Romantic forebears and contemporaries like the late Howard Nemerov, a great reader of natural hieroglyphics and unlettered poetry, who takes an easy fanciful notice of alphabets inscribed in the air by blue swallows or incised by skaters' blades on frozen ponds. But Graham, almost everywhere else, even more surely thwarts such comparison.

Nemerov was always clear in his doubleness. Looking at the swallows "divide the air / In shapes invisible and evanescent," he tempts himself and us with the possibility of meaning in nature:

> Thus helplessly the mind in its brain
> Weaves up relation's spindrift web,
> Seeing the swallows' tails as nibs
> Dipped in invisible ink, writing.

But his mind, trained by William of Occam, knows it must look at the world "emptied of speech" because "the spelling mind / Imposes with its grammar book / Unreal relations on the blue / Swallows." To read the world as the *liber naturae* is a dream whose usefulness has long since passed, but Nemerov constantly entertains such nostalgias. He wants to see writing everywhere (in the invisible ink of swallows, in skaters' blades on ice), and where he sees writing he wants meaning (in Chinese ideograms he cannot understand). He loads his potent epigram pregnantly: "Still, the point of style / is character" ("Writing").[4]

Graham frustratingly spurns the discursive clarity of Nemerov and his entire generation. Regardless of the genuine, wrenching, and dramatic changes that she has made in her books—correcting, undoing, and revising earlier work—one element remains constant: her visual delight in the world is matched by an opposing resistance to the visible. She has revived the grand ambitions of poets like Wordsworth, Eliot, and Stevens but has also undercut the very ground that made those ambitions possible. She asks us to see the world anew. Description is one element among many, but one she will neither rely on wholly nor do without.

Just when a reader might think that Nemerov's blue swallows or their cousins have appeared, Graham works a turn on the Romantic preoccupation with bird flight and birdsong. She devotes as much energy, throughout her poetry, to looking at birds as to listening to them, thereby evincing at least an equal sensitivity to the visible as to the audible.[5] Here, for example, is the beautiful ending of "Existence and Presence" (*Materialism*, 142) in the same volume, in which she conducts a soliloquy on a hillside and seems to see at twilight the figure of Diana the huntress, followed by ambiguous flocks:

An alphabet flew over, made liquid syntax for a while,
diving and rising, forking, a caprice of clear meanings,
right pauses, unwrapping the watching-temptation—
then chopped and scattered, one last one chittering away,
then silence, then the individual screeches of the nighthunters
at dusk, the hollows sucked in around that cry.

Failing even to identify the kind of bird, Graham jumps instinctively to the level of the abstract, the intellectual. She does not so much "describe" the flock as attempt to "read" it, but whatever clarity of meaning it possesses goes unspecified and finally disappears. The experience of the event is more important than its accurate description. And not only does she refuse to describe but she also, characteristically, refuses to moralize or to mourn. Seldom has the experience of the natural world resulted in so little human emotion.

Even writing itself suffers a fate worse than in Nemerov's lovely dreams. In "Penmanship" (*Hybrids*, 31), the alphabet becomes a landscape on the page in the eyes of the young learner, each letter contributing to the ongoing development of a visual image that metaphorically resembles a natural one. For a moment in midpoem, Graham loses herself in an imagined seascape ("flooded lowlands, topsoil gone downstream, the ocean / flashing her green garments, many-stemmed and / many-headed") before personifying the twenty-six letters as a school of fish whose major impulse "is for normalcy, marriage," that is, for correctness. But poet and poem drift off into an inconclusive reverie (with an explicit allusion to the labials and gutturals in Stevens's "The Plot Against the Giant"), as if to acknowledge that such dreams can never be realized:

> these labials and gutturals narrowing their aim,
> shedding the body for
> its wish, a pure idea, a thought as true as
> not true, water
>
> lilies, water-
> striders. . . .

Regardless of the real, wrenching, and dramatic changes that Graham has made in her books, each of which corrects, undoes, and revises the previous ones, one element remains constant: she must discover or grapple with ways of handling her ambivalent responses to Romanticism and its American modernist inheritors.

* * *

The title of the first poem in Graham's first book ("The Way Things Work," *Hybrids*, 3) might invite thoughts of celebration, on the principle of Richard Wilbur's "The Beautiful Changes"; instead, the poem moves from fluidity, transition, a Romantic principle of harmony, to electricity, mechanics, tangibility. The first line extends from the generalized title:

> is by admitting
> or opening away.
> This is the simplest form
> of current: Blue
> moving through blue;
> blue through purple;
> the objects of desire
> opening upon themselves
> without us;
> the objects of faith.
> The way things work
> is by solution,
> . . . .
> The way things work
> is that we finally believe

they are there,
common and able
to illustrate themselves.
Wheel, kinetic flow,
rising and falling water,
ingots, levers and keys,

. . . .
The way things work
is that eventually
something catches.

Admitting, solution, belief, catching: the poem ends on a note of almost random chance. Eventually some hook or ratchet takes hold, stapling us to a universe that might as well do without us. Whereas most interested observers of the processes of the natural or physical world tend to take delight in the manifold operations of a clockwork universe, or of an organically unfolding unity, of the visible evidence of an indwelling spirituality, Jorie Graham has maintained so skeptical a stance from the beginning (beneath all the stylistic changes in her poetry) that we may reasonably call her the least hedonistic, least delighted, least sensuously fulfilled of descriptive poets in spite of the lush outpourings of gorgeous details and ecstatic feelings that fill her work.

Like all but one of her books, *Hybrids* has a cover illustration by a painter. In this case, it is one of Mark Rothko's color-field oils. Graham has always been drawn to painting as a subject and an analogy, but "For Mark Rothko" proves that from the start Graham has never tried to be a conventionally ekphrastic poet. Instead of "describing" one of Rothko's paintings—a challenge to any poet's potential wish to represent the nonrepresentational (see Chapter 5)— Graham makes an homage to him by proceeding deductively from the idea of a color in Rothko to the specific scene she observes from her window:

Shall I say it is the constancy of persian red
that permits me to see
this persian-red bird
come to sit now
on the brick barbecue
within my windowframe.
    (36)

Nature, we assume, imitates art or, rather, one kind of experience (the memory of a Rothko painting) prepares a viewer for another kind of sighting, one that changes before one's eyes as the bird disappears from view:

When I look again he is gone.
He is easy to imagine
in flight: *red extended flame,*
I would say, or, *ribbon*
torn from a hat
rising once

before it catches on a twig,
or, *flying painted mouth*
but then how far
have we come?
He could fly now
into a moment of sunlight

that fell from the sun's edge
ten thousand years ago,
mixed in with sunlight
absolutely new.
There is no way to understand
the difference. Some red

has always just slipped from
our field of vision, a cardinal
dropping from persian to magenta to white so slowly
in order that the loss
be tempted,
not endured.
      (36–37)

The idea of color dominates the poet's imagination, as does the way color slips from shade to shade, moment to moment in time, and along a visual spectrum in space. Something comes into view and then vanishes, leaving imagined traces in the perceiver's eye. The last stanza suggests vision's eternally transitional qualities, so beautiful that they invite us to repeat the process of perception and memory (one possible implication of the verb "tempted") rather than lament the loss of beauty. As in "The Way Things Work," where blue moved through blue through purple, here Graham refuses to settle for an elegiac response to change and loss.

The visible world has always inspired in Graham a deeply ambivalent set of responses. On the one hand, it attracts her; on the other, she deeply distrusts it. As I mentioned in Chapter 1, seventy years ago, in his famous introduction to the idiosyncratic *Oxford Book of Modern Verse*, Yeats claimed that he and his generation wanted to revolt "against irrelevant descriptions of nature." Graham hews to the same path of resistance: "irrelevant" may be for her synonymous with "perceptually accurate" or "deeply committed" or "carefully witnessed." Her contemporary Mark Doty poses and answers the question: "What is description, after all, / but encoded desire" ("Description," *Atlantis*), and in another poem from the same volume ("Two Ruined Boats"), he makes a comparable gesture of reparation and restitution: "Description is itself a kind of travel, / And I can study all day in an orient / of color."[6] Such ease of formulation, clarity of purpose, and delight in sensuous participation must appeal to that part of Graham's temperament and upbringing that comes from years in France and Italy, dedicated looking at real and painted landscapes, and physical self-awareness. But increasingly she has come to resist the orient of color in favor of blanknesses, interstices, gaps and lacunae. Here, for example, is the opening of "Room Tone" (*The End of Beauty*, 73):

> Turn around (wind in the sycamore).
> Did you see that did you hear that (wind in the
> _____ _____ _____?) can you touch it,
> what *can* you touch? will you
> speak back to me,
> will you look up now, please?
> Dear reader, is it enough for you that I am thinking of you
> in this generic sort of way,
> moving across the page for you that your eyes move,
> moving in and out of these rooms that there be a *there*
> for you?

Leaving things out rather than putting them all in—omission instead of inclusion—becomes as much a tool for the wordsmith as the painter, as both John Ashbery (at the start of *Three Poems*) and James Merrill (in such experimental lyrics as "Losing the Marbles" and "Self-Portrait in Tyvek™ Windbreaker") have proved.[7] The source of such flamboyant economies in the twentieth century has been the Ezra Pound of mock-imagism, but in excerpts such as this one Graham shows how omission, like fragments and asides, possesses its own dramatic usefulness. In this case, Graham wishes to reconstruct an earlier scene, an erotic pairing of lovers (one of them, perhaps, the poet herself, who remains, however, curiously removed from her own reminiscence), but what resonates most powerfully is her inability to retell, to reimagine, to describe with anything like fluency. Like John Ashbery and Charles Wright, Graham uses narrative (which is an element like air or water, or description) in her poetry but never tells a story in its entirety.

Instead, interruption, echoes from *Paradise Lost*, repeated phrases, hallucinated questions of and reminders to the reader amass almost musically to inhibit, frustrate, and finally to destroy all sense of both narrative and description itself. The poem ends:

> and here is the daylight now, look,
> and this a lifted hand up into it,
> and a name repeated slowly to indicate _____,
> and here the one (half-cup of?) breath being exchanged by the two
>   two bodies,
> the one breath back and forth and back and forth until they're
> dizzy
>   they're
> making themselves sick, in the white room, in the
> (as in the land of darkness yet in light) white room, so white,
> (and fansie that they feel
> divinitie within them breeding wings) how white? (wherewith to
>   scorn
> the earth)
> and freedom (click) and minutes (click) and
> (under amazement of their hideous change)
> something like what's called *being-born* (click, click
>   (75–76)

Leisurely storytelling and description have given way to the nervousness of candid snapshots. Whether such a technique can ever be judged as more than experimental or other than frustrating to either poet or audience is less important than its temporary usefulness to a woman who resists the very impulses that most strongly inspire her: the impulses to narrate and to describe. Graham wishes to achieve depiction through other means.

The goal of beauty becomes, in this transitional volume, its completion, and Graham tries to use the "end" to justify several radical means. Her perverse daring allows her to title a poem "Description" (*End of Beauty*, 11) and then to locate a natural sight within a frame constructed of both experience and myth, and to animate the whole as though it were a story narrated or filmed. The poem seems to deposit Tristan and Isolde in an industrialized, midwestern blight. And yet it begins as a sight caught from a passing train window (a frame, in other words, that always resists stasis):

> Meet me, meet me whisper the waters from the train window and
>   the small skiff adrift
> with its passenger, oarless, being pulled in by
> some destination, delicate, a blossom on the wing of
> the swollen waters.

The passenger is floating "down through the air-killed reeds, / past the refinery," and only the echo of Wagner-filtered-through-Eliot ("Waste / and the empty / the sea") tells us that the poet's mind has invested the scene with mythic possibilities by reading into a glimpsed vision some mythic adjustments.

But even this focus needs readjusting, as the poet ends by losing sight of the skiff and its passenger and also by merging Tristan and Isolde with the figures of Orpheus and Eurydice, another pair of lovers referred to throughout the volume:

> ... Westward strain the eyes,
> eastward the ship flies, the rudderless boat, the sleepy
> passenger mortally
>
> wounded. How far will he go pulled in by the listening of that far
>   shore?
> And as she approached, unable to see any body
>   within,
> she heard to her heart's delight a lovely harp,
>   a sweet voice,
> and as long as he harped and as long as he sang
>   she never stirred to
> save him.
>   (13)

The provocative breaking-up and breaking-down of story and scene has for Graham a psychological analogy: the volume contains five partial self-portraits, each of which figures the author in terms of a mythic pair: Apollo and Daphne, Adam and Eve, Demeter and Persephone, Orpheus and Eurydice, and (a variant) Penelope weaving and unweaving. Identity is fragmented, doubled, reconditioned; neither self nor story retains the satisfying fulfillments that we expect myth and description to provide.

Graham has apparently forsworn discursiveness. Even other kinds of continuities, especially syntactic and grammatical ones, have evaporated in

The End of Beauty (to be restored, partially, later on). In an interview she attempts to justify her experiments with endings and her wish to move beyond Western notions of language and eschatology: "I'd like to find a kind of language—or *action* in language (form, in other words) which would . . . be more like the painting or the stage-event than the label to it. The ritual rather than the *use* it's put to."[8] Although many poems from all of her books retain titles that seem more like labels ("Self-Portrait," for example) or explanations than events, it is also clear that Graham wishes to push language into realms analogous to those explored and then created by the action painting of Pollock and other Abstract Expressionists. Whether a poet can ever realize this dream of a field of linguistic action is doubtful: if the experience of reading such jagged, partial, often uncompleted utterances yields only a sense of action or ritual, but no sense of ending or purposefulness (even Kant's "purposefulness without purpose"), then the dream serves a need for the dreamer but not for the recipient.

Even to frame Graham's purpose in terms of dreams takes us to an area of intersection with a poet whom we would not immediately think of as a stylistic precursor: Elizabeth Bishop. Once more, the comparison with so devotedly a "descriptive" poet as Mark Doty brings out Graham's peculiar manipulation of her poetic inheritance. Where Doty actually pays homage to Bishop's marine scenes (replacing Provincetown for Nova Scotia) and to the famous seal of "At the Fishhouses," everywhere gently insinuating his allegiance to Bishop's famous observant eye and her painterly spirit, Graham attaches herself to the darker, existential side of Bishop's temperament: not to her imagery, her syntax, or her humor, but to the failures that lie on the other side of her successes.[9] Acknowledging the liminality of Bishop's poetry, its preference for border states (one thinks of "Cape Breton," "The Bight," "At the Fishhouses," "In the Waiting Room," inter alia), Graham responds to these poems' enactment of the ways "the ineffable erodes the known, and the known makes inroads into the ineffable."[10] There is no great leap from Stevens, at the intersection of the visible and the invisible, to Bishop—or Graham—at the threshold between the known, the knowable, and the unknown. *Erodes*, of course, is a Graham word, not a Bishop one. What to Bishop were ideologically innocent acts of description becomes for her successor something else: "Description is an attempt to go out into it and come back changed. . . . [Not in description itself] but in the cracks of it, the thing emerges. You have to undertake an act which you know is essentially futile, in the direct sense: the words are not going to seize the thing. But leaks in between the attempts at seizure is the thing, and you have to be willing to suffer the limits of description in order to get it."[11] Graham suggests that all meaning is accidental and beside the point, a thing uncovered during the adventure.

Graham makes reading difficult deliberately, in part for political reasons. We have been inured, she says, to the possible distortions and lies of language through politics and advertising. She is as skeptical of labels and "uses" as she is of terminations. Paradoxically, this postmodern skeptic, who distrusts Western notions of closure, and eschatology in general, sounds like an echo, at century's end, of T. S. Eliot at its start: she aims for "the dissociated sensibility restored to wholeness by the act of reading. . . . [I] had to go back to the line, had to contend with all the implications of the line, not just the sentence."[12] But Graham extends an even older tradition than that of Eliotic high modernism and its nostalgias for a premodern temper of wholeness of culture and personality. As with the great English gardens of the eighteenth century, modeled after the paintings of Poussin and Claude, themselves based on the pastoral imagery of Theocritus and Virgil, in much of Graham's poetry the look of landscape often seems filtered through, or *as*, the look of painting. Where the field of action and observation is strenuously, though often opaquely, depicted, we cannot be sure whether we occupy a reading space intended to put us in mind of or within the frame of a painting or an external scene. Graham manages to internalize all of her spaces even while seeming to respond to something outside of herself.

For Graham, "reality" itself is liminal: the real exists *between* or *among*, never *within*. Thus her series of self-portraits as X and Y. And thus, also, her sympathy with Eurydice ("Orpheus and Eurydice," *The End of Beauty*, 18):

—what she dreamed

was of disappearing into the seen

not of disappearing, lord, into the real—

Because, as Helen Vendler has observed, the present is the time of lyric, everything in Graham seems to rush into a continuous present even in those moments when she adheres to a narrative impulse to recount past events.[13] Nothing can be caught entire; nothing can be seen, understood, or transcribed entire. The impulse to describe and to narrate gives way, breaks down, and surrenders to greater forces, because time moves more swiftly than one's ability to capture or even register it. "Here it is, *here*, the end of beauty, the present" ("The Lovers," 64): the origin of the title phrase of this volume presents ending and culmination as always in medias res, unreachable, unstoppable.

Nevertheless, Graham contains within herself both a closet painter and a closet metaphysician. She wishes to capture a scene, especially to register the connections, however tentative, between the visible and the invisible (which we may read as the "spiritual"). When Persephone emerges from the underworld (in "Self-Portrait as Demeter and Persephone," *The End of Beauty*, 62):

> The first thing she saw when she surfaced was the wind
> wrapping like a body round the stiff stripped trees
> that would bend more deeply into that love if they could
> to accompany its eagerness young wind its rage
> if they weren't so perfect if they weren't so shorn.

Such Romantic wistfulness seems like an updating of both Shelley ("Hymn to Intellectual Beauty") and Keats ("In Drear-Nighted December"). What Shelley calls "the awful shadow of some unseen Power" emerges as Persephone, fresh from the embrace of Pluto, imaginatively populates the natural world by seeing the unseen as an erotic force, enwrapping and inspiring the trees that want to respond, but that in their early spring leaflessness cannot open themselves to the wind's caresses. Like Keats, Graham looks on vacancy and performs an imaginative act of reparation, in this case, an anticipation of later fruitfulness when the wind, though still not literally visible, will fulfill—and be fulfilled by—the responsive, clothed trees.

The poem registers an act of reparation, of discovering and then filling emptiness. "Pollock and Canvas" (*The End of Beauty*, 86–87), a medley of speculations, reflections, and quotations from the painter, quotations from God to Moses, an envoi from a Renaissance lyric, epitomizes Graham's wrestling with the problem of description, of technique in general, in painting and, by extension, in poetry. The theme is fullness and emptiness, completion and separation; the technique is simultaneously aggregative and disjunctive. Unlike William Blake, who adoringly welcomed the binding line that gives form and shape, whether in drawing or in epigram, Graham can neither accept nor fully evade the confinements of ending. The third part of the poem begins:

> Where does the end
>   begin?
> where does the lifting off of hands become
>   love,
> letting the made wade out into danger,
>   letting the form slur out into flaw, in-
>
> conclusiveness? Where does the end of love
> begin? (Where does *that* love begin?)

And then He rested, is that where the real
making
   begins—the now—Then He rested letting in chance letting in
any wind any shadow quick with minutes, and whimsy,
   through the light, letting the snake the turning
in.

The question exists on the artistic, the erotic, and the religious planes. For
Graham, all creation (God's, Pollock's, her own) starts with the promise of satisfaction but invariably ends with the admission of the serpent into the garden.
Form slurs into flaw; inconclusiveness is itself broken between lines, spilling
over linguistic borders. Graham fears both beginnings and endings. "Form's
what affirms," says the self-parodying James Merrill in his "The Thousand
and Second Night,"[14] but for Graham form oozes, melts, blends, drips, in the
way Pollock's paintbrush never touches "at any point, / the still ground" (81).
Graham's quicksilver forms affirm the shadowy boundaries between speech
and writing, self and other, narrative and lyric, center and periphery, finitude
and expansiveness. The arena of her poems exists, like that of Pollock's drip
paintings, in the great gap "between." Frames exist to be broken.

When Ashbery announces, in "Self-Portrait in a Convex Mirror," that
"Today has no margins, the event arrives / Flush with its edges, is of the
same substance, / Indistinguishable," he embodies the charming—sometimes
goofy, sometimes exasperating—random continuum of his own work and its
renderings of time's fluidness.[15] If time is his central element, space is Graham's: her painterly obsession inclines her to an experience of the world that
both visualizes (attempts to see) and surveys (attempts to map) it through
lineation. In the same way that Charles Wright's extended and broken lines
reproduce the canvasses of Cézanne, Graham's even more jagged syntax and
lineation approximate the thoroughly nonrepresentational effects of Pollock
and other Abstract Expressionists.

Her readers have always sensed that Graham's turn toward open forms,
longer lines, less "organically" composed and ended poems has liberated her
from the more artful closure of the lyrics in her first two volumes. What
interests me, on the other hand, is the constancy of her ideas rather than the
changes in her techniques. As Elaine Scarry has written, with reference to a
letter from Coleridge to William Godwin in 1800, "The end of the century
is a period in which the performative and the descriptive often become for
a time indistinguishable."[16] In her ongoing performances, Graham has been
unable to avoid description.

Even in *Hybrids* the problem could not be solved. And it was—as it
remains—intimately allied with the nature and notion of framing. As counter

to the frame, that which binds, surrounds, limits, and defines, Graham has always posed what we may call the "blur," which is not just something that smashes a frame but, instead, any principle of occluding, oozing, or dimming crispness of perception. She evidently takes seriously Stevens's aphorism that the poem must make the visible a little hard to see. Forms and color, like perception itself, melt. Voice interrupts; parentheses interrupt.[17]

Graham does not see: if she did, she would have clear direct objects of vision. Instead, she must look *at, toward,* above all, *through.* "To look" is never a transitive verb, no matter how much one wants it to be. The prepositions make a frame. Graham began her career as a poet who wanted to look through, at, and toward, and occasionally she used her looking as the means of reaching an ending, of coming upon moral certitude. In "I watched a snake" (*Erosion,* 34–35), she performs a maneuver so characteristic of another *kind* of poet that its unusualness in her oeuvre stands out. Here is a poem thoroughly within the Romantic or neo-Romantic tradition, in which observation leads to emblem making. The snake, threading its way through the grass behind the house, visible then invisible, becomes a conventional simile:

> This must be a perfect progress where
> 　　movement appears
> to be a vanishing, a mending
> 　　of the visible
>
> by the invisible—just as we
> 　　stitch the earth,
> it seems to me, each time
> 　　we die, going
> back under, coming back up. . . .
> 　　It is the simplest
>
> stitch, this going where we must,
> 　　leaving a not
> unpretty pattern by default.

The human analogy allows her to end on a note of triumph, with the kind of generalization that her later work eschews, along with conclusion:

> . . . Passion is work
> 　　that retrieves us,
> lost stitches. It makes a pattern of us,
> 　　it fastens us

to sturdier stuff
  no doubt.
  (35)

Everything about this poem is easy: the Romantic move from observation to application to moralizing; the clarity of simile; the offhand diction ("it seems to me," "a not / unpretty pattern," "no doubt"); the effort to allow description to convey human passion by sequestering the observer much as the snake sequesters itself in its work to capture a "blue- / black dragonfly"; the epigrammatic nugget ("Desire // is the honest work of the body, / its engine, its wind") that would sit more comfortably in the finished work of Nemerov or Richard Wilbur than in Graham's later, more explosive confrontations with nature, with description, and with herself.

Looking at something, especially within a frame or from the protective backing of a frame (a speaker gazing outside *through* a window), is a standard procedure in Graham's poetry and is often complemented by an insistence on "being looked at" or being seen. Always, as she announces at the start of "Framing" (*Hybrids*, 35), "Something is left out, something left behind." Only by framing does history occur. Looking at an old photo of herself, seeing herself through the frame of a portrait and a temporal one as well, Graham also enjoys looking out, where she cannot be seen, as in "Self-Portrait" (46), a love poem in the same volume:

> After fresh snow I'll go up to the attic and look out.
> My looking is a set of tracks—the first—
> a description of the view
> that cannot mar it.

New snow occasions metaphoric action—writing—an assault on the landscape. She inscribes her traces on the snow without (or so she thinks) physically altering the scene but affecting it anyway. The provocation of the snow distinguishes Graham from Ashbery, who is always more passive a persona and a respondent in his poetry. In "Self-Portrait in a Convex Mirror," for example, there are the beautiful, unexpected lines about snow following upon the discovery that whereas we think we have "surprised" the painter, or the work of art, in actuality it's the other way around ("he has surprised us / As he works"):

> . . . The picture is almost finished,
> The surprise almost over, as when one looks out,
> Startled by a snowfall which even now is

> Ending in specks and sparkles of snow.
> It happened while you were inside, asleep,
> And there is no reason why you should have
> Been awake for it, except that the day
> Is ending and it will be hard for you
> To get to sleep tonight, at least until late.[18]

Unlike Graham, Ashbery feels no need to make actual or metaphorical tracks in the snow, which has come unannounced, silent and secret, interrupting our sleep patterns but proffering warmth and minor comfort. Ashbery is a poet of reverie; Graham, a poet of engagement.

As she announces in "Still Life" (*Hybrids*, 51), looking out from a window at a wintry scene beyond:

> For at the windowpane
> we are the heroes
> leaving home to journey out over the visible, that trusty fabric,
> and are the heroines
>
> staying behind.

For Graham, whose Rilkesque pronouncement "the patience of the visible / is the invisible" ("The Slow Sounding and Eventual Reemergence Of," *Hybrids*, 58) exposes both her spiritual longings and her impatience with waiting, the poet seems a still, free spirit attached to the world but never quite at home in it. The final poem in *Hybrids*, summarizing her various obsessions throughout this book (and the later ones), shows us the shifting panorama composed of external nature, internal reality, and the invisible spiritual world to which both aspire through a painted or depicted world. An elaborate image emerges linking birds, their feathers, pens, writing, protection against and aspiration to the invisible, in a form that echoes nursery rhyme as well as scripture. Although not nominally a "descriptive" poem, opening with a categorical equation ("The bird is an alphabet"), "A Feather for Voltaire" (66–67) presumes looking and describing as the basis for the connections and turnings it makes. Graham concludes her first book with a statement of heroic, almost theological purposefulness:

> A feather,
> pulled from the body or found on the snow

can be dipped into ink
to make one or more words: *possessive, the sun.* A pen
can get drunk,
having come so far, having so far to go—*meadow,*
in vain, imagine
the pain

and when he was gone then there was none

and this is the key to the kingdom.

Writing may well be both the best revenge and also the only access we have
to the invisible. Emptiness, as in a wintry landscape, or a feather left by a
now departed bird, or a solitary woman, invites or demands filling, first by a
looking, then by an assault on the invisible through writing. These assaults,
though nominally changed in their form, provide the basis for Graham's
subsequent books.

I have already termed "being looked at" the obverse of looking. At its
most inviting, such an impulse from the natural world inspires our assaults
upon it, as in Graham's offhand remark: "the day tries harder to be *really /
seen*" ("Event Horizon," *Materialism*, 51). But as it does, it also can quietly
menace us as a kind of payment for our own emotional disequilibrium. In the
remarkable, sonnet-like "Act III, Sc. 2" (*Region of Unlikeness*, 66), a climactic
dramatic moment between two people is figured in terms of their surround.
"Look she said this is not the distance / we wanted to stay at": her request for
intimacy is unheeded, met with silence, "*waiting*," and even her casual "Look"
at the start of line 1 turns out to anticipate the intensity of looking, and being
looked at, that stills the couple literally at the midpoint of the action (e.g., III,
2), which is also the poem's end:

> Then the you, whoever you are, peering down to see
>   if it's done yet.
> Then just the look on things of being looked-at.
> Then just the look on things of being seen.

That things being looked at have their own "look" means either that an animism underlies the world, or (at least as likely a possibility) that Graham's
speaker (here and elsewhere) displays the kind of paranoia that would inspire
her to look and suspect that the external world knows it is being looked at.
Dickinson's field of gazing grain and Stevens's "the way things look each

day" are her transcendental forbears. It is significant that the poem that succeeds this one is entitled "Immobilism" (*Region*, 67) and begins with an act of vigorous looking that is stopped in its tracks:

> The eye in its socket sweeps over the withered field.
> It slides over the still place.
> Stays.

The "fast" eye, neither "translator" nor "intruder," according to Graham's denials, although a "prisoner," works hard to survey the wintry landscape, running, leaping, counting, and astounding nature. That which "cannot look back" at one moment becomes animated the very next when the clicking-camera-eye surveys the landscape it "owns": "The two white metal chairs look at each other" (69). Such diction must do more than mean simply that the two chairs face one another (as if even "facing" ever obliterates the animation implicit in the things of this world); instead, it gives us, as do the nervous pace, lineation, and syntax of this rendition of surveillance, the potential sense of our being looked at in return by those things we are observing. Graham chose as epigraph to this section of *Region of Unlikeness* an appropriate aphorism of Nietzsche; "It is a sad, hard but determined gaze—an eye that looks out" (63).

The work of looking, of trying to connect the world to God's shadow, admits of no conclusion. Like Graham's unhedged boundaries and broken frames, the poem is open-ended because the quest for sight is like the quest for salvation, and the poet is as skeptical of aesthetic finalities as she is of religious certitudes. The poem ends as it had begun. The eye (never absolutely identifiable as the antecedent of "it") skirts nervously into oblivion beyond the frame:

> It darts, it stretches out along the dry hard ground,
> it cannot find the end, it darts, it stretches out—
>   (70)

Although "Immobilism" is relatively open-ended, it repeats with variations a theme and technique that Graham had used to good advantage in *Erosion*, her "art" book, filled with homages to painters and the processes of visualization. In "Scirocco" (*Erosion*, 8–9), she takes what might be the occasion for an ordinary touristic poem and converts it into a religious exploration of the way what we look at looks back at us. The title wind blows over Keats's apartment in the Piazza di Spagna, but it evades description itself, working itself through us:

... Who is
   the nervous spirit
of this world
   that must go over and over
what it already knows,
   what is it

so hot and dry
   that's looking through us,
by us,
   for its answer?

This personified wind, "working the invisible" (i.e., both for it and through it), fingers the dry leaves around the plaza, touching even the grapes that have begun to grow on the terrace arbor. Soon, these will soften and "enter"

our world, translating
   helplessly
from the beautiful
   to the true. . . .
Whatever the spirit,
   the thickening grapes

are part of its looking.
   (9)

Looking at us, the world wants us to receive it, mend it, and calm it. Seldom does Graham pay such explicit homage to a traditional trope, even when converting the wind-as-spirit into a dry desert plague, and in her later poetry she will turn away from such neat conclusions as she creates here, but even early on our transactions with the world—our looking at it—are met by its looking at and through us. On the lookout ourselves, we are always observed.

"Is there a new way of looking?" Graham asks ("Notes on the Reality of the Self," *Materialism*, 3), placing the question significantly at the start of her most literary book. But this is the essential question she has asked implicitly all along. The poem begins with a descriptive phrase ("Watching the river, each handful of it closing over the next, / brown and swollen") whose very personification brings nature into close companionship with its onlooker. But right after the query Graham reverts to the language or at least the imagery of

Hybrids: "Is there a new way of looking / valences and little hooks—inevitabilities, proba- / bilities?" Everywhere she wants mechanical as well as organic connections or the promise of them. When she quotes a phrase from Jeffrey Hamilton on George Oppen in "Steering Wheel," we know she is borrowing in order to affirm one of her central tenets: "we have to regain the moral pleasure / of experiencing the distance between subject and object" (5). Everywhere Graham wants to engage with the physical world, the world of her perception, but at the same time she wants to experience the moral pleasure of keeping it at arm's length.

Framing allows her to relish both sides of her temperament, the sensuous and the puritanical. When she observes "the day unfolding its stern materialism" ("In the Hotel," *Materialism*, 7) it is her own sternness that is at issue. She can neither fully evade nor fully enjoy the sensuous world. Hence, in "Steering Wheel" (*Materialism*, 5–6) we have a unique twist on her own tropes of framing, revising as well the parable of Plato's Cave: she watches the world in reverse, as she looks into her car's rearview mirror as she backs out of the driveway. The frame of the mirror exists only to frustrate, not to contain, as what is witnessed is swirling leaves, suctioned into an updraft along with someone's hat from down the block. The poet moves out of the driveway watching a framed or reflected scene, which, far from stationing or capturing the things of this world, obeys its own laws of movement as well as gravity:

> —me now slowly backing up
> the dusty driveway into the law
> composed of updraft, downdraft, weight of these dried
>   mid-winter leaves,
> light figured-in too, I'm sure, the weight of light,
> and angle of vision, dust, gravity, solitude,
> and the part of the law which is the world's waiting,
> and the part of the law which is my waiting,
> and then the part which is my impatience—now; *now?*—
>
> though there are, there really are,
> things in the world, you must believe me.

This is a kind of desperate, daring updating of the trope of the fallen leaves that is scattered from Homer to Howard Nemerov.[19] It also demonstrates Graham's unwillingness ever fully to let go of the things of this world, trapped as she seems to be in a paradoxical Limbo always in motion.

In 1987, Graham observed in an interview, "In my physical experience of reality, I feel the presence of another world, whether we think of it as *the world in the instant before we perceive it,* or *the dead,* or *the invisible.* There are different terms for it: where the angels are. I feel most alive in the particular enterprise which involves sensing the translation of the invisible world into the visible."[20] Thomas Gardner quotes this quasi-religious, quasi-Stevensian claim, which looks forward to Graham's use of angels in *The Errancy* (1997); he then remarks, especially of the poems in *The End of Beauty,* that they try to locate themselves "actively in what Graham calls the 'slippage' of language which renders unstable the delicate, wisteria-scented surfaces we call beauty."[21] This instability has proved a leitmotif throughout her career. When she says (in the long poem "Manifest Destiny," *Materialism,* 97) that "What's ical slides through," she means both that it appears and disappears from sight. Framing is an inevitable tool for any shaper, especially one with an eye for art; it also offers the chance to test the waters, to hold nectar in a sieve, to capture or name the ephemeral, the invisible, the unnameable. It is for this reason (among others) that Graham chooses to begin some poems inductively, with observation, and others deductively, working from abstraction to individuation. "Young Maples in Wind" (*Materialism,* 136), quoted above, begins as a "descriptive poem," nervous fragments, quicksilver detail:

> Green netting set forth;
> spectrum of greens a bird arcs through; low and
>   perfect
> postponement.
> The wind moves the new leaves aside—as if there were
>   an inventory
> taken—till they each wink the bit of light
> they're raised into.

Such attention to the visible shows that the Wordsworthian eye still lives in the contemporary scene. Alternatively, we have the beginning of the adjacent poem, "Opulence," whose title is exemplified by the plant that is semi-described throughout. "The self-brewing of the amaryllis rising before me" (134): here the fragment initiates less observation of the trumpet-plant than an occasion for self-reflexiveness and a meditation *on* self-reflexiveness.

This looking—at the world and at the self—has dangerous consequences, which Graham often wants to avoid. In "The Surface" (*Materialism,* 143), she begins with simple observation in an equally simple grammar: "It has a hole in it." "It" is a river surface, but not until the poem's penultimate line do we get a complete sentence rather than a fragment. Instead, Graham articulates a world of breakage, a river "ribbonning, twisting up" and an internal river "of my attention laying itself down" upon the river, which becomes at last an

article of permanence and a constant flux, with its "slowed-down drifting performances / of the cold / bed." At the end, "I say *iridescent* and I look down. /
The leaves very still as they are carried" (143). The severe focus on the leaves
amounts to little, because they continue to evade her mental or physical grasp.
Permanence is possible only in the finality of death and in the grammatical
presence of the final (verbless) phrase. The poet's pronouncement: Do we take
it as command, observation, or wish? This she will not say, but the final line
exemplifies the cost exacted of such a vision. The shining the poet observes
glints from the dead leaves, which are borne away. Nothing stays. Framing
fails in the same way that verbs fail: the containments of language cannot do
justice to the temporal processes of observation.

Although *Materialism* and *Region of Unlikeness* were identified as breaking with many of Graham's earlier patterns of composition and her themes,
in fact the same tenacious holding onto and somewhat reluctant letting go of
the world, a looking at and a looking away from it, inform even the poems in
Erosion, which is nominally her "art" book. Such breaking away—breaking of
a frame, erosion, and blurring—explains why "San Sepolcro" (2–3) stands first
in the volume. Piero's Madonna del Parto, that exquisite painting depicting the
pregnant Virgin, housed until recently at a little temple in Monterchi, perfectly
centers the poet's interest in process of many sorts. The poem locates the painting within the poet's life (its first half describes her house and landscape) before
effecting a transition that cuts between stanzas, levels of diction, and theme:

> There's milk on the air,
>   ice on the oily
> lemonskins. How clean
>   the mind is,
>
> holy grave. It is this girl
>   by Piero
> della Francesca, unbuttoning
>   her blue dress,
> her mantle of weather,
>   to go into
>
> labor. Come, we can go in.
>   It is before
> the birth of god. No-one
>   has risen yet
> to the museums, to the assembly
>   line—bodies

and wings—to the open air
   market. This is
what the living do: go in.
   It's a long way.
And the dress keeps opening
   from eternity

to privacy, quickening.

The mind, that holy grave, a repository of images and thoughts alive as well as dead, contains or recollects all it has seen and witnessed. It becomes the living maid about to go into labor, recalled by the poet as an invitation to the person she is addressing. The Virgin is about to give birth; Christ is about to come out of his mother's body, just as the tourists are about to enter the small chapel. The living are always going in, somewhere, somehow, to a chapel like an eternal grave that is also an eternal womb. As the "dress keeps opening," so does the moment of Mary's lamentation. The poem ends:

   Inside, at the heart,
is tragedy, the present moment
   forever stillborn,
but going in, each breath
   is a button
coming undone, something terribly
   nimble-fingered
finding all of the stops.
   (3)

A viewer of the painting realizes that birth is a moment and part of a process; we bear witness to its just-about-to-happen, its already-having-begun, its always-already-having-happened. Although I earlier referred to Graham as a poet of space rather than of time, clearly in these early poems she tries to explore and to blur the boundaries within and between these two primary categories.[22]

Boundary becomes the great subject of this volume. The catastrophic floods of 1966 that ruined the art treasures of Florence gave the teenage Graham a firsthand look at overflowing and erosion of several sorts (she participated in the relief efforts) and also offered her a retrospective understanding of how the self "is an act of / rescue / where the flesh has risen, / the spirit / loosened" ("In What Manner the Body Is United with the Soul," 14). From the start Graham looked carefully at the world, and at art, but noticed the

ways things fell apart, melted, or abraded through the visible. Her attraction
to the liminality of Elizabeth Bishop appears early, in a poem called "Wanting a Child," whose setting is a tidal estuary, "the living echo . . . of some great
storm far out at sea, too far / to be recalled by us / but transferred / whole
onto this shore by waves, so that erosion / is its very face" (29). Crossing the
bar laterally, as she does here, or vertically, as she does in "The Age of Reason"
(*Erosion*, 19–20), Graham can never get enough of exploring:

> How far is true
>   enough?
> How far into the
>   earth
> can vision go and
>   still be
>
> love?
> . . . . .
>   There is
> no deep
>
> enough. For what we want
>   to take
> inside of us, whole orchard,
>   color,
> name, scent, symbol, raw
>   pale
>
> blossoms, wet black
>   arms there is
> no deep enough.

Graham here alludes to but then goes beyond the delicate imagist petals on
a wet black bough that Pound made famous as a meager dose of "the thing
itself." Her greed for possession forces her to look and to gather; her sense of
the inadequacy of all efforts at capture or recollection inhibits and frustrates.
In a poem called "Tragedy," in which the poet from her window watches her
neighbor across the yard in *her* window frame, she observes: "Then she and
I, / each at our gap, / sustain the visible" (28).

Sustaining the visible means, in part, being sustained by it (just as looking, as I have suggested, often complements being looked at), but it also means
that visible objects are "beautiful interruptions" of consciousness, jagged lines of

light coming into one's sight ("Still Life with Window and Fish," 32). While Graham often positions herself inside looking out, or about to enter an interior space like the chapel at Monterchi, the outside world often seems to want to come inside and to penetrate the inner space of a domestic scene or the poet's own consciousness. She loves "it in here where it blurs, and nothing starts or / ends, but all is / waving, and colorless, / and voiceless" (32). Likewise, in "For John Keats" on the occasion of visiting his grave in the Protestant Cemetery in Rome, Graham repeats her preference: "We live up here // by blurring boundaries, calling it *love, the present moment,* or / *the beautiful*" (50–51).

Graham may share with both Bishop and Stevens a double allegiance to landscapes: raised in Italy and trained to love the richness of its countryside and its art, she responds as a connoisseur of lushness to its warmth and color. ("We are too restless / to inherit / this earth," she announced in "Still Life with Window and Fish" [33]). That is her "south," her Key West. Her "north," the Iowa landscape she inhabited for more than a decade until she moved to Cambridge in the later 1990s, offers a cleaner, barer image of reality. Like that native Iowan Amy Clampitt, Graham respects the empty spaces of the prairie. The title poem of this volume praises dissolution—things falling apart or down—rather than growth. In "For John Keats" she could not find the dividing lines between the plots in the cemetery: "we break every / enframement, being / entirely // transitive" (50). Erosion is a version of more sudden breakings: a slow dissolution or blurring rather than a rapid one. The title poem prepares us for the "The Sense of an Ending," not only an appropriate conclusion to *this* volume but also a preparation for *The End of Beauty* in its themes and methods.

"The Sense of an Ending" has (mostly) an American setting and opens, like many of Graham's poems, with an entire section of phrasal, almost verbless units, describing and setting a scene in northern California. She tests the limits of the visible; it always disappoints her. Neither does it grant access to things themselves, nor does it deliver access to the realm of the invisible. The poem contains what will become Graham's signature methods: an anecdote or two, a fugal intertwining of various elements, a reminiscence (a memory of going to a Roman eye clinic to correct blurred vision), meditation on an abstraction. The leitmotif is enclosure, whether of a plant, a walled garden, or a caged wolf, and how the promises of enclosure are undone: "Because the body must open / for its world // so that we know there is a wall / beyond which we can't go" (*Erosion*, 79). As with paradise, a walled garden, so with the caged wolf: there is a thin line between containment and imprisonment.

Graham's style features fragments and ellipses as indexes of boundaries and the slippages between them. Thus, the title essentially gives onto the opening line and demands that we fill in an essential element, as: "The sense of an ending . . . [is best heard] . . . There in the sound of a chainsaw winding down" (78). The last section begins in the same way: "Or [you might find the sense of an ending] where the draft is from an unseen / gap" (82). The conclusion, redolent of Platonic/Virgilian myths of birth and rebirth, suggests that unborn human souls are greedy "to be born," that even the smallest amount of time here is "better than any / freedom, any wholeness" (83). Nothing, in other words, surpasses the demand for life, which necessarily means definition, enclosure, surrounding, and termination. The poem itself concludes with a revelation. It is almost as if the poet is surprised that she could come down so assertively on the side of lived life. The sense of an ending ensures the sense of a beginning. Rather than freedom and expansive wholeness, the poet comes to prefer

> . . . this heaviness, this stilled
>
> quickness, this skin, this line
> all the way round and sealed into the jagged island
>
> form, the delicate
> ending, better, even for an instant, even if never brought
>
> further than term
> into this broken mewing, this dust of lilacs, cawing
>
> ravens, door just slamming, someone
> suddenly home in this lie we call blue light.
>   (83)

What M. H. Abrams long ago defined as the Romantic nature lyric, a poem meandering from a specific beginning in time and place, through meditation and recollection back to its origin as its terminus, here gives shape to Graham's own poem, winding at its close to the details with which it began.[23] To end a discussion of Graham with this poem is unfair, of course: seldom afterward does termination come as easily to her. Her own jitteriness, her wariness when it comes to determining limits, gets the better of her, as I have shown. But the new way of looking forces itself continually on and through this poet, whose subject matter—the relation of body to soul, the visible to the invisible—ought to place her among the poets of sexual and religious bliss instead of those whose skepticism undercuts happiness, poetic closure, and even the satisfactions of "just looking" (as Charles Tomlinson put it) and rendering what one has seen. Because "what's *real* slides through"

("Manifest Destiny," *Materialism*, 97), any sense of an ending is tentative, hopeful, and delusory at best.

NOTES

1. Wallace Stevens, *Opus Posthumous*, rev. and ed. Milton Bates (New York: Knopf, 1989), 193, 196.

2. Ernest Hartley Coleridge, ed., *The Letters of Samuel Taylor Coleridge* (Boston: Houghton Mifflin, 1895), 2: 558–559.

3. Jorie Graham, "Young Maples in Wind," in *Materialism* (New York: Ecco Press, 1993), 137. All references to Graham's work are cited in the text. The other volumes included in this discussion are *Hybrids of Plants and of Ghosts* (Princeton: Princeton University Press, 1980), *Erosion* (Princeton: Princeton University Press, 1983), *The End of Beauty* (New York: Ecco Press, 1987), and *Region of Unlikeness* (New York: Ecco Press, 1991). Graham's books of the past decade, which I do not discuss in this chapter, are *The Errancy* (New York: Ecco Press, 1997), *Swarm* (New York: Ecco Press, 2000), and *Never* (New York: Ecco Press, 2003).

4. Howard Nemerov, "Writing" and "The Blue Swallows," in *The Collected Poems of Howard Nemerov* (Chicago: University of Chicago Press, 1977), 203, 397.

5. In a forthcoming essay, "Jorie Graham Listening," I discuss the changes in Graham's ongoing engagements with birds, their flight, and their songs. See Thomas Gardner, ed., *New Essays on Jorie Graham* (Madison: University of Wisconsin Press, 2005).

6. Mark Doty, *Atlantis* (New York: HarperPerennial, 1995), 5, 90.

7. See Thomas J. Otten, "Jorie Graham's _____s," *PMLA* 118 (2003): 239–253, for the fullest discussion of Graham's lacunae, which Otten calls "a material idiom of mediation, a repertoire of images and substances that shape and reflect back to us our understanding of social bonds, and affective ties, of what is between us" (250).

8. Thomas Gardner, *Regions of Unlikeness: Explaining Contemporary Poetry* (Lincoln: University of Nebraska Press, 1999), 216–217. Gardner includes both an interview with Graham (214–237) and a critical essay about her ("Jorie Graham's Incandescence," 168–213).

9. In "Repetition and Singularity," *Kenyon Review* 25, no. 2 (2003): 149–168, I discuss Graham's debt to Bishop in her latest volume, *Never*.

10. Gardner, *Regions of Unlikeness*, 230.

11 Ibid.

12. Ibid., 233, 235.

13. From almost the start, Graham has found a champion in Helen Vendler. See Vendler's *Soul Says: On Recent Poetry* (Cambridge, Mass.: Belknap Press of Harvard University Press, 1995), 212–256; *The Breaking of Style: Hopkins, Heaney, Graham* (Cambridge, Mass.: Harvard University Press, 1995), 71–95; and *The Given and the Made: Strategies of Poetic Redefinition* (Cambridge, Mass.: Harvard University Press, 1995), 84–130.

14. James Merrill, *Collected Poems* (New York: Knopf, 2001), 185.

15. John Ashbery, *Selected Poems* (New York: Viking, 1985), 200.

16. Elaine Scarry, "Counting at Dusk (Why Poetry Matters When the Century Ends)," in Elaine Scarry, ed., *Fins de Siècle: English Poetry in 1590, 1690, 1790, 1890, 1990* (Baltimore: Johns Hopkins University Press, 1995), 25.

17. See Adrienne Rich's 1966 poem, "Necessities of Life," in *Collected Early Poems* (New York: Norton, 1993), 205, for another example of the relation between oozing or melting in painting and fluctuations in personal identity; for Rich, all boundaries are—or were at that point in her work—permeable. I have already discussed interruption as a structural, formal, and thematic device in the work of James Merrill. See "Breaking the Mirror: Interruption in the Trilogy," in David Lehman and Charles Berger, eds., *James Merrill: Essays in Criticism* (Ithaca: Cornell University Press, 1982), 186–210. What D. H. Lawrence long ago referred to as the breakdown of the old stable ego has produced some of the most interesting poetic experiments of the past four decades.

18. Ashbery, 195.

19. See Nemerov, "For Robert Frost, in the Autumn, in Vermont," 405, on the trope of the fallen leaves.

20. Thomas Gardner, "Accurate Failures: The Work of Jorie Graham," *The Hollins Critic* 24, no. 4 (October 1987): 2.

21. Ibid., 6.

22. See Bonnie Costello, "Jorie Graham: Art and *Erosion*," *Contemporary Literature* 33 (1992): 373–395, for a discussion of the way the poems in *Erosion* enact a modernist concern with aesthetic wholeness.

23. M. H. Abrams, "Structure and Style in the Greater Romantic Lyric," in Frederick W. Hilles and Harold Bloom, eds., *From Sensibility to Romanticism* (New York: Oxford University Press, 1965), 527–560.

LANGDON HAMMER

Hall of Voices: Richard Howard

In a 1973 essay on Emily Dickinson, given pride of place as the first piece in *Paper Trail*, Richard Howard meditates on the impulse to normalize Dickinson's eccentricities of presentation and sensibility. Mischievously, he proposes that we see those eccentricities as analogous to "perversions." "It was Freud," he writes, "who first taught us that a perversion is the opposite of a neurosis, that homosexuality, for instance, is not a problem but the solution to a problem." He goes on to explain what this might mean for a reader: "The one generalization I should care to hazard as to how we should respond to literature is that when we are troubled—bored, provoked, offended—by characteristic features of a writer's work, it is precisely those features which, if we yield to them, if we treat them as significance rather than as defect, will turn out to be that writer's solution to his own problems of composition and utterance." This principle, Howard adds, he derived from Jean Cocteau, who two decades earlier had advised him as follows: "Ce que les autres vous reprochent, cultivez cela: c'est vous-même (What other people reproach you for, cultivate: it is yourself)." Besides being a strategy for making one's way in a French salon, this was also, Howard saw, a plan for writing poetry, and he used it to become what he praised Dickinson, in her very different way, for being: a reproachable writer.

From *Parnassus: Poetry in Review* 29, nos. 1/2 (2005): 97–117. © 2005 by *Parnassus: Poetry in Review*.

Reproachable? As *The Silent Treatment*, the title of his newest book of poems, playfully suggests, Howard is alive to the potential for insult, umbrage, and counter-attack in our dealings with each other. In particular he is attuned to the ways that people express or defend themselves against the hatred of Jews and gays, and to the isolating sacrifices required of the artist. He often reminds us that to make art is to risk giving offense, no less than other kinds of human singularity or difference do. The reproachable singularity he himself has cultivated is that of an immensely cultivated man. An obsessive reader, a lover of modern art, and a tireless expert in almost every other form of culture as well, Howard expects the reader to keep up with him; while he may explain and even tutor, he never provides notes to guide us through his work. In one poem he has Proust say, with some pique, "I don't see why / people can't look things up, I always do" ("Love Which Alters"). His poetry continually invites us to "look things up."

Howard's style, instantly recognizable, is learned, recursive, hypotactic, wise-cracking, arch. It is tempting to call it a camp style, and to explain it as a reflex of his homosexuality, that "problem" which Freud taught him to view as a "solution." But this would be to miss what is most daring and distinctive about it. That is, his homosexuality is less likely to scandalize the reader today than what he calls his "verbality." So while it matters that he is gay, it also matters that he worked as a lexicographer in the Fifties, and that he is a prolific and important translator of French literature and literary theory. The perversity of his poetry is the perversity of a style made out of the dictionary, the museum, and the library.

Howard doesn't write manifestoes or position-pieces—or perhaps he is always writing them, but only in the guise of lavishly sympathetic appreciations of other writers and artists. He has introduced, as *Paper Trail* reminds us, the work of many poets, including Frank Bidart, Norman Dubie, and J. D. McClatchy, and he has written on Rodin, Twombley, Mapplethorpe, and Brassaï, among visual artists. Yet the book also includes one defense of Howard's work, "Sharing Secrets," an essay written nineteen years after "A Consideration of the Writings of Emily Dickinson." Here an older Howard, now the senior poet, narrates an encounter with a quasi-allegorical figure, a "young woman at Bard College," who tells him: "I don't like your poems . . . ! don't like them because there's too much history in them." Aware that he is being accused of sexism, among other things, Howard tries to acknowledge some of her objections: "My critic was, if I may say so, kicking against the pricks. For surely my poetry as she heard it was all clanking and clattering, scratchy and thorny with the intimation, the positive insistence, of facts, features, names of occasions and even—history indeed!—with dates, the very data of circumstance. And was such a thing, ontologically ripped from the gossip column, the chronicle, the matrix of our records of each other which the French so wisely call commérage—was such a thing poetry?" Howard argues that his work is poetry, of course, but not before his young critic has told him: "Fuck off."

This conversation at Bard, whether real or only semi-real, points to our current distance from the intellectual world in which Howard came of age. That would be the world of Columbia College in the late Forties and early Fifties, where he was a student of, among others, Lionel Trilling and Mark Van Doren (whose poetry is the topic of an essay in *Paper Trail*) and a friend of Allen Ginsberg, Anthony Hecht, and John Hollander. Postwar New York had succeeded Europe's ruined capitals as the bearer of Western culture. The enormous value of that culture, of artworks, archives, and the lives recorded in them, was freshly affirmed in the light cast by the terror and destruction of the war. There was for Howard and others of his generation an opportunity to claim, but also a responsibility to conserve, what had not been lost. Howard's camp decadence is crossed with this keen seriousness of purpose.

Hence his affronted response to a culture that is no longer interested in history. The debate in "Sharing Secrets" is made ridiculous by the ignorance of his interlocutor. (She: "There never was a woman who wasn't oppressed by history." He: "Never? Not even Queen Elizabeth?" She: "Which Queen Elizabeth?" He: "Oh, you know, Queen Elizabeth the First, of England . . . in the Renaissance?" She: "When was the Renaissance?") Howard knows that there are other and more formidable parties to address, however, including poets of his own age such as W. S. Merwin, John Ashbery, and Mark Strand, and younger poets influenced by them. "Sharing Secrets" was published in 1992, but I doubt Howard would want to modify its claim that American poetry has become "a poetry of forgetting" whose practitioners "rise against the form in which they are writing; their burden is to lose the gifts of order, recovery, convergence upon an end so that all might begin again; their burden is their aspiration to gainsay, to despoil the self of all that had been, merely, propriety." It is deemed acceptable, Howard observes, and even courageous, to "forget"—by which he means to proceed in poetry without "givens," without ceremonial verse forms, without a sense of (either comforting or agonized) repetition. On another level, Howard himself perhaps feels in danger of being forgotten.

"Save it all," he contrives for Mrs. William Morris to say at the beginning of "1915: A Pre-Raphaelite Ending, London," one of the dramatic monologues in *Untitled Subjects*, which won the Pulitzer Prize in 1970, and which remains, if not his finest book, then his most distinctive and characteristic. Like most of his speakers, Jane Morris, looking over a box holding a lifetime's accumulated documents, speaks for the poet too. The central and surprising fact of Howard's singularity is that his cultivation of it meant opening his poetry to manifold voices. "Save it all" is the imperative that motivates his recovery of speakers such as Mrs. Morris—with a sense that there is something important of himself to be saved along with her and her past. She continues:

> you do not know
> the value things will come to have until
> the world grows dim around you, and your things
> —however doubtful in the changing light,
> things are what you have
> left. And all you have.

In this essay I will consider what Howard has saved of himself, of his poetical "things," in *Inner Voices*, and what he has now added to that selection in his most recent book, *The Silent Treatment*. The point won't be to quash or ignore the objections of his "Bardic hostess," but to see whether the "defects" she finds in his poetry can direct us to its "significance."

Having heeded Cocteau's advice and cultivated what seemed most himself, Howard has created a body of work whose characteristic concerns and procedures are apparent even in his early poems. Take for example "An Old Dancer," a poem from *Damages*, his second book, published in 1967. The poem is an apostrophe to Martha Graham, and it begins with an epigraph from her: "Because there is only one of you in all of time . . . the world will not have it . . ." A quotation as epigraph, or a framing name or date or dedication, is typical of Howard, who often begins his poems by locating them, noting the givens—"the very data of circumstance"—from which they take off. This particular quotation comes from a memoir by Agnes de Mille in which Graham is quoted as saying about the dance: "There is a vitality, a life force, a quickening that is translated through you into action, and because there is only one of you in all time, this expression is unique. And if you block it, it will never exist through any other medium and will be lost. The world will not have it. It is not your business to determine how good it is . . . It is your business to keep it yours, clearly and directly, to keep the channel open." Graham's emphasis on the dancer's uniqueness (and, by implication, solitude), along with her notion of the dancer as a "medium" for a "vitality" that would otherwise be lost, makes her sense of vocation a model for Howard's. But when, in the epigraph, he isolates those two phrases—"Because there is only one of you in all of time" and "the world will not have it"—from the rest of her statement, he changes Graham's meaning: He stresses not the world's potential loss, but its censure and refusal, of that uniqueness.

The poem, which responds to a late performance by the dancer in the light of many previous, begins:

> Your props had always been important:
> Preposterous poignards, rings and thorns,
> Things without a name you fell upon
> Or through. Now they are your props indeed.
> Take that iron prong you dangle from,
> Strung up, slung like a sick animal
> Who used to rise as straight as any tree
> Without such corporal irony.
> Propped then, you make no bones, or only
> Bones, of husbanding your strength. For strength
> Was your husband, and you're widowed now.
> The face that was a mask of wonder
> Wizens into the meaninglessness
> Of some Osaka marionette,
> And there is properly little more
> That you can do for us than think.

Idealizing, admiring, the poet who beholds the aging dancer is also coolly objectifying. The power of his description lies in his elaborate phrasing. To get the portrait right, Howard must get his terms right. These he approaches as if they had a particular truth to disclose, beginning with "props." He gets at what the word might mean by allowing its parts to return in other words—first "important," then "preposterous" and "poignards." These in turn generate new sounds, new graphemes: "rings," "thorns," and, combining these, "things"—as the "g" and "n" in "poignard" are reversed. These return in "prong," "dangle," "strung," and "slung," at which point the progress of these letters and sounds yields up, as if by its own insistent logic, a disturbing image of the dancer "Strung up, slung like a sick animal." Meanwhile Howard has made a discovery: Props are at last . . . only props—not what the performer holds up but what holds up the performer, who has been manipulated by the "life-force" like a Bunraku puppet. This twist, this reversal, amounts to a "corporal irony" in two senses: because it testifies to the iron law of the body's decay, and because the image of that law is the "iron prong" the dancer "dangles" from.

The fate of the aging artist is a theme of the later Yeats, whose "Sailing to Byzantium," with its images of an old man as "A tattered coat upon a stick" and the soul "fastened to a dying animal," is clearly on Howard's mind here. Yeats himself emerges at the end of the poem, where Howard returns to and develops the implications of that image in the first stanza of the young dancer rising "as straight as any tree":

> What you were a whole theater
> Has become. What have you lost by that
> Exchange, save as the tree loses by
> Giving up its leaves and standing bare?
> O Dancer, you have lost everything,
> Shuddering on your iron gallows-tree.
> Bane, bone and violence, you answer
> Yeats in kind, unkindest witch of all:
> "We know the dancer from the dance" by age,
> By growing old. The dance goes on,
> The dancers go, and you hang here
> Like stale meat on your dead steel branch,

The Yeats Graham answers is, of course, the poet who asks the famous questions at the end of "Among Schoolchildren":

> O chestnut tree, great rooted blossomer,
> Are you the leaf, the blossom or the bole?
> O body swayed to music, O brightening glance,
> How can we know the dancer from the dance?

Howard thinks nothing of introducing another poem into one of his, and doing so in a teacherly way. It is as if Yeats's poem had been behind this one to begin with—as if Howard had turned to Graham precisely to answer Yeats's question. The move, however, is not pedantic; it leads through art toward a recognition of the limits of art. This comes as a simple human truth: "'We know the dancer from the dance' by age, / By growing old." Because it is rhetorically self-conscious, in other words, Howard's answer takes apart Yeats's rhetorical question, just as Howard takes apart his own. "What have you lost . . . ?" Answer: "everything." In the end the "straight" tree turns into "stale meat" on a "steel branch."

Howard discovered his trademark poetic form, the dramatic monologue, in *Untitled Subjects*, the book that followed *Findings*. The poems from this book remain, now as when they first appeared, overwhelming in their technical virtuosity and their intense quality of imagining. Howard extends the strategy of address used in "An Old Dancer," endeavoring to speak not to but as or for his subjects: When these poems do not take the form of monologues, they are narrated from a character's point of view in indirect discourse. Yet this heightened intimacy comes with increased historical distance, as Howard reaches back into the nineteenth century for his subjects. The dead, already alive only on the page, seem available for Howard's imagining as the living are not. Robert Browning, the obvious model for Howard's ventriloquism, reflects on this effect in a long monologue, "November 1889":

> what is dead or dying
> is more readily apprehended by us
> than what is part of life.
> Nothing in writing is
> easier than to raise the dead.

In part this is the case simply because that is how the dead exist for Howard—in writing. *Untitled Subjects* is a book made out of other books—above all out of letters, diaries, memoirs, biography, history. These genres suggest forms for his poems. In particular, Howard often casts his monologues as letters, as writing rather than speech, and the distinction is important. There is magic and drama in his recovery of historical voices, but what he is imagining is precisely the work he is himself engaged in—the effort to put language on the page, to speak in writing.

"I am in the wrong period!" exclaims the young archaeologist in a somewhat later Howard poem, "A Natural Death." Just so, Howard's poetry itself seems "in the wrong period," at least from certain angles. Part of the éclat of *Untitled Subjects* derived from its demand that the reader plunge with the poet into the past. Its poems range in imagined occasion from a letter by Philippe-Jacques de Loutherbourg in 1801, applying to Lord Elgin for a commission to copy the Parthenon marbles, to the aged Mrs. William Morris addressing her spinster daughter during World War I. Together they radiate from a moment when the august, classic, heroic past still seems an approachable ideal, and yet when the disasters and dismantlings of the modern are coming into view. This transitional moment is dated and depicted in "1891: An Idyll":

> A storm is coming, but the clouds are still
> no more than a classic custard in the west,
> no closer than the sun, still august, shining
> through the dishevelled branches of an oak
> as if there were no darkness gathering
> itself together round the scene's edges,
> although the gulls come sideways, suddenly
> white against the cliffs, loud in their anger.
> It is the Isle of Wight, and Tennyson's Tree

... under which are sitting two old men,
the Laureate and the Signer painting him;
and being read to, both of them, by Hallam
Tennyson out of a green book, The Golden Bough,
published this year of the first Electrocution
(America's riposte to Gallows and Guillotine)
and the last of Parnell: it is 1891.

There is history here, but imagination too. As Howard explains at the end of the poem, this scene, of George Frederick Watts ("the Signor," the renowned nineteenth-century English portraitist) painting Lord Tennyson ("the Laureate"), is being photographed by Julia Margaret Cameron—even though the pioneering photographer had in fact died in 1879 (Tennyson's death was near: 1892). Howard wants Cameron in the picture, taking a picture of her own, because he wants his image to include the technology that has already begun to supplant old Watts's oil paint: Photography is just as much a part of the "coming storm" as the primitivism of Sir James George Frazer's anthropology, America's electrocutions (think of the lightning brewing in those clouds), and the break-up of the British Empire, as adumbrated in Parnell's Irish nationalism. But to put Cameron in, Howard must defy chronology and go back to an earlier decade when she, Watts, and Tennyson were together on the Isle of Wight. What Howard cares about here is not so much fact as a deep stratum of cultural history which is accessible only with the assistance of fancy. What he creates is a mental scene, where the Victorian and the modern interpenetrate, the one emerging from the other like a storm from the clouds in the Western sky. It is the special kind of historical truth that art can represent.

Howard's immersion in this pre-modernist moment makes his work hard to place among the postmodernisms of his contemporaries. His involvement with historical personages and the dramatic monologue form are opposed to confessional poetry and to the various poetries of romantic selfhood promoted by Harold Bloom and Helen Vendler. His high polish and seeming realism also set his work against the alternative to these autobiographical modes that is the post-Pound avant-garde. And yet Howard has something in common with both of these broadly defined schools. To begin with, he owes an obvious debt to Pound, who also read Henry James and Browning deeply, and who made translation his crucial theme and practice in The Cantos, that many-voiced "poem including history." The fussy eloquence of his phrasing calls into question, moreover, the presumed naturalness of the speaking voice, as only experimental poetry is supposed to do—even while he remains committed to the representation of specific voices and speakers, and to the possibility of constituting a self in language.

Howard's poetry is not usually discussed in relation to post-structuralist literary theory (it must seem too old-fashioned for that), but it might well be, and particularly in relation to the works of Roland Barthes, whom Howard knew and translated. For example, in his virtuoso commentary on Balzac, *S/Z*, Barthes makes a distinction between "readerly" and "writerly" texts: The one is realist in nature, defined by its referential function, by the story it tells, while the other is modernist, reveling in the priority of its semiotic codes. Howard furnished a preface to the English edition of *S/Z* (he was not the translator), now reprinted in *Paper Trail*, in which he discusses Barthes's use of these terms. Unlike the polemicizing Barthes, however, Howard does not choose sides. He proposes instead that "what is authentically writerly can become readerly"—that, in effect, modernist semiosis and realist representation can be, and even need to be, reconciled. Howard summarizes Barthes's point: "All telling modifies what is being told, so that what the linguists call the message is a parameter of its performance . . . what is told is always the telling."

Whether or not Barthes would agree with this statement, it tells us something about Howard's own inclinations and aims as a poet, and it suggests a way to position his work in its period. When Howard set out to reconcile the semiotic and semantic dimensions of poetic speech, he tried to solve a basic—perhaps the basic—problem confronting postwar writing: how to recover, after modernism's "writerly" revolution, the traditional practices of storytelling and theatrical self-presentation. His solution was to return to the point at which these dimensions of the verbal began to come apart—a prolonged, half-real, half-imaginary moment sometime between 1842, when Robert Browning wrote "My Last Duchess," and 1876, when Mallarmé wrote "L'Après-midi d'un faune" (Howard's translation of which is included in *The Silent Treatment*), or else 1897, when the same poet wrote in "Crise de vers" that, "L'oeuvre pure implique la disparition élocutoire du poète, qui cède l'initiative aux mots, par le heurt de leur inégalité mobilisé? ("The pure work implies the disappearance of the poet as speaker, ceding the initiative to words, which are mobilized by the shock of their differences.") In Howard's work, it is as if Browning were writing Mallarmé's poems, and Mallarmé Browning's.

Although he is no confessional poet, Howard is an autobiographical one, albeit of a curious kind. What he shares with us is his life as a reader and spectator, simultaneously projecting himself into and absorbing the lives and works he studies and relishes. As he frankly puts it in his *Paris Review* interview, "My good monologues are good because the monologuist is me." Certainly the reader will observe that Howard's people tend to sound related, and that they all sound like him; in fact, those poems in his "own" voice can sometimes seem flatter, less animated, less distinctively like Richard Howard than his dramatic monologues. But verisimilitude is not the point. "It seems to me," he says in the same interview, "I choose (or with luck invent) characters whose register I know I can coax—even force—into mine." Or it may be that some projection is necessary in order to go inside himself, that he needs these voices to find his own "register." Wallace Stevens, another master for Howard, especially in his sense of verbal play, speaks of this phenomenon in his "Adagia": "When the mind is like a hall in which thought is like a voice speaking, the voice is always that of some one else." Howard's work constantly literalizes this remark. We can say of his characters what he says of Hofmannsthal's in "Beyond Words": that they are "merely / the others of him." When we hear "their" voices, then, we must remember that we are hearing his, but also that his is a creation of theirs—of his reading, reverberating in mental space. In this sense, all the voices of *Inner Voices* are "inner."

The difficult but entertaining drama enacted by his characters amounts, therefore, to a version of Howard's own effort "to find lines of verse that would articulate and exemplify my struggles with meaning." Although Howard deploys numerous forms, the one that readers will likely think of as distinctively his is a twisting, sinuous syllabic poem, in some cases with, but just as often without, stanza breaks. His poems in this form look like Marianne Moore's, but where her eccentric syllabic designs crystallize a highly individual perspective, Howard uses his syllabics to accommodate many speakers. What he takes from Moore is her sense of verse as an arbitrary contrivance, a vivid show, to which the poet submits as to a painstaking discipline. In "November, 1889," an example of this form, Howard's Browning declares, "I am not interested in art. / I am interested in the obstacles / to art"—and the enjambment, enforced by the pattern, emblematizes those "obstacles." Formally, Howard's syllabics allow for speech that unrolls like Victorian blank verse, without predetermined periods. But unlike blank verse, the form has built-in expansions and contractions that make for suspension, even suspense, in the unfolding of syntax across the line-breaks. Repeatedly effecting semantic delays through enjambment, it permits Howard to put on a verbal performance that, for all his loquaciousness, includes plenty of what Henry James called "hanging fire."

So "verse" for Howard typically doesn't mean accentual-syllabic meter or rhyme. Rather, it means what its root does in Latin, "turning": It is an "old ceremonial of keeping, of returns and recuperations," enacted "on the lathe of prosody" (this from an introduction to the poetry of—Howard would not want us to miss the pun—Turner Cassity). But verse as a process of turning around and back is also allied with the semiotic play we saw in "An Old Dancer," where the energy is dispersive as well as recuperative, full of quibbles and queries, nervously undoing whatever has just been said. Howard's manner includes both impulses. His verse as it appears on the page, whether wrapping around in serpentine syllabic patterns or repeating intricate, jagged stanza designs, mirrors the double action of looking into language, of moving ahead by turning around, that goes on throughout his work.

This turning movement is also reflected in the rhetorical figures that Howard favors. For example, chiasmus, in which verbal elements repeat and exchange positions. The effect, as in "An Old Dancer," can be of a serious irony, a poignant turnabout:

> Propped, then, you make no bones, or only
> Bones, of husbanding your strength. For strength
> Was your husband, and you're widowed now.

At times it is as if Howard simply could not resist a good bad joke: "a stocky body in a body stocking" ("A Commission"), a "grizzled chin and chiseled grin" ("The Masters on the Movies"). At other times this type of movement seems to generate large-scale thematic and formal designs. Not chiasmus precisely, but rhetorical inversions and reversals of various kinds contribute to the structure of "Dorothea Tanning's Cousins" a meditation on the artist's odd, comic sculptural forms made of "synthetic fur over cotton stuffing, wood base, 60 x 25 x 21 inches." (Tanning's piece appears on the cover of *Trappings*.) Howard reads those synthetic forms as the entangled bodies of two lovers. The "lathe of prosody" turns here with a vengeance:

> She came to him in dreams, as he to her
> in waking. And that was how they would meet,
> ever wrong from the start, however right
> for the act, melting
> together yet somehow sadly apart,
> orifices certainly unmatched to
> protuberances, although affording
> opportunity,
> it appeared, in the oddest places; no
> completion but the striving, the struggle,
> the melancholy abandonment of his
> strain, her stratagem:
> eventually, then, it came down to
> this immense tedium, another name
> for all our tenderness, solicitude.
> Ready and waiting,
> but the hope forlorn, the motive foregone:

> she tyrannically submissive to
> his compliant despotism, he yielding
> over and underneath
> to her surrender—her victory his
> peculiar triumph.

The unsettling symmetries of division-in-unity come to seem like the inevitable figure for erotic relations, as if they inhered in the necessarily unfulfillable desire for human union. To desire someone, it seems, is to be turned both toward and against that person. Predictably, the poem's concluding moral turns on a cliché: "With enemies like themselves . . . what lovers need friends?"

As this example suggests, when he is playing with language, Howard is searching for proverbs, epigrams, practical truths. These range from simple negations—"Having / Things your way is not really having them" ("On Hearing Your Lover is Going to the Baths Tonight")—to more complex reversals and paradoxes:

> only when you leave
> Will you know where you are
>   ("Sandusky—New York")

> Deep secrets hide in surfaces
>   ("Beyond Words")

> we are not ourselves
> until we know how little
> of our selves is truly our own
>   ("Beyond Words")

In these cases, Howard turns a word or idea until it comes around to mean something like its opposite. In other cases, he puns on multiple meanings of the same word or phrase. The effect can be of resignation—"Even the flags had . . . flagged" ("Love Which Alters")—or affirmation, as in "Still life is still life" ("Concerning K"). The device makes for a powerful conclusion when it appears at the end of a poem, where the poet seems to have made a concession and seen the wisdom of not attempting to do more. For instance, in "Beyond Words," where Howard quotes Hofmannstahl:

> in an early
> poem he said, "and yet, to say
> 'evening' is to say much." It is evening.

Or in "Venetian Interior, 1889":

> Nothing but
> darkness abides, darkness demanding not
> illumination—not from the likes of us—
> but only that we yield. And we yield.

The neatness of these rhetorical gestures gives a feeling of rightness, necessity, closure. Thus the writerly text, Howard might say, becomes a readerly one: The quibbling comes to rest, and a memorable dignity is achieved. But the semiotic is a festive, unruly force in Howard's work, and just as often his wordplay is open-ended and carnivalesque. It produces perfect howlers, such as "a Jew d'esprit" ("1881: A Beatification") and "Cleveland was our mother-in-lieu" ("Decades"); anagrams such as "a manatee must emanate" ("The Manatee"); and parodic literary echoes, as of Baudelaire: "I read you, mon semblable, mon Pierre!" ("At the Monument to Pierre Louÿs"). Howard knows that, like any speaker, he is threatened by bathos, the unwitting double entendre that reveals one to be under the control of one's words, rather than the reverse. So he always tries to get there first by acknowledging all the potential words within his words. This creates a verbal environment in which the sounds of Howard's speech themselves seem to say something beyond or behind what he is saying; and his writing, as it attends to that subliminal speech, becomes a process of listening.

This attitude toward language rests on a fundamental Freudian faith in the therapeutic power of speech, expressed in the title of Howard's *Talking Cures* (2002). The idea is that language has something it wants to tell us—if we only listen patiently enough, if we give it the freedom, but also observe the rules, that are necessary for it to speak. When it does, we hear or say what we did not know was in us—a "secret." The dramatic monologue as a genre is characterized, Howard remarks, by "the necessity of the secret that the speaker, who does not know it, must reveal," and in this way the form exemplifies, for Howard, poetry's potential for truth. The secret may be merely sexual, a spiritual mystery, or something of both. To perceive it, Howard explains in "Sharing Secrets," demands from us a "passivity ... a trust, a confidence in what Yeats names a natural momentum in the syntax, a cumulus he said enabled a poem to carry 'any amount of elaborate English.'" Reader and writer, like analyst and analysand, must trust in language to such a degree that words are released to their "natural momentum," or as Mallarmé would put it, to their own "initiative." "The confidence shared," Howard goes on, gathering momentum himself, "the saving grace, if that is what it is, is all in the capacity of language itself—compulsively qualified, idiosyncratic in address, entirely given over to conventions and observed usages and allusive reliances—to carry the impulse, the effort of the poem (the received memory, the history of Western consciousness, not to put too fine a point on it) by the energeia which words hold within themselves, by the dynamics they generate 'among one another' line by line rather than one at a time—by a secret plot."

The Silent Treatment might seem to retract this promise. That phrase, "the silent treatment," suggests first of all a killing comeback, the cold shoulder that trumps all talk. At the same time, as the title of the successor volume to *Talking Cures*, it suggests something else again: that silence might itself be a treatment, a cure. That the silence Howard is concerned with here is not outside language but within it, the deep secret language has to divulge, is suggested by the book's title poem. It is an ekphrastic poem about a white marble relief by the sculptor Natalie Charkow Hollander entitled "Nine Caves & Their Inhabitants," which is pictured on the cover. (*Talking Cures* and *The Silent Treatment*, both printed by Turtle Point Press, are beautifully designed books.) Charkow's "caves" or panels show "mute figures," discernible barely if at all. Their solitude and ours mirror each other, as Howard reads the work, reminding us of what we should have known to start with: that "everyone's backs are always to us." In this case, it is as if the artworks had turned its back to us, revealing not a secret scene but a veil, "a perforated snowy shroud." The artwork is a "relief," in the punning sense that Howard emphasizes, because it relieves us of the fantasy of ever moving past that veil. Speaking of the sculptor's marble "caves," but articulating a principle that holds for his monologues as well, he concludes, "only a hidden life is there / to be looked for, not found." The far side of representation, the very back and bottom of things, rises before us as its sublime white surface.

Once silence is seen as essential to it, speech becomes something we can never get around. "What we say," Howard says in *Paper Trail*, "structures instinct and generates the scripts in which experience and sensation, in themselves, are registered and understood." As a consequence, "history does not merely touch / language, it takes place in it" ("Oracles"). To say that there is too much history in Howard's poems is therefore to say that there is too much language in them, a language too aware of its own processes and protocols, its roots and branches, and burdened by the "received memory" of its history of speakers. The objection to his subject is also an objection to his style. They are the same thing. And when we view Howard's poetry in this way, the features that seem to risk, or even invite, reproach—its insistent learning, its knowingness, its punning "verbality," its relentless performance—come to seem, as he says of Dickinson's "defects," the "solution" to specific "problems of composition and utterance."

"Oracles," the poem from which I just quoted, is a résumé of Howard's ideas about poetic language, and a fitting place to bring this discussion to a close. First collected in *No Traveller* (1989), it is Howard's longest poem (25 pages, 807 lines) and possibly his best monologue. The speaker is an aged Hellenist, a German, who lectures to young students and older researchers on an unnamed Greek isle, "once the place of prophecy," where "a Scholars' Retreat" has been established now. She is "no oracle" herself, but an expert in the history of oracles, and thus a model for the role of mediator and explainer that Howard often assumes in his poems. But the rational, edifying, demystified discourse of scholarship takes on, in her, oracular powers of its own. Not here, she begins,

> I must be out of the wind,
> under something—otherwise
> I cannot light these insipid weeds
> alleged to be cigarettes.

Other Howard poems begin similarly: with a conspiratorial or imperious gesture that establishes a relationship to the listener by beckoning him—it is a him here, a young man—to take up with the speaker an oblique position, partly concealed, "under something." Speaking out of the decay of her body (her heart requires a machine to keep it going), the woman is like a Yeatsian character at the limits of existence, or Graham in "An Old Dancer"; and, being a true Howard character, she can't speak without reflecting on how people speak:

> my condition
> —that is what I have, a condition—
> is serious, but neither
> fatal nor severe; it is merely
> something that I remember
> on certain occasions, like a poem
> (what we say about ourselves
> is always poetry)

As usual, there are diverting reversals, transpositions, repetitions:

> So I am taken aback
> or perhaps it is forward—at least
> I am stirred up
> Proof of pleasure is pleasure itself—

groggy by night
and gaga by day
Appearances are apparitions!

The young man remains silent except as she speaks for him, anticipating or rephrasing his comments. It is like the psychoanalytic transaction, only here the older authority, the analyst, does the talking, amusing and instructing the young man—the reader's surrogate, holding him spellbound or "entranced." Her topic is the history of prophetic speech in Greece, beginning with the *pythia*:

At Patara, she would be
chained inside the temple after dark
so the god could get at her,
enter her—his medium, his lips . . .
(It was the first witticism
I ever made in English without
translating: for the priestess
to be entered was to be entranced—
entrance was enhancement . . .)

The young man wants to know about "Pythian replacements— / boys for virgins . . ." in the period of prophecy's decline. These "Unofficial oracles / —by rights a contradiction in terms—" could be consulted outside the temple, "'at home,'" where the god would be invited by "erotic / excitement." So, Howard implies, the erotic replaced the sacred. The words of such a boy, "witlessly murmuring / under your touch," might amount to "oracles, / reliable ones, in the highest / inspirational manner," but it was no longer precisely a god speaking:

Of course you heard in the words he spoke
only what was already
in you, but to know what was in you
you needed the words spoken,
and for this the motions of "passion"
were indispensable.

The eliciting of sacred speech, improvised outside the temple, becomes a model for poetry, in which we hear our own words spoken by others; as Howard puts it, "my good monologues are good because the monologuist is me." But again we need to stress the otherness of that "me." The speaker of

"Oracles" understands it clearly, and she points up the relation of her own speech to that of the "Unofficial oracles" when she lectures her young man on the relationship between them:

> When you believe I am I and she
> is she, you are unconscious;
> when you believe I am she and she
> is I, you are cognizant . . .

To be conscious in Howard's poetry is to be "cognizant" of the otherness of one's self and the presence of one's self in the voices of other people.

As the Hellenist dismisses her young man, we can hear the poet preparing to take leave of us, his readers:

> We have been fortunate.
> I really have enjoyed your visit—
> you must know: with you I seem
> to hear myself speak as a stranger
> —without recognizing myself.
> Only after you are gone shall I
> discover that it was . . . I.

In an elegy for James Boatwright, Howard speaks of "the loneliness / produced by culture, of culture's dreams," by which he means the solitude that poetic communication arises from and returns to, as imaged in "The Silent Treatment," or described in "Oracles." Like Martha Graham's uniqueness, it is a poignant but not a pitiable condition. The Hellenist recognizes that "it was . . . I"; we could also say the opposite—that, in the presence of her listener, her "I" was "it." While she was speaking, she joined herself to the impersonal force, the "energeia," of the language she spoke, and she shared with her listener its secrets, not hers. This has been Howard's own project for more than forty years.

ADAM KIRSCH

The Modern Element in Criticism

The twentieth century, besides its more serious crimes, must be held responsible for poetry's neurotic obsession with the modern. Ezra Pound was the first victim of this sickness, declaring in 1917 that "no good poetry is ever written in a manner twenty years old." This principle condemned poetry, like a decrepit mansion, to constant renovation. Each generation had to find its own way of being up-to-date, from William Carlos Williams ("A new *Zeitgeist* has possessed the world") to Charles Olson ("Verse now, 1950, if it is to get ahead . . . must, I take it, catch up"), all the way down to Alice Fulton ("Synthesis and unity are fundamentally premodern concepts. . . . [A] truly engaged and contemporary poetry must reflect this knowledge").

But just as the Puritan could never be sure he was one of the elect, so the twentieth-century poet could never be certain he was writing in the way that "the age demanded" (as Pound put it in *Hugh Selwyn Mauberley*). His only hope was to recognize the state of grace from outward signs, which meant brandishing his modernness like a placard. So in style, too, the stakes of newness were constantly being raised. Pound demanded "direct treatment of the 'thing,'" and Williams announced "we are *through* with the iambic pentameter"; Olson looked to "possibilities of the breath, of the breathing of the man who writes," while Fulton plumps for "asymmetrical or turbulent composition."

From *The Modern Element: Essays on Contemporary Poetry*, pp. 322–29. © 2008 by Adam Kirsch.

As a result, the poetry criticism of the last century often sounds like a madhouse, with each patient floridly expounding his delusion. To understand how we got to this point, it is necessary to go back to the beginning of modern thought about poetry, which lay in the Renaissance's return to Plato—a return which was also an overturning. For Plato, poetry was suspect on both ethical and ontological grounds. The charge that it "feeds and waters the passions," however, is no longer likely to dismay any reader of poetry. More challenging is the Platonic accusation that poetry is deficient in its very being.

In the *Republic*, Socrates argues that poetry should be held in contempt because it is "third in the descent from nature." Only the Ideas, what Yeats called the "ghostly paradigms of things," are essentially real. Actual, concrete objects—a bed, a tree, a ship—merely copy that ideal reality; and fictions, poetic or painterly, only copy the copies. Even though *poiesis* means "making," Plato denies that the poet is "a creator and maker." At best "the tragic poet is an imitator, and therefore, like all other imitators, he is thrice removed . . . from the truth."

There are two ways of braving this Platonic contempt for poetry. The first is Aristotle's, and might be called pragmatic. In his *Poetics*, Aristotle denies that there is a suprasensible realm of Ideas, insisting that our ordinary world is the only reality. And he honors poetry as an artful imitation of that reality. There is no disgrace in such imitation, because, as he points out, "imitation is one instinct of our nature." Moreover, because poetic imitation is deliberate and not slavish, poetry actually improves on reality, "making a likeness which is true to life and yet more beautiful."

Such a poetics honors the poet for accurate and subtle knowledge of the world and human life, and it values style as the means by which the poet communicates that knowledge. It follows that when the Aristotelian mind turns to criticism, as in the neoclassical essays in verse and prose of Dryden, Pope, and Johnson, it will attend mainly to practical rules and concrete observations, confident that—as Pope wrote in his *Essay on Criticism*—"Those RULES of old discover'd, not devis'd, / Are Nature still, but Nature Methodiz'd."

The other way of looking at poetry, which became dominant in the early nineteenth century and remains deeply influential, is the Romantic. The Romantic critic agrees with Plato that there is a divine realm, of which our world is a flawed reflection. But instead of scorning poetry as an imitation of the lower world, the Romantic worships it as a means of direct access to the higher. Not philosophy but poetry becomes the ladder on which we ascend to the heavens. If this is a contradiction of Plato, it is no less alien to Aristotle, since it removes poetry from the realm of worldly understanding and secular skill. Instead of an art, poetry becomes a magic.

Sir Philip Sidney made the first approach toward this idea, significantly tying his "Defense of Poetry" to a subversive reading of Plato as "of all philosophers . . . the most poetical." Sidney praises poetry exactly insofar as it is not an imitation of life: "to borrow nothing of what is, has been, or shall be; but range, only reined with learned discretion, into the divine consideration of what may be and should be." The poet is not only not "third in descent from nature," but, "lifted up with the vigor of his own invention, doth grow, in effect, into another nature." And like every subsequent Romantic critic, Sidney sees meter as, at best, a mere garment of poetry's spiritual body: "Verse being but an ornament and no cause to poetry, since there have been many most excellent poets that never versified."

The Romantics of the early nineteenth century continued to disparage verse in theory, though they never abandoned it in practice. In the preface to *Lyrical Ballads*, Wordsworth lamented that "confusion has been introduced into criticism by this contradistinction of Poetry and Prose, instead of the more philosophical one of Poetry and Matter of Fact, or Science." Poetry, on this view, is not metrical language, but a form of superior wisdom: "Poetry is the first and last of all knowledge—it is as immortal as the heart of man." It follows that one earns the title of poet, not by writing verse, but by spiritual excellence, "a more comprehensive soul than [is] supposed to be common among mankind." No wonder that, as Coleridge recalled in *Biographia Literaria*, "Mr. Wordsworth's admirers . . . were found too not in the lower classes of the reading public, but chiefly among young men of strong ability and meditative minds, and their admiration . . . was distinguished by its intensity, I might almost say, by its *religious* fervor."

This religious conception of poetry shifts its focus from the poem, an object with certain formal qualities, to the poet, who writes to express his extraordinary soul. Only in this light can we understand the strange pronouncements of Coleridge, that "a poem of any length neither can be, or ought to be, all poetry"; of Shelley, that "a man cannot say, 'I will compose poetry' . . . when composition begins, inspiration is already on the decline"; or of Emerson, that "when we adhere to the ideal of the poet, we have our difficulties even with Milton and Homer." Poetry, it seems, is not poems; it is not a skill practiced by the poet; and it cannot be found in even the greatest poets of the past. It has become a name for a mystic experience that can never be more than approximately described, as in Shelley's Platonic rhapsody: "A poet participates in the eternal, the infinite, and the one; as far as relates to his conceptions, time and place and number are not."

Probably no poet today would repeat Shelley's creed word for word. But the modern understanding of poetry is still profoundly influenced by Romanticism, if only because modernism and postmodernism were dialectical responses to it. Modernism, under the (more modest and useful) name of Symbolism, came to French poetry before English. But the French Symbolists were themselves influenced by an American, the much-misunderstood Edgar Allan Poe. And Poe's essay "The Philosophy of Composition" was a torpedo aimed directly at Romanticism and its religious pretensions.

Far from being "the first and last of all knowledge," Poe claims, a poem is simply a technology for producing aesthetic sensations. When we think we are being elevated by a poem, we are really just being stimulated by "some amount of suggestiveness—some undercurrent, however indefinite, of meaning. It is this latter, in especial, which imparts to a work of art so much of that richness . . . which we are too fond of confounding with the ideal." By divorcing poetic pleasure from all ethical and metaphysical concerns, Poe returns our focus to the poem itself, which now becomes only a pattern of stimuli—as he demonstrates in his cold-blooded account of writing "The Raven."

Filtered through Symbolism, this became the dominant understanding of poetry among the American modernists. It had a profound influence on Pound, Eliot ("The effect of a work of art upon the person who enjoys it is an experience different in kind from any experience not of art"), and Stevens ("A poet's words are things that do not exist without the words"). In the New Criticism of the 1930s and 1940s, the idea was reduced to an academic doctrine. "The meaning of poetry," Allen Tate declared, is "its 'tension,' the full organized body of all the extension and intension that we can find in it." Or, as the young Yvor Winters put it, the poem "is not a means to any end, but is in itself an end."

The poetry criticism of the mid-twentieth century was largely an attack on this modernist principle, which had begun to seem like the arid formalism of what Kenneth Rexroth called a "Reactionary Generation." "No avant-garde American poet," Rexroth declared in 1957, "accepts the . . . thesis that a poem is an end in itself, an anonymous machine for providing aesthetic experiences." Instead, the influential poets of the 1950s and 1960s advanced a new ideal of the poem as a faithful record of experience. This ideal received different inflections at the hands of different poets. For Charles Olson it is the outer world that must be recorded ("Objectism is the getting rid of the lyrical interference of the individual as ego, of the 'subject' and his soul"), while for Denise Levertov it is the inner sensation ("The sounds, acting together with the measure, are a kind of *extended onomatopoeia*—i.e., they imitate, not the sounds of an experience . . . but the feeling of an experience, its emotional tone, its texture").

In their hatred of artifice and their loyalty to individual perception, the experimental poets of the mid-century often sound like Romantics. But in fact, they resemble the Romantics only as a double-negative resembles a positive. For they were not in search of transcendence, only of authenticity. Indeed, the American generation that came after the modernists could most accurately be called the Authentic poets. Not to falsify one's personal experience, even or especially in the name of art, is their great principle. The poem, it follows, is only a means of synchronizing the reader's experience with the writer's. "The poem," Frank O'Hara wrote, "is at last between two persons instead of two pages."

It is in the pursuit of such authenticity that these poets made the great refusal about which the Romantics only speculated: the immolation of meter, rhyme, and form. They took Emerson's notion of a "meter-making argument" more seriously than Emerson himself, turning "the metric movement," in Levertov's words, into "the direct expression of the movement of perception." For just the same reason, Olson praises the typewriter, which allows the poet to "indicate exactly the breath, the pauses, the suspensions even of syllables." Here is the aggressive egotism of authenticity, which does not simply hand the poem over to the reader, but compels the reader to follow the writer's most detailed instructions. And here too is its puritanism, its hostility to pleasure. For meter, like all artifice, finds pleasure in the gratuitous, and the gratuitous is the enemy of authenticity.

Today, the poetics of authenticity is securely established. There have been isolated dissents from it, but no comprehensive rejection. Yet it should be clear by now that this poetics has thoroughly failed. It has made it more difficult for poets to produce major work, and its critical legacy is remarkable only for intellectual crudity and rhetorical violence. The sound of the critical madhouse is a thousand utterly authentic voices, all talking at once.

In the last twenty years, however, poets and critics have done little to challenge the ideal of authenticity. Instead, the most influential of them have turned from literary questions to sociological ones, focusing on the shortcomings of the institutional poetry world. In this category belong Robert Pinsky's thoughts on "poetry gloom," Donald Hall's on the "McPoem," and Dana Gioia's famous question, "Can Poetry Matter?" But the success or failure of American poetry is not determined by institutions—M.F.A. programs, publishers, magazines. Like any poetry at any time, it will compel recognition only by becoming great.

If criticism can make any contribution to this goal, it is to help us break free from the post-Romantic dialectic that obsessed American poetry in the twentieth century. For there is a saner, more sophisticated, more humane tradition in criticism: the pragmatic tradition of Aristotle and Horace, Johnson and Arnold. If we embrace it, we will not need to look to poetry for transcendence, or to flee into aestheticism when transcendence fails, or to flee into authenticity when aestheticism fails. We will be able to see how the twentieth century gave us poets of humane insight—Hardy, Frost, Moore, Larkin, Lowell—as well as poets of otherworldly magniloquence and hectic experimentalism. And if we are fortunate, our poetry will come to understand the full implications—ethical, intellectual, and aesthetic—of Horace's seemingly simple formula:

> Of writing well, be sure, the secret lies
> In wisdom: therefore study to be wise.

Chronology

1921   Richard Wilbur born in New York City.

1925   Gerald Stern born in Pittsburgh. Maxine Kumin born in Philadelphia.

1927   John Ashbery born in Rochester, New York. W.S. Merwin born in New York City. Galway Kinnell born in Providence, Rhode Island.

1928   Donald Hall born in New Haven, Connecticut. Philip Levine born in Detroit.

1929   Adrienne Rich born in Baltimore. John Hollander born in New York City. Richard Howard born in Cleveland.

1930   Gary Snyder born in San Francisco.

1934   Wendell Berry born in Henry County, Kentucky. Mark Strand born in Prince Edward Island, Canada; lives most of his life in the United States.

1935   Charles Wright born in Pickwick Dam, Tennessee. Jay Wright born in Albuquerque.

1936   C.K. Williams born in Newark, New Jersey. Lucille Clifton born in Depew, New York.

1938   Charles Simic born in Yugoslavia and moves to the United States as a teenager.

191

1939	Stephen Dunn born in New York City.
1940	Robert Pinsky born in Long Branch, New Jersey.
1941	Billy Collins born in New York City. Stephen Dobyns born in Orange, New Jersey. Robert Hass born in San Francisco.
1942	Sharon Olds born in San Francisco.
1943	Louise Glück born in New York City. Nikki Giovanni born in Knoxville, Tennessee.
1945	Kay Ryan born in San Jose, California. Philip Schultz born in Rochester, New York.
1950	Edward Hirsch born in Chicago, and Jorie Graham born in New York City.
1952	Rita Dove born in Akron, Ohio.
1953	Mark Doty born in Maryville, Tennessee.
1957	Richard Wilbur awarded Pulitzer Prize in Poetry for *Things of This World*.
1970	Richard Howard awarded Pulitzer Prize in Poetry for *Untitled Subjects*.
1971	W.S. Merwin awarded his first Pulitzer Prize in Poetry for *The Carrier of Ladders*.
1975	Gary Snyder awarded Pulitzer Prize in Poetry for *Turtle Island*.
1976	John Ashbery awarded Pulitzer Prize in Poetry for *Self-Portrait in a Convex Mirror*.
1981–82	Maxine Kumin serves as Consultant in Poetry to the Library of Congress.
1983	Galway Kinnell awarded Pulitzer Prize in Poetry for his *Selected Poems*.
1987	Rita Dove awarded Pulitzer Prize in Poetry for *Thomas and Beulah*. Richard Wilbur is Poet Laureate Consultant in Poetry from 1987 to 1988.
1989	Richard Wilbur awarded Pulitzer Prize in Poetry for his *New and Collected Poems*.

1990	Charles Simic awarded Pulitzer Prize in Poetry for *The World Doesn't End*. Mark Strand is Poet Laureate Consultant in Poetry from 1990 to 1991.
1993–94	In 1993, Louise Glück is awarded Pulitzer Prize in Poetry for her collection *The Wild Iris*. From 1993 to 1995 Rita Dove is Poet Laureate Consultant in Poetry. In 1994 Robert Hass is named Poet Laureate of the United States.
1995–97	In 1995, Philip Levine is awarded Pulitzer Prize in Poetry for his collection *The Simple Truth*. From 1995 to 1997,Robert Hass is Poet Laureate Consultant in Poetry. In 1996, Jorie Graham is awarded Pulitzer Prize in Poetry for her collection *The Dream of the Unified Field*.
1997–2000	Robert Pinsky is Poet Laureate Consultant in Poetry. In 1998, Charles Wright is awarded Pulitzer Prize in Poetry for *Black Zodiac*. In 1999, Mark Strand is awarded Pulitzer Prize in Poetry for *Blizzard of One*. In 2000, C.K. Williams is awarded the prize for *Repair*. From 1999 to 2000, Rita Dove, Louise Glück, and W. S. Merwin serve as Special Bicentennial Consultants.
2001–03	Billy Collins is Poet Laureate Consultant in Poetry. In 2001, Stephen Dunn is awarded Pulitzer Prize in Poetry for *Different Hours*.
2003–04	Louise Glück is Poet Laureate Consultant in Poetry.
2006–07	Donald Hall is Poet Laureate Consultant in Poetry.
2007–08	Charles Simic is Poet Laureate Consultant in Poetry. In 2008, Robert Hass is awarded Pulitzer Prize in Poetry for *Time and Materials* and Philip Schultz is awarded the prize for *Failure*.
2008	Kay Ryan named Poet Laureate Consultant in Poetry.
2009	W.S. Merwin is awarded Pulitzer Prize in Poetry for *The Shadow of Sirius*.

Contributors

HAROLD BLOOM is Sterling Professor of the Humanities at Yale University. He is the author of 30 books, including *Shelley's Mythmaking, The Visionary Company, Blake's Apocalypse, Yeats, A Map of Misreading, Kabbalah and Criticism, Agon: Toward a Theory of Revisionism, The American Religion, The Western Canon,* and *Omens of Millennium: The Gnosis of Angels, Dreams, and Resurrection. The Anxiety of Influence* sets forth Professor Bloom's provocative theory of the literary relationships between the great writers and their predecessors. His most recent books include *Shakespeare: The Invention of the Human,* a 1998 National Book Award finalist, *How to Read and Why, Genius: A Mosaic of One Hundred Exemplary Creative Minds, Hamlet: Poem Unlimited, Where Shall Wisdom Be Found?,* and *Jesus and Yahweh: The Names Divine.* In 1999, Professor Bloom received the prestigious American Academy of Arts and Letters Gold Medal for Criticism. He has also received the International Prize of Catalonia, the Alfonso Reyes Prize of Mexico, and the Hans Christian Andersen Bicentennial Prize of Denmark.

MARJORIE PERLOFF is a professor emerita at Stanford University and a scholar in residence and lecturer at the University of Southern California. She has written many titles about poetry, including *Differentials: Poetry, Poetics, Pedagogy* and *21st-Century Modernism: The "New" Poetics.* She has been president of the Modern Language Association.

STEPHEN PAUL MILLER is a professor at St. John's University. In addition to publishing books of poetry, he is the co-editor of *The Scene of My Selves: New Work on New York School Poets.*

BARBARA L. ESTRIN, professor emerita of Stonehill College, specializes in early modern literature and modern poetry. Her books include *The Raven and the Lark: Lost Children in Literature of the English Renaissance* and *Laura: Uncovering Gender and Genre in Wyatt, Donne, and Marvell*.

ROGER GILBERT is a professor at Cornell University, where he teaches courses in American poetry. He co-authored *Consider the Radiance: Essays on the Poetry of A. R. Ammons* and co-edited *The Walker's Literary Companion*.

ANTHONY HECHT was a poet who in 1968 won the Pulitzer Prize for Poetry and who served as Poet Laureate Consultant in Poetry to the Library of Congress between 1982 and 1984. For many years he taught at the University of Rochester, and he taught at several other prestigious institutions as well.

LINDA GREGERSON is a professor at the University of Michigan. Her publications include books of poetry and other titles such as *Negative Capability: Contemporary American Poetry*. She has contributed to many journals.

DAVID BROMWICH is a professor at Yale University. Among his publications are books on Wordsworth and Hazlitt and a collection of essays on modern poetry.

WILLARD SPIEGELMAN is a professor at Southern Methodist University who writes about and teaches the English romantic poets and American poetry of the twentieth and twenty-first centuries. He is the editor of *The Southwest Review,* and his works include *How Poets See the World: The Art of Description in Contemporary Poetry* and *How to Read and Understand Poetry*.

LANGDON HAMMER is chairman of the English department at Yale University. His research and teaching focus on modern and contemporary poetry. He is a reviewer of poetry for the *New York Times* and poetry editor of *The American Scholar.* He is the editor of *Hart Crane: Complete Poetry and Selected Letters*.

ADAM KIRSCH is a poet and critic. His work includes books of poems and the nonfiction collection *The Modern Element: Essays on Contemporary Poetry*. He was book critic for the *New York Sun* and has written regularly for magazines.

Bibliography

Baker, David. *Heresy and the Ideal: On Contemporary Poetry*. Fayetteville: University of Arkansas Press, 2000.

Baker, Peter, ed. *Onward: Contemporary Poetry and Poetics*. New York: Peter Lang, 1996.

Barillas, William. *The Midwestern Pastoral: Place and Landscape in Literature of the American Heartland*. Athens, Ohio: Ohio University Press, 2006.

Bartlett, Lee. *Talking Poetry: Conversations in the Workshop with Contemporary Poets*. Albuquerque: University of New Mexico Press, 1987.

Bertram, Vicki. *Gendering Poetry: Contemporary Women and Men Poets*. London; Chicago: Pandora; Chicago: Distributed in the USA by Independent Publishers' Group, 2005.

Blazer, Alex E. *I Am Otherwise: The Romance between Poetry and Theory after the Death of the Subject*. Normal, Ill.: Dalkey Archive Press, 2007.

Bloom, Harold, ed. *W.S. Merwin*. Philadelphia: Chelsea House Publishers, 2004.

Brunner, Edward J. *Poetry as Labor and Privilege: The Writings of W.S. Merwin*. Urbana: University of Illinois Press, 1991.

Bryson, J. Scott. *The West Side of Any Mountain: Place, Space, and Ecopoetry*. Iowa City: University of Iowa Press, 2005.

Bryson, J. Scott, ed. *Ecopoetry: A Critical Introduction*. Salt Lake City: University of Utah Press, 2002.

Byers, Thomas B. *What I Cannot Say: Self, Word, and World in Whitman, Stevens, and Merwin*. Urbana: University of Illinois Press, 1989.

Chevalier, Tracy, ed. *Contemporary Poets*. Chicago: St. James Press, 1991.

197

Cook, Eleanor. "On John Hollander's 'Owl.'" *Philosophy and Literature* 20, no. 1 (April 1996): 167–76.

DuBois, Andrew. *Ashbery's Forms of Attention*. Tuscaloosa: University of Alabama Press, 2006.

DuPlessis, Rachel Blau, and Peter Quartermain, ed. *The Objectivist Nexus: Essays in Cultural Poetics*. Tuscaloosa: University of Alabama Press, 1999.

Fletcher, Angus. *A New Theory for American Poetry: Democracy, the Environment, and the Future of Imagination*. Cambridge, Mass.: Harvard University Press, 2004.

Frazier, Jane. *From Origin to Ecology: Nature and the Poetry of W.S. Merwin*. Madison, N.J.: Fairleigh Dickinson University Press; London: Associated University Presses, 1999.

Fredman, Stephen. *Poet's Prose: The Crisis in American Verse*. Cambridge, England; New York: Cambridge University Press, 1990.

Gardner, Thomas. *A Door Ajar: Contemporary Writers and Emily Dickinson*. Oxford; New York: Oxford University Press, 2006.

———. *Regions of Unlikeness: Explaining Contemporary Poetry*. Lincoln: University of Nebraska Press, 1999.

Gardner, Thomas, ed. *Jorie Graham: Essays on the Poetry*. Madison: University of Wisconsin Press, 2005.

Gray, Timothy. *Gary Snyder and the Pacific Rim: Creating Countercultural Community*. Iowa City: University of Iowa Press, 2006.

Gregerson, Linda. *Negative Capability: Contemporary American Poetry*. Ann Arbor: University of Michigan Press, 2001.

Haralson, Eric, ed. *Reading the Middle Generation Anew: Culture, Community, and Form in Twentieth Century American Poetry*. Iowa City: University of Iowa Press, 2006.

Herd, David. *John Ashbery and American Poetry*. New York: Palgrave, 2000.

Hix, H. L. *Understanding W.S. Merwin*. Columbia: University of South Carolina Press, 1997.

Hoeppner, Edward Haworth. *Echoes and Moving Fields: Structure and Subjectivity in the Poetry of W.S. Merwin and John Ashbery*. Lewisburg, Pa.: Bucknell University Press; London; Cranbury, N.J.: Associated University Presses, 1994.

Jackson, Richard. *Acts of Mind: Conversations with Contemporary Poets*. University: University of Alabama Press, 1983.

Karagueuzian, Catherine Sona. *No Image There and the Gaze Remains: The Visual in the Work of Jorie Graham*. New York: Routledge, 2005.

Kelly, Lionel, ed. *Poetry and the Sense of Panic: Critical Essays on Elizabeth Bishop and John Ashbery*. Amsterdam: Rodopi, 2000.

Keniston, Ann. *Overheard Voices: Address and Subjectivity in Postmodern American Poetry*. New York: Routledge, 2006.

Kern, Robert. "Mountains and Rivers Are Us: Gary Snyder and the Nature of the Nature of Nature." *College Literature* 27, no. 1 (Winter 2000): 119–38.

Kirby, David. *Mark Strand and the Poet's Place in Contemporary Culture.* Columbia: University of Missouri Press, 1990.

Langdell, Cheri Colby. *Adrienne Rich: The Moment of Change.* Westport, Conn.: Praeger, 2004.

Lea, Sydney, ed. *The Burdens of Formality: Essays on the Poetry of Anthony Hecht.* Athens: University of Georgia Press, 1989.

Lindsay, Geoffrey. "'Heirs of an Humiliating Splendour': Richard Howard and Contemporary American Poetry." *Wascana Review of Contemporary Poetry and Short Fiction* 36, no. 1 (Spring 2001): 71–89.

Longenbach, James. "Richard Howard's Modern World." *Salmagundi* 108 (Fall 1995): 140–63.

Mark, Alison, and Deryn Rees-Jones, eds. *Contemporary Women's Poetry: Reading/Writing/Practice.* Houndmills, Basingstoke, Hampshire; New York: St. Martin's Press, 2000.

Marshall, Tod. *Range of the Possible: Conversations with Contemporary Poets.* Spokane: Eastern Washington University Press, 2002.

Murphy, Margueritte S. *A Tradition of Subversion: The Prose Poem in English from Wilde to Ashbery.* Amherst: University of Massachusetts Press, 1992.

Murphy, Patrick D. *A Place for Wayfaring: The Poetry and Prose of Gary Snyder.* Corvallis: Oregon State University Press, 2000.

Nelson, Cary. *Our Last First Poets: Vision and History in Contemporary American Poetry.* Urbana: University of Illinois Press, 1981.

Nelson, Cary, and Ed Folsom, eds. *W. S. Merwin: Essays on the Poetry.* Urbana: University of Illinois Press, 1987.

Nelson, Howard, ed. *On the Poetry of Galway Kinnell: The Wages of Dying.* Ann Arbor: University of Michigan Press, 1987.

Nicosia, James F. *Reading Mark Strand: His Collected Works, Career, and the Poetics of the Privative.* New York: Palgrave Macmillan, 2007.

Perry, Carolyn. "Contemporary Poetry." In *The History of Southern Women's Literature*, edited by Carolyn Perry and Mary Louise Weaks, pp. 467–77. Baton Rouge: Louisiana State University Press, 2002.

Raisor, Philip, ed. *Tuned and Under Tension: The Recent Poetry of W.D. Snodgrass.* Newark: University of Delaware Press; London; Cranbury, N.J.: Associated University Presses, 1998.

Ratiner, Steven. *Giving Their Word: Conversations with Contemporary Poets.* Amherst: University of Massachusetts Press, 2002.

Scigaj, Leonard M. *Sustainable Poetry: Four American Ecopoets.* Lexington: University Press of Kentucky, 1999.

Smith, Eric Todd. *Reading Gary Snyder's* Mountains and Rivers Without End. Boise, Idaho: Boise State University, 2000.

Stein, Kevin. *Private Poets, Worldly Acts: Public and Private History in Contemporary American Poetry.* Athens: Ohio University Press, 1999.

Stitt, Peter. *Uncertainty & Plenitude: Five Contemporary Poets.* Iowa City: University of Iowa Press, 1997.

Tarlo, Harriet. "Provisional Pleasures: The Challenge of Contemporary Experimental Women Poets." *Feminist Review* 62 (Summer 1999): 94–112.

Templeton, Alice. *The Dream and the Dialogue: Adrienne Rich's Feminist Poetics.* Knoxville: University of Tennessee Press, 1994.

Trawick, Leonard M. *World, Self, Poem: Essays on Contemporary Poetry from the "Jubilation of Poets."* Kent, Ohio: Kent State University Press, 1990.

Tuten, Nancy Lewis, ed. *Critical Essays on Galway Kinnell.* New York: G.K. Hall; London: Prentice Hall International, 1996.

Vendler, Helen. *The Breaking of Style: Hopkins, Heaney, Graham.* Cambridge, Mass.: Harvard University Press, 1995.

Vincent, John Emil. *Ashbery and You: His Later Books.* Athens: University of Georgia Press, 2007.

Wheeler, Lesley. *Voicing American Poetry: Sound and Performance from the 1920s to the Present.* Ithaca: Cornell University Press, 2008.

Acknowledgments

Marjorie Perloff, "Apocalypse Then: Merwin and the Sorrows of Literary History." From *W. S. Merwin: Essays on Poetry*, edited by Cary Nelson and Ed Folsom. Copyright © 1987 by the Board of Trustees. Used with permission of the author and the University of Illinois Press.

Stephen Paul Miller, "Periodizing Ashbery and His Influence." From *The Tribe of John: Ashbery and Contemporary Poetry*, edited by Susan M. Schultz, © 1995 by the University of Alabama Press. Reprinted as "Literature in a Convex Mirror (Chap. 4)," in *The Seventies Now*, pp. 139–219. Copyright © 1999 Duke University Press. All rights reserved. Used by permission of the publisher.

Barbara L. Estrin, "Re-Versing the Past: Adrienne Rich's Outrage Against Order." From *The American Love Lyric after Auschwitz and Hiroshima*. Copyright © 2001 by Barbara L. Estrin. Originally published by and used by permission of Palgrave Macmillan.

Roger Gilbert, "Contemporary American Poetry." From *A Companion to Twentieth-Century Poetry*, edited by Neil Roberts. Copyright © 2001 by Blackwell Publishers. Reproduced with permission of Blackwell Publishing Ltd.

Anthony Hecht, "Treasure Box." From *The New York Review of Books*, vol. 48, no. 16. Reprinted with permission from *The New York Review of Books*. Copyright © 2001 NYREV, Inc.

Index

203